For Penny, the light of my life

Praise for *The Wit and Wisdom of William Hamilton*.....

Other works by William Hamilton

Fiction:

Co-written with Penny R. Hamilton as William Penn:

The Grand Conspiracy (2001)

The Panama Conspiracy (2003)

The Berlin Conspiracy (2010)

JFK: The Umbrella Conspiracy (2013)

Non-fiction:

"The Decline and Fall of the Joint Chiefs of Staff," *US Naval War College Review*, April, 1972.

"The Influence of the American Military Upon United States Foreign Policy," 1965-1968, University of Nebraska, 1978.

"The Uncounted Enemy: A Vietnam Deception," *World Media Report*, Spring, 1987.

THE
WIT AND WISDOM
OF
WILLIAM HAMILTON:

THE SAGE OF SHEEPDOG HILL

A Selection From Almost 2,000 Weekly
"Central View" Newspaper Columns

William Hamilton

Pegasus Imprimis Press
Lake Granby, Colorado

Cover photo by: Amy Taborsky

Graphics of curtain and masks from:
www.123rf.com/profile_andreykuzmin,
www.123rf.com/profile_elnur

The Wit and Wisdom of William Hamilton: The Sage of Sheepdog Hill
First Edition

ISBN-13: 978-0692949276
ISBN-10: 0692949275

TABLE OF CONTENTS

INTRODUCTION

Some readers skip Introductions, going right on to the first page of the text. That is perfectly fine; however, some Introductions tell you most of the material that is in the book and you might even be able to pass a quiz about the book just based on reading the Introduction.

Relax. This book doesn't come with a test at the end. It can be read from front-to-back or even from back-to-front. And you can skip around all you wish.

The first of the "Central View" newspaper columns appeared in 1982 in the SUN Newspapers of Lincoln, Nebraska. Because Lincoln is situated only 168.5 miles from the geographical center of the United States, the publisher suggested the name: "Central View." When Penny (AKA Wonder Wife) and I moved full-time to Colorado in 1992, the title "Central View" moved along with us to Colorado where we built a home high on the side of a terminal moraine left by a receding Ice Age. Although we are now located 486.4 miles west of the geographical center of the U.S., the name of the column remains: "Central View." And, in terms of political orientation, the column remains just right of the political Center.

The terminal moraine overlooks Lake Granby, which at 7,200 acres or 11.4 square miles, is Colorado's second-largest man-made lake. Because we love Old English Sheepdogs and also love our unique and equally lovable, Tibetan Sheepdog, we named the moraine: Sheepdog Hill.

Since 1982, almost 2,000 "Central View" columns have been written and published in newspapers around the nation. Hopefully, each column contains at least one fact previously unknown to the reader and/or looks at facts in an unusual, sometimes humorous, way and strives to do so without being overly politically partisan. The goal is to reach open, not closed minds. For reasons of space, this volume only contains about one-percent of the newspaper columns published since 1982. See: www.central-view.com "Past Columns" for all the newspaper columns written since 1999.

In the early years of "Central View," newspaper editors were fine with 650-word opinion columns. But, as print advertising revenues declined due to Internet competition, space for news and opinion pieces declined as well. Consequently, the columns produced in later years are about 530 words in length. Some of the columns have been edited for space, clarity and, in some cases, for context. For the most part, the columns are arrayed in chronological order; however, not in all cases. If you encounter: NB, the abbreviation for Nota Bene (note well), look for an attempt to add clarity or historical context.

Going forward: We begin this collection of newspaper columns at the end of the 20th Century and at the beginning of the New Millennium, the 21st Century. While many people had high hopes for the new century, actions taken and not taken in the previous decade would light a long, smoldering fuse that would blow up on 9/11, 2001, and then spew its way on to 2008 and the worst financial crisis since the Great Depression of the 1930s. The financial crisis of 2008 would make possible the election of President Barak Hussein Obama. The eight years of the Obama Administration would lead to one of the greatest political upheavals in American political history: the election of President Donald. J. Trump.

Finally, this collection of newspaper columns begins with the year 1999 and ends within the year 2017. Also included are some articles that were published in *USA Today*. Thus, the period covered includes the end of the Clinton Administration, the two terms of George W. Bush, the two terms of Barack Hussein Obama, and the first months of the presidency of Donald J. Trump. As the book's cover suggests, during this period, our nation has experienced both comedy and tragedy, and continues to do so.

William Hamilton

CHAPTER ONE

PERSONAL IRKS, QUIRKS, AND MEMORIES

SUMMER: THE MOTHER OF INVENTIONS

It's enjoyable to write columns in the summer because you know no one is paying attention anyway. That gives one the freedom to drop subjects such as War and Peace and replace them with matters that are really important.

For example, I've always wanted to invent devices and ideas that would rank my name right up there with the great inventors such as Galileo, Edison, Bill Clinton, and Al Gore. Here are some samples:

I'd invent house shoes that always land right-side-up when you drop them on the floor. I hate it when they land upside-down and I can't get my feet in them. You see, you could mount a gyroscope in each shoe like the gyros pilots use in airplanes to help them keep the wings level. As the shoes fall, the gyro keeps them right-side-up.

I'd invent a holder for paper towels that would keep the paper from rolling too fast and spewing paper towels all over the kitchen. I'd put an inertial reel inside the towel holder somewhat like the reel that keeps your auto seatbelt from unwinding too fast when you make a sudden stop or crash.

I'd invent a TV remote with an imbedded photoelectric cell and when the cell doesn't get enough light, it sets off an alarm. That way, if the TV remote gets in among the bedclothes or falls down behind the seats in the sofa, it will let you know where it is.

I'd invent a dog collar that fires an anchor bolt and chain into the ground when your dog starts to run away and won't come back. One press of a remote command device and the dog finds him or herself staked to the ground until you can catch up.

I'd invent a telephone/answering/fax machine that automatically shuts itself down at 9:00 p.m. At any time, however, it would detect and tell those annoying telephone marketers in the kindest possible way where to place their products so they do not become exposed to daylight.

I'd invent a grocery store cart that when left blocking the aisle sets off a loud siren and then broadcasts the name of the person who blocked the aisle out over the store's public-address system. You see, when you grip the handle of the cart with your fingers, it reads your fingerprints, gets your name from the FBI files and then stores your name in memory just in case you block the aisle with your cart and you deserve to be publicly humiliated by a public-address announcement.

I'd invent a lighted sign for above the rear license plate that flashes banner messages in several foreign languages telling people who tailgate to "back-off." This would be very useful in New York City or Washington,

D.C. where taxi drivers are required to know Farsi but are forbidden to understand English.

I'd invent a limpet mine that detaches from your car and attaches, as they whiz by, to cars that don't dim their high beams. To avoid innocent injuries or deaths, the limpet mine wouldn't explode until the rude driver reaches his or her garage and shuts off the engine.

I'd invent a car with gas-filler ports on both sides. That way it wouldn't make any difference which way you pull up to the gas-pump island.

I'd invent a limpet mine that attaches to cars that park at the gas-pump island in such a thoughtless way that they block access to the pumps by other motorists. It would work just like the limpet mine for those who don't dim their high beams.

I'd invent a Happy Hour clock for the bar area that shows it is 5:00 p.m. in all the world's time zones.

I suppose there are hundreds of other equally useful devices waiting to be invented. If the summer lasts long enough, maybe I'll get around to inventing them as well.
©1999. 906

THINGS TO DO IN THE MOUNTAINS

Our Rocky Mountain home is literally at the end of the snowplow route, the electric line, and the telephone line. As the only year-round residents of our small subdivision, the only person we may see for weeks is the county snowplow operator.

We always advise our invited guests to come up in a four-wheel or all-wheel drive vehicle. As Wonder Wife is prone to say: "It's a great place to live, but you wouldn't want to visit here."

In summer, our splendid isolation is not without its frustrations most of which are caused by *uninvited and lost* motorists who somehow manage to make it up our road. It is all I can do to keep from inflicting a variety of practical jokes on such folks. Fortunately, Wonder Wife keeps most of my impulses in check.

For example, at night or even at first light when I am walking our dog, anyone venturing up our narrow, one-lane road will find me clad only in pajamas. Wonder Wife says I will be embarrassed when some motorist rounds the bend and I am caught, like a deer, in the headlights.

Fortunately, I have given that circumstance some thought and I have it all worked out. When these intruders finish turning around in our cul-de-sac, I plan to approach the driver and smuggle him or her a note that says: "They have taken away my clothes and I am being held here against my will. Go for help!"

My other thought is to don a sheriff's uniform. When the uninvited are struggling to negotiate our tiny cul-de-sac, I would simply walk over, admonish them for failing to heed the "Dead End" and "No Trespassing" signs and issue them a phony ticket.

Wonder Wife says "N.O." to both ideas. She fears I will be taken seriously and the motorist or hiker or biker will send for the Sheriff. The local Sheriff is a personal friend and Wonder Wife would like for us to remain on speaking terms. She also nixed my leaping on their cars in a bear costume.

Now and then, telephone marketers call offering to deliver one of the Denver newspapers to our door every day, to include Sunday. I used to tell such callers we weren't interested and try to terminate the call. If the caller refused to take "no" for an answer, I sometimes say I am blind and ask if they could deliver a Braille edition.

But I have found it is more fun to start giving the caller directions on how to deliver the paper. I start the directions where the pavement ends and the gravel road begins. I suggest that for the next half mile they will need a four-wheel drive vehicle. Then, if they make the extreme hairpin curve up into our subdivision, I suggest they switch to an all-terrain vehicle for the next quarter-mile. After that, I recommend cross-country skis for the final two-tenths of a mile. Without fail, the caller decides to withdraw his or her offer of newspaper delivery.

Clinging to the mountainside above our house is a huge rock about 30-feet long, 30-feet high and 30-feet wide. If it were to detach from the mountainside and roll down, it would obliterate half of our house on its way into the lake down below.

Both guest bedrooms happen to look out and up at this enormous rock. Some of our overnight guests have expressed a fear of being crushed in their sleep. My inclination is to get some very thin saplings about 15-feet long and lean them up against the rock as if they were placed there to keep the rock from rolling downhill. Then, when guests ask me if the rock has shown signs of rolling down, I could say, in all honesty: "No, not since we propped it up with those saplings." Wonder Wife likes that one.

©1999. 911

THE BRADY CHECK NEEDS A REALITY CHECK

Recently, this observer traded in some firearms we no longer need for another weapon I really don't need either. The new firearm is just like the one carried by James Bond -- a .380 Walther PPK semi-automatic pistol. Of course, *everyone* really needs one of those.

Actually, there is a little more to the story than a desire to own 007's weapon of choice. When I was an intelligence agent stationed in West Germany, we were required to fire our sidearms once a year. Sometimes, we had to share the firing range with our German counterparts. Just as sailors know that anytime two sailboats are headed in the same direction that a race ensues, anytime armed men meet on a firing range a marksmanship contest takes place.

Unfortunately, my partner and I were armed with 2.0-inch barrel .38 Smith & Wesson revolvers. Our German intelligence counterparts sported the 3.2-inch barrel .380 Walther PPK and the German criminal police had the 3.9-inch barrel Walther PP.

When it comes to the firing range, longer barrel length really does make a difference both in aiming and due to the increased number of twists (spin) received by the round before it leaves the barrel. That, plus the fact that my partner and I never practiced between these annual contests, placed us at a distinct disadvantage. Suffice it to say our West German friends shot rings around us.

Call it a case of barrel envy if you will; however, a brand-new Walther PPK is now properly secured in our home. But the most interesting part of trading for the PPK was filling out Alcohol, Tobacco and Firearms Form ATF F 4473 (5300.9) Part I, also known as the Brady Check.

The upper part of the form asks for the kind of personal data that we all provide on most any government form. But, surprisingly, giving your social security number or your alien registration number or your military ID number is optional.

Obviously, I passed the Brady Check. But here are some of the actual questions you are supposed to answer with either a "yes" or a "no" in order to complete the form. Let's skip the innocuous questions and begin with question d.

d. Are you a fugitive from justice?

e. Are you an unlawful user of, or addicted to, marijuana, or any depressant, stimulant, or narcotic drug, or any other controlled substance?

f. Have you ever been adjudicated mentally defective or have you been committed to a mental institution?

g. Have you been discharged from the Armed Forces under dishonorable conditions?

h. Are you an alien illegally in the United States?

i. Have you ever renounced your United States citizenship?

j. Are you subject to a court order restraining you from harassing, stalking or threatening an intimate partner or child of such partner?

k. Have you been convicted in any court of a misdemeanor crime of domestic violence?

The list goes on and on. But, let's face it. No criminal is going to answer these questions truthfully unless he or she gave a truthful answer to question f. and admitted to being mentally defective.

But I think the Brady Check is incomplete. If an applicant actually entered "yes" as the answer to questions dealing with being a fugitive from justice or being a user of illegal drugs or being an alien illegally in the United States, I think the Brady Check should be amended to add an instruction that says:

"If you answered 'yes' to questions d., or e., or h. above, please place your hands on the table in front of you, move your feet back away from the table so the majority of your weight is resting on your hands and spread your feet as far apart as you can. Kindly remain in that position until the police come to take you into custody where you so rightfully belong."

©2001. 1009

THE ROUNDABOUT: DID WE LOSE THOSE TWO WORLD WARS?

The late, great humorist Robert Benchley was fond of saying: "The world can be divided into two kinds of people: Those who divide the world into two kinds of people and those who do not." This observer likes to say that the world is divided into two kinds of people: Those who prefer Order and those who like Chaos. Fortunately, those who prefer Order outnumber those who like Chaos. Slightly.

Speaking of Chaos, in the small town that lies about ten road miles to the south of our little cabin in the woods, the subject of a traffic roundabout has come up. My colleague, Dave Barry, claims the United States fought World Wars I and II to prevent the imposition of the metric system upon the United States. We lost on that point. But I always thought we fought World Wars I and II to prevent us from being forced to suffer roundabouts.

For almost a decade, Wonder Wife and I lived, off and on, in Europe where we experienced roundabouts first hand. To understand what a roundabout looks like from above, go to your sink, turn the tap on full blast, allow the sink to fill with water, pull the plug and watch as the water swirls around and around down the drain. But there is one MAJOR difference between watching a roundabout from above and watching your sink: The roundabout has very tiny drains. When there is even a modest inflow of traffic, the roundabout overflows.

But there is a MINOR difference. Roundabouts rotate counter-clockwise, while water rotates clockwise in drains north of the Equator. But I digress.

The reason roundabouts clog up with traffic is because of a rule called: The Priority of the Right. In France, it's *Priorite de la droite*. In Italy, it's *Priorita della destra*. But, in any language, the result is the same: Chaos followed by gridlock.

When we lived in Europe, vehicles entering the roundabout from the right had the right-of-way. Meaning, vehicles already inside the roundabout must give way and they are then often trapped inside the circling traffic and could not break out to the perimeter so they could reach one of the exits to escape the whirling, imploding madness before it grinds to a halt.

But, for our adopted hometown, this phenomenon could have some economic benefits. When roundabouts are flowing freely, the alert motorist must crank his or her neck rapidly right and left to avoid being hit from either side. This will benefit sales from the nearby drug store for neck ointments, balms and braces.

But, once the inevitable gridlock occurs, the nearby 7-11 store could erect a viewing platform on its roof and charge admission to people who want to view the grid-locked roundabout from above. Sales of soft drinks and coffee will zoom.

Fortunately, the local clinic is nearby to treat the wounds that grid-locked motorists often inflict upon each other. These wounds are the result of digital communications, genealogy and physiology. The outraged motorists sometimes communicate their anger by displaying the center digit on one hand at each other while calling into question each other's genealogy and urging each other to perform anatomically impossible acts.

Experienced roundabouters wear sneakers because they do less damage to car hoods when nature forces motorists who are, shall we say, less continent than others to walk across the tops of cars seeking a restroom.

Teenagers could augment their allowances so they can obtain necessities, such as tongue and nose rings, by walking across hoods to reach sneakerless motorists who will pay big bucks for the relief afforded by the in-car delivery of a Piddlepac™. The nearby sandwich shop could hawk tons of subs to the stranded.

Finally, operators of construction cranes can find work lifting out the Rosetta Stone vehicle that will unlock the tangled mass of vehicular metal and allow it to flow freely.

This observer can't wait to drive in town and climb that observation platform. Ah, Chaos. Ah, Nostalgia. It will seem like old times in France and Italy.
©2002. 1037

IN MEMORIAM: HIS FINEST HOUR

One of the downsides of living to age 95 is that very few of the people who know all the things you did are still around. How many people know that William A. Hamilton, Jr., who left us on June 19, 2002, could play five musical instruments quite well, spoke Spanish as a boy, was a champion tennis player, was an excellent amateur magician, a crack rifle shot, a serious fisherman, and a hero of World War II?

Sir Winston Churchill characterized the struggles of the British people in World War II as: "Their Finest Hour." For William A. Hamilton, Jr., World War II was his "finest hour" as well.

After World War II began and both Europe and Asia were in flames, William Hamilton yearned to join his younger brother who was fighting out in the Pacific. But there were five obstacles in his way.

He was 36-years-old -- well beyond draft age. He was married. He had a child. He was occupying what was called a war-critical job. And, he was classified as 4-F -- physically unfit for active service. Four of these disqualifying factors could, however, be waived at the discretion of the individual. He waived all four.

But when he went to the Navy recruiting office to volunteer for active duty, he had to take a physical. When the physical was over he was told that, due to his sinus problems, he was classified as 4-F.

William Hamilton was not about to be 4-F for long. So, at his own expense, he had a surgeon cut open some passages in his sinus cavities. At the time, a very painful operation. But the result was good. And, after healing, he was able to change his physical classification from 4-F to 1-A and join the United States Navy as a volunteer.

Because he was a college graduate, the Navy wanted him to enter officer training. But he felt the war would be over before he could graduate. So, he trained as a signalman and joined the fleet almost right away. In all, he served 21 months.

He served 13 months of sea duty on two different Liberty Ships as part of the Navy's Armed Guard Program. Liberty ships needed to be protected from enemy attacks from the air and by submarine and they needed to be integrated into the Navy-escorted convoys. To do that, the Navy assigned signalmen and gun crews to protect these merchant ships. So, when William Hamilton was not on duty on the bridge making or receiving signals for the ship's captain, he was the loader on the crew of a 40mm anti-aircraft gun. Off the shores of Iwo Jima and Okinawa, his crew brought down two Mitsubishi bombers.

During these kamikaze attacks, he was almost killed. Not once, but twice. One Japanese aircraft attacked the bridge with 20mm cannons, but he was saved from being killed by a heavy steel bulkhead. On another occasion, a Japanese torpedo plane broke through the anti-aircraft defenses and launched a torpedo that was headed straight for the middle of his ship. But the torpedo tumbled as it hit the water and did not run straight and true. Instead, it dove under the ship and disappeared. Had the torpedo not tumbled, it would have made a direct hit with disastrous consequences.

At war's end, the Navy asked him to stay on as a commissioned officer. But his heart was at home with his wife and family and the people of Caddo County. So, he came home with a chest full of campaign ribbons and battle stars for his service in the Pacific. Some lesser men tried to avoid the war. But William Hamilton, Jr. overcame five obstacles in order to sail in harm's way. That truly was his finest hour.

©2002. 1056

TEN PET PEEVES

Out here in the woods, we never stay up late enough to watch David Letterman; however, we do know he is famous for his ten-item lists of various things. In that spirit, here is this observer's most recent list of: Pet Peeves.

10. Disorganized people in the grocery checkout or other lines who don't have their stuff together. Only AFTER their groceries are tallied and bagged do they even begin to look for their check book which they have trouble finding and, of course, nothing on the check has been entered in advance – not even the date. These are often the same people who get into the 15-item express line with a gazillion items.

9. People who block the grocery store aisles with their carts. Women, in particular, seem to have this territorial imperative. I think they do it to send a message to us males who do grocery shopping which is: "Look buster, this is female terrain. Go home and do something useful like cleaning the garage."

8. People who leave their shopping carts anywhere they please rather than returning them to the store or placing them in a storage rack.

7. People who arrive early for a dinner party. To get everything ready by the appointed hour is a struggle for many hosts and hostesses. To be descended upon by guests in the middle of the mad flurry of last-minute preparations is a crime deserving of capital punishment. The 8th Amendment prohibition against "cruel and unusual" punishment should not apply in such cases. Emily Post says to arrive about ten minutes after the appointed hour. Surely, she has been elevated to sainthood by now.

6. People who say they are leaving and then linger on and on, half-in and half-out the front door. In the military, the custom was that once you bid your host and hostess farewell, you moved out smartly.

5. People who block the moving sidewalks in airline terminals instead of standing on the right side of the moving sidewalk so others (who might be rushing to catch their flights) can pass by on the left.

4. People who get on airliners dressed for the beach in shorts, tank tops and sandals. In an off-airport landing (otherwise known as a crash) they are the first to become incapacitated and taking care of them then becomes a burden on those who had enough common sense to wear long pants, long sleeve shirts and sensible shoes and can act as first-responders.

3. People who get on airliners and place their carry-on bag in a storage bin BEHIND where they are sitting instead of in front. Duh. When it is time to deplane, they have to go backwards to get their bag thus blocking the outward flow of passengers.

2. People who call on the phone without giving their name at the outset of the conversation. Perhaps, they have such large egos that they think everyone knows who they are or they think their voice is so special that no one should forget it or, maybe, good manners just were not part of their home curriculum. As our population ages, hearing loss is more common and we need to be mindful of that.

1. And finally, (drum roll) People who say they use email and then never check for their messages. MicroSoft Outlook Express has a feature whereby the sender can request a message receipt that reveals the time and date when recipients open their messages. Some folks, to whom this observer has sent what, by any measure, were important messages may not open them for weeks. When that happens, they get email capital punishment: deletion from the email address book. Apparently, city dwellers who get their mail delivered to their door rely less on email than those who live far from a post office or where RFD is not readily available. For rural/mountain America, email is becoming the essential means of written communication.
©2002. 1062

CLICHÉS: HOW TO AVOID THEM LIKE THE PLAGUE

Writer's Digest says writers should avoid clichés like the plague. So, one morning, fresh as a daisy, I decided to get down to brass tacks and write a column without a single cliché. But, knowing that two heads are better than one, I asked Wonder Wife (she earned a Ph.D. in Communications) if I should try to make my clichés as scarce as hen's teeth.

She said clichés can be helpful in getting one's point across and I should not throw the cliché baby out with the pedantic water. If, however, I'm unwilling to let sleeping dogs lie, she said I should put my money where my mouth is and step up to the plate.

Obviously, she wasn't going to give me help on a silver platter. So, I let her words go in one ear and out the other, even though I knew avoiding clichés wouldn't be a piece of cake. So, I turned, like a bat out of hell, to the Internet, where I found just what the doctor ordered. I don't mean to let the cat out of the bag; however, the Internet reveals many writers who use more clichés than Carter has little, liver pills.

Realizing I was on a roll and could meet my editor's deadline in the nick of time, I was determined not to throw in the towel or let my shorts get wrapped around the axle. Besides, some editors are dumber than a box of rocks and, if you make them think you've been burning the midnight oil, they'll say encouraging things like: wake up and smell the coffee or, even better, the check's in the mail.

Even though I know you can't judge a book by its cover, I also did research at a bookstore. I noticed a certain author's book was selling like hotcakes, so I decided when in Rome to do as the Romans do and jumped on the band wagon to buy his book. Even though people were fighting like cats and dogs over the book; I bit the bullet and bought the last copy, leaving others, not only green with envy, but as mad as hornets.

One disappointed customer wouldn't take no for an answer. But, as a rule of thumb, I've found if you let people take an inch they will take a mile. So, I told him he was making a mountain out of mole hill. Finally, this guy made me a deal I couldn't refuse. After all, a penny saved is a penny earned. Besides, when I glanced at the preface, it was all Greek to me.

I could tell he was chomping at the bit to buy the book. But, being honest as the day is long; I didn't want to put my foot in my mouth by giving him the whole nine yards about how the book would make him happier than a pig in, well ...dirt.

I was reluctant to go out on a limb; however, knowing that he who hesitates is lost, I bet him dollars to donuts that the book would make him feel like a kid in a candy store. Still, not wanting to count my chickens before they hatched and not about to take any wooden nickels, I was pleased when he paid me a King's ransom in cash and left.

With my column deadline nearing, it became clear as crystal that I would only make it by the skin of my teeth because I was finding that ridding my work of clichés was putting me between a rock and hard place. Yet, if I failed, I wouldn't cry over spilled milk. But, to be safe rather than sorry and not wanting to be caught a day late and dollar short or to be barking up the wrong tree, I checked the work of another writer by the name of William Shakespeare. He wrote that, "All's well that ends well."

©2007. 1301

MEMORIES OF TONY SNOW: JOURNALIST EXTRAORDINAIRE

In summer of 1989, Novosti (the Soviet Press Agency) invited 12 American journalists to tour the USSR. At the time, yours truly was editor-in-chief of *The Capital Times* of Lincoln, Nebraska. My wife, Penny, was special-features editor and a Lincoln radio and TV personality. Somehow, she and I were selected to join ten other American journalists for 17 days of interviews with senior Soviet officials.

As our group assembled at New York's JFK Airport, we were introduced to a quiet, shy, handsome, young man who, at the time, was editorial-page editor for *The Washington Times*. His name was Tony Snow. Tony, to the regret of everyone who, later, knew him or knew of his work on radio, as a speech writer for President George H.W. Bush, as the seven-year host of Fox News Sunday, and as press secretary for President George W. Bush, died last Friday of colon cancer, at age 53.

The ring master for our group of 12 was the irrepressible essayist and novelist, Larry Moffitt. Larry sent me off to buy a supply of duty-free whisky to be used to "influence" certain friends Larry knew from his previous ventures behind the Iron Curtain. Tony Snow was dispatched to buy as many cartons of Marlboro cigarettes as the law would allow. None of us smoked; however, the cigarettes would prove indispensable in dealing with customs inspectors and getting Moscow taxi drivers to stop for us. Larry showed us how to pack the cartons of cigarettes inside our suitcases so the Soviet customs inspectors would be able to set them aside and then "forget" to put them back.

The most exciting part of the trip for me was getting through KGB passport control at Moscow's Sheremetyevo Airport. In an earlier life, I had operated in Europe under a variety of names and with a variety of passports. Would the computer being used by the KGB officials say I should be denied entry or even arrested? Fortunately, he gave me the same bored look that he gave to Penny, Tony, Larry and the others. I was in.

Tony was the kind of guy who put the word "gentle" into gentleman. But he was no pushover. One evening our group, AKA the Dirty Dozen, (the City of Moscow had shut down the central hot-water plant for repairs), was invited to a Russian wedding. Vodka was flowing. The Russians were dancing. Then, a really huge and very drunk Russian came over to our table to pick a fight. In a flash, Tony, who was 6-foot-two and very fit, was in between our table of superannuated journalists and the bellicose Russian. I think the Russian was grateful that his comrades pulled him away before Tony could deck him.

In Moscow, Novosti provided a small carry bus to take us (and our KGB minder) to interview the senior officials Novosti wanted interviewed. Tony wanted to interview "real" Russians, so he induced one of us to pretend a wasp bite. During the ensuing confusion, Tony slipped off the bus in search of "real" Russians. When he discovered Tony was missing, our minder almost fainted.

One night near Minsk, we were hosted at dinner by the director of a Collective Farm. As a youth, our host had been badly wounded by the Nazis. An old Babushka (grandmother) nursed him back to health with fermented mare's milk. Recounting that story, the director made us toast her memory with a shot of fermented mare's milk. Yuk.

As the senior journalist (in age), I jumped up to offer a response-toast -- but with vodka. Tony caught on to my ploy. He followed immediately with a vodka toast. Then, the rest of the Dirty Dozen caught on and we kept the vodka toasts going around the table to the point our vodka-addled host forgot all about any more toasts with fermented mare's milk. Whew.

Tony Snow was someone you never forget. We just wish he could have stayed with us a lot longer.

©2008. 1379

COMPUTER JIHAD: READY, AIM, AND BLAST AWAY

Recently, someone got so frustrated with his computer that he took it outside and blasted the computer eight times with his pistol. Apparently, the computer had not developed enough Artificial Intelligence of its own to know that its very existence was in mortal danger and to take evasive action.

At the very least, you would think the computer would have figured out a way to call the bogus "Hands up!

Don't shoot" videos from Ferguson, MO, down out of the Cloud and run them on its display screen. Moreover, a really smart computer would know if its owner is a big supporter of the First Amendment. In that case, the computer might quickly display photos of free-speech advocates Pamela Geller and Dutch parliamentarian Geert Wilders. Of course, the downside of featuring the sponsors of a Mohammad cartoon contest would be the risk of having the images of Geller and Wilders blasted by Islamic jihadists.

So, it is not easy being a computer these days. In our household, we have two desktop PCs, a tablet, an ordinary cell phone, and a smarter-than-I-am phone. The most irritating behavior of the PCs is when you are ready to shut down and go to bed and the PCs decide to download the latest updates to their programs. You are faced with the choice of sitting there, delaying your bedtime for an hour or so while the updates download or going to bed and leaving the computer on all night. And, even though the computer claims it will shut itself down, can you really trust it like we do the light inside the refrigerator?

Windows Live Mail and Windows Explorer have this odd behavior of shutting themselves down now and then. Usually right when you are in the middle of some e-mail or search you think is important. Sometimes, volumes of text will disappear from Windows WORD, forcing a "global search" to find out where it went.

My PC keeps suggesting that a trip to Nigeria would be a good thing. Once in Nigeria, I could claim billions of dollars due me from a mining claim I never knew I owned.

To prove I am the rightful heir, all I have to do is wire $500 to a banker in Nigeria. Or, I could fly to Scotland and take up the title I supposedly inherited from the 14th Duke of Hamilton. With all due respect to Nigeria, Scotland has more appeal. The Duke was the first pilot to fly over Mt. Everest and he was Commodore of the Scots Royal Air Force during World War II. So, both being pilots, maybe we are related?

The tablet computer gets little use. It came with one of those touch-screen operating systems. I had to download a program that makes it look like the keyboard and mouse system of yesteryear. Still unsatisfactory.

The problem is that those computer geniuses in Seattle or Silicon Valley have to keep earning their fabulous salaries. So, instead of leaving well enough alone, they dream up "improvements" to operating systems that are working just fine. Don't they understand how many computers they are placing in front of firing squads? How callous of them.

©2015. 1788

BRIT HUME IS BACK

The return of the Emmy Award-winning, Brit Hume, to prime time at Fox News Channel brings back a fond memory of a huge favor that Hume did for a relatively unknown writer from fly-over land. Back in May, June, and July of 1987, the televised Iran-Contra Hearings were commanding a huge viewing audience. Coincidentally, there was the prospect, albeit dim, that yours truly, the then editor-in-chief of *The Capital Times* of Lincoln, Nebraska, might become a commentator for *USA Today.*

Seeking a break-through news story, and without any official press credentials, I lined up in the hallway of the Russell Senate Office Building along with the hoard of folks trying to get inside the ornate hearing room's tiny visitors' gallery. The sergeants-at-arms would count off the number of people to be let in to take the places of the folks being let out. Each group only got to stay inside for a few minutes before being hustled back out. To be able to file a credible story, I knew a stay of several hours would be needed.

Brit Hume, whom I had only seen as the ABC-TV Capitol Hill correspondent, came to my rescue. When the time came for me to be let in, I caught the eye of the only familiar face amidst the rows of credentialed reporters, that of Brit Hume. Brit, in his smiling, avuncular way, came ambling over. I whispered my name and said I was trying to place a piece in *USA Today.* As if we had known each other forever, Brit put his arm around my shoulder as he explained to the sergeant-at-arms that Bill, his journalist-colleague, would be sitting all day with him in the press gallery.

Thanks to Brit Hume, I got the full flavor of the media circus known as the Iran-Contra Hearings. Back at my home newspaper, I used satire to report that, due to some kind of TV-switching error, I had witnessed the Presidium of the USSR conducting a show trial of some

American intelligence agents who had been caught trying to overthrow a Soviet-backed regime in Central America.

Apparently, the piece was okay. The satire appeared in *USA Today* on July 3, 1987. Following that, I enjoyed 24 years of completing dozens of assignments for the nation's most widely-circulated newspaper. For example, in December, 1990, when Soviet Vice President Gennady Yanayev led a coup to overthrow Mikhail Gorbachev, my then *USA Today* editor, Sid Hurlburt, recalled that my wife and I had, a couple of years earlier, interviewed Gennady Yanayev in Yanayev's Moscow office. Sid let me opine that the hopelessly alcoholic Yanayev could not organize a one-car parade and that his coup would fail within hours. On our prediction, *USA Today* scooped the rest of the world press by several days.

But it was Brit Hume, and my long-time editor at *USA Today*, Sid Hurlburt, and *USA Today* founder, the late Al Neuharth, who provided the kind of opportunities that most writers from fly-over land rarely receive. Forever grateful to them all; I am especially indebted to Brit Hume. *NB: Following the election of 2016. Brit reverted to his role as a Fox contributor.*

©2016. 1855

This article appeared in the July 3, 1987 issue of USA TODAY

"AS THE WORLD TURNS" ON OUR TV SCREENS

Lincoln, Neb -- The other morning, my favorite TV soap opera was interrupted. Usually, studio switching errors are to blame. But this particular error was different.

My TV screen showed 26 officials sitting behind high desks. Evidently, it was the Presidium of the USSR. Doubtless, the proceedings were being conducted in Russian. But, through some miracle of translation, the audio came through in English.

Apparently, the Soviets had caught some U.S. agents trying to overthrow a Soviet-backed regime in Central America. Some members of the Presidium seemed hopping mad, and the rest looked like they needed a vodka break.

Watching closely, I began to understand why the Presidium was so upset. Evidently, these U.S. agents had pulled off a scam in which they jacked up the prices on some weapons sales, and then used the profits against Soviet interests.

Part of the money had gone to gain the release of some U.S. hostages. Other money went to support anti-communist insurgents in Nicaragua.

This made the Presidium angry because, at some point in the past, the Presidium had announced the Boland Doctrine. The Boland Doctrine is, however, not to be confused with the Brezhnev Doctrine. The Brezhnev Doctrine says: Once a nation goes communist, it must remain in the Soviet orbit forever. The Boland Doctrine says the USA must be prevented from even trying to interfere with Soviet takeovers -- specifically, in the Western Hemisphere.

Many of the Presidium members seemed intent on proving that the president of the USA was behind these efforts to stop the spread of communism. Gee, I said to myself, I certainly hope so.

I was about to call the TV station to complain about my soap opera being pre-empted, when one of the captured U.S. agents (a retired general I think), stunned the Presidium with some pretty cheeky answers. If I were captured by the enemy, I hope I'd have the nerve to stand up to them like that.

When the Presidium wasn't picking on the captured U.S. agents, they would say ugly things about someone called Colonel North. Evidently, this North chap had hurt the communists a lot. Colonel North, however, was not yet on camera. I suspect they were working him over before dragging him in.

Unfortunately, just as the show trial was getting interesting, my soap opera reappeared. I suppose the Soviets found their switching error and were ashamed to let the world see what really goes on inside the Presidium.

I know I wouldn't want the world to see some of things that go on in our Congress.

GROWING UP DIVERSE: WHAT'S IN A NAME?

For this writer, growing up in an area of cultural diversity was a "built-in" blessing. While we had families whose ancestors came from the British Isles, Germany, Poland, Spain, Africa, and Scandinavia, our main claim to fame was that our town was and is known as the: "Indian Capital of the Nation."

Back in those times, we thought we were getting to play Cowboys and Indians with real Indians; however, after the Political Correctness Movement came along, it turns out that we had actually been playing Cowboys and Native Americans. We just didn't know it at the time.

Actually, "Indian" was a misnomer by Christopher Columbus arising from the fact that naval navigation *circa* 1492 A.D. did not have the benefit of timepieces able to withstand the rigors of shipboard life and, therefore, they could not measure Longitude, i.e. how far a ship had been sailing in either a westerly or an easterly direction.

Columbus did, however, know his Latitude (distance between the North and South Poles). The Greek geographer/mathematician, Claudius Ptolemy (90-170 A.D.), solved that part of the navigation problem long before the time of Columbus. Ptolemy figured out how to measure the angle between the true horizon and the sun and, from that angle, derive one's Latitude between the North and South Poles.

However, precise Longitude could not be determined until 1773 when the Englishman, John Harrison, perfected his marine chronometer -- a relatively rugged sea-going clock that allowed sailors to know how long they had been sailing from the Prime Meridian at Greenwich, England. Back in 1492, Columbus had no idea how long he had been sailing westward. He mistook the islands of the Caribbean for India and named the natives: Indians. (For more on Longitude: See: Dava Sobel's *Longitude: The True Story of a Lone Genius Who Solved the Greatest Scientific Problem of His Time*.)

All this Indian versus Native American stuff seemed of little concern to my grade-school chums who actually preferred to be thought of according to their tribal names which could be: Kiowa, Comanche, Western Delaware, Wichita, Arapahoe, Caddo, or Apache. As kids were wont to do back then, we thought it was a fun thing to become blood brothers.

We probably got the idea from the Saturday picture shows which featured a lot of Cowboys and Indians. Not Cowboys and Native Americans. Some of my Kiowa and Comanche pals decided it would be a good idea to make me a blood brother. This involved nicking our wrists with a knife (careful not to do any real damage) and mixing a few drops of our blood. The idea appealed to me because some of my chums had some really cool names such as: Running Deer or Running Bear or Running Beaver or Running Fox. But, because I suffered from allergic rhinitis, I was afraid they were going to call me: Running Nose.

Fortunately, my pals must have been psychic. They could not have known that years later, after taking a test called: the Myers-Briggs Personality Inventory, yours truly would be classified as an INTJ which stands for: Introverted, iNtuitive, Thinking and Judgmental. In other words, a person who acts more on intuition, who is driven rapidly to come to conclusions and takes action rather than worry about how many angels can dance on the head of a pin. In short: a person who makes quick decisions and then crashes forward into almost every endeavor.

Somehow, my Kiowa and Comanche chums perceived those traits already and they named me: Crashing Boar. Or, was it: Crashing Bore? In any event, they never made that clear. Of course, readers are free to make up their own minds about that.

©2011. 1538

FOX WATCH: A LESSON FOR US ALL

Once again, we are empty-nesters. The fox family that used the cave underneath the huge rock directly behind our house departed. Either that, or the ground squirrel we now see examining the fox den must have a death wish.

Several weeks ago, Wonder Wife saw this sweet, little fox face peering out from the darkness of the cave. Increasing our surveillance, we began to see four kits in all. Three of them were very robust, one of them sickly. By the dawn's early light, we sometimes saw the male bringing food to the den. When she was well enough, the vixen shared in the food-gathering chores, mostly in the evenings.

One morning, the vixen brought all four kits down from the cave and out onto our gravel driveway. While the father fox supervised the healthier kits at play -- learning how to leap and pounce on each other -- the vixen lay down to encourage the sickly kit to nurse. Unfortunately, that was the last time we saw the sickly kit.

All too soon, the remaining kits were teenagers exhibiting the unfocused, wandering ways of teenagers. Those drew quick corrections from the vixen and/or the father fox. One of the kits who was obviously the alpha male or the alpha female spent much more time lying just outside the entrance to the den than did the other kits. As a result, when one of the parents returned to the den carrying something to eat, the alpha kit was first in line for chow. Charles Darwin at work.

As the kits grew stronger, we could tell the alpha kit was trying to decide if it was time to face the world on its own terms. Was it time to break the loving bonds of family and venture out into the unknown world? We just happened to be watching when the alpha kit left the den for good and trotted determinedly out our driveway. We were proud and sad. We hated to see that brave alpha kit go.

Initially, all that giving birth, feeding, and kit-rearing caused the vixen, like new mothers everywhere, to look pretty bedraggled. But the last time we saw her, her coat looked much better and the spring was back in her step. Yesterday, the father fox was sitting on a small rock at the far end of our driveway. He seemed lost in thought as if he were thinking about how they grow up all too quickly and then they are gone. Well, almost gone.

We take comfort in the fact that our house seems to be in the center of their approximately two-mile-radius range. We also know that the adolescents, even though now out on their own, often linger within the range to help with the raising of the next litter.

The Red Fox, (*Vulpes fulva*) will be mating again next year sometime between January and March. If we are lucky, come spring, the vixen will return to the cave underneath the huge rock behind our house and the fox family will, once again, provide us with several weeks of viewing enjoyment.

Granted, chicken farmers, voles, mice, and ground squirrels do not share our enthusiasm for the Red Fox; however, the *Vulpes fulva's* careful parenting, supervised play, and their loving and cooperative family life should be a role model for us all.

©2012. 1630

UPDATE: THE FOX FAMILY

Based on reader response, the adventures of the fox family -- living a mere 30 yards from our house -- are of great interest. As fox-savvy readers know, once kits are old enough to leave the den, it is unusual for them to return. But it's not like the mother's complaint: "You never call. You never write." The adolescent kits tend to stay within a two-mile range of the family den. Sometimes, they even come back to help with their parent's next litter.

And it's not like we are trying to invade the privacy of this fox family. But they seem so close we can almost touch them and, without trying, we can see right into their den. Speaking of privacy, there is a Hummingbird hanging around our front deck. It keeps looking into our windows. Each year, the Hummingbirds fly all the way up from Nicaragua. We can't tell if these are Democrat Hummingbirds or Sandinista (communist) Hummingbirds or if they are drones sent here by the current regime. Fortunately, it is too tiny to be armed. But it may be beaming photos back to Big Sis in D.C.

Back to the foxes: We all know the economy is bad and not likely to improve between now and November 6, 2012. That probably explains why one of the kits has had to move back into the family den. He's the one we dubbed: Homeboy. He is not the kit we figured out was the Alpha Male. The other two kits remain unnamed and are, so far, unaccounted for.

Each evening, after the entrance to the den is in the cooling shade of the big rock; Homeboy lies at the entrance to the den and takes a nap. That was until recently when the economy got so bad that Alpha Male decided to return home as well. Poor Homeboy was napping when Alpha Male announced his return by pouncing on a startled Homeboy.

Nevertheless, they seem to get along quite well. Each morning they are up early, practicing their stalking and pouncing skills on each other. If we had those Olympic scoring paddles, we would award Homeboy a 9.8 and Alpha Male a 9.9. But, like too many Olympic scores, that would be very subjective. Still, we admire their pouncing because we understand it is essential to their work at rodent control around our house.

Of course, Homeboy and Alpha Male are so precious we want to feed them. But, if we put them on welfare, they will no longer work at hunting for Rodent-Fil-A. Then, the potentially disease-carrying rodent population would soar. Also, with no need to work, the omnivorous foxes might get into cannabis – the gateway drug. Common sense says welfare recipients should be drug-tested and we don't know how to do that with a fox.

Too bad Homeboy and Alpha Male can't understand English so we could explain the wisdom of former President Bill Clinton (D) when he signed a law that welfare recipients had to either be in job-training or be out looking for work.

Sadly, we have not seen the kits' aging parents in some time. We pray they have not fallen victim to one of the death panels of the current regime. It's still okay to pray. Right? Right?

©2012. 1636

REJECTION: THE FEAR OF EVERY WRITER

For many years, the back page of *Writer's Digest* featured a contest that asked readers to make believe that they were the publishers who had the bad judgment to reject submissions by some of the world's greatest authors. The contest was called: "Reject a Hit." Recently, this writer finally decided to submit a Reject a Hit based on Frederick Forsyth's *The Day of the Jackal*, only to be rejected because *Writer'sDigest* decided to drop Reject a Hit and replace it with a different type of writing contest. Rather than discard it, my Reject a Hit submission is this week's "Central View."

Pegasus Imprimis Press
8 Herbert Crescent
Knightsbridge, London
September 30, 1971
Dear Mr. Forsyth,

Thank you for your recent submission of your manuscript *The Day of the Jackal.*

    While the idea of a manhunt conducted across France to intercept an assassin employed by the *Organization l'Armée de Secrète* to assassinate French President Charles de Gaulle is intriguing, it is my duty to inform you that former French President Charles de Gaulle was never assassinated. As every French school boy knows, President de Gaulle died in his sleep on November 9, 1970, in his home in *Colombey-les-Deux-Églises.*

    Should your work ever find a publisher or be the plot of a motion picture, which we seriously doubt, any knowledgeable reader or viewer would know that President de Gaulle was never assassinated. No reader is going to be captivated by a plot which could not possibly be true -- past, present, or future. As our junior reader said, "We know the climax already, the plan fails."

Based on the biography you attached to your manuscript, it appears that holding onto a steady job is not one of your strengths. You have been a RAF fighter pilot, an amateur bull-fighter, a small-market newspaper reporter, worked for a news agency, been a free-lance journalist, and now, you purport to be a novelist.

But, because our junior staff reader says your writing has a certain authentic ring, as if you actually experienced some kind of paparazzi pursuit of President de Gaulle, we might entertain future submissions; provided that they have some sort of basis in fact.

Looking toward our list for next year, we might be interested in a novel about Nazis who were never brought to justice or, perhaps, a novel detailing the gruesome work of mercenaries in Africa. Meanwhile, forget about *The Day of the Jackal*. Try to find a steady day job.

Sincerely,
Howard Hutchinson
Editor-in-Chief
Pegasus Imprimis Press

©2016. 1839

THE TIBETAN SHEEPDOG, OR NOT?

A few years ago, Wonder Wife, working with Tracy's Dogs of Texas, rescued a one-year-old male canine of undetermined breed. With his bushy tail carried over his back, and his blue-black tongue, we suspected one or more of his ancestors might be a Chow. DNA testing proved inconclusive. But his friendly, regal bearing caused us to name him: Prince.

Of all the canines recognized by the American Kennel Club, the Tibetan Terrier and Prince look most alike; however, Prince is twice the size of the typical Tibetan Terrier. Moreover, Prince exhibits more the guardian behavior of the Old English Sheepdog than that of a terrier. In order to suit both his looks and his behavior, we call Prince: a Tibetan Sheepdog. Wonder Wife made business cards for Prince, implying that Prince is the world's only Tibetan Sheepdog.

But now, we have our doubts. A recent re-reading of John Masters' World War II classic, *The Road Past Mandalay* (1961), uncovered the following account of when John and Barbara Masters were hiking above 12,500 feet in the Himalayas:

"...Marmots whistled at us from every stone, and we came upon two shepherds, with their flock, living in a stone shelter which they willingly shared with our porters. Their dogs were Tibetan sheep dogs, huge beasts of the chow family, their coats so thick and matted that even a leopard would have a hard time sinking his fangs through them; and they wore collars made of solid steel, with triple

rows of spikes, hand-beaten and sharpened, six inches long.

"The shepherds told us that these two dogs had killed a leopard down the valley only a month earlier. The dogs eyed us coldly, slow growls rumbling in their deep chests, as ready to kill us as any leopard, if we had come to harm the sheep. When we patted them they looked very puzzled. One tried to wag his tail but he really didn't know how to, and almost threw himself over. Affection was something they had never known, or had forgotten. They were guardians. But they came back for more, and I pulled the thick coats and pushed the heavy heads this way and that in a flood of sympathy. I had something to tell them about our common lot, if only I could speak to be understood..."

Of course, our Prince has known nothing but affection and, in the world of tail wagging, Prince is so proficient there is no danger of him falling over. But now, we are faced with the realization that Prince might not be the world's only Tibetan Sheepdog. Did John and Barbara Masters encounter Prince's ancestors long ago high in the Himalayas? Is our gentle, loving, yet protective, Prince a descendant of those brave guardians of Himalayan sheep?

We don't have any sheep for Prince to guard and we don't have any snow leopards, only mountain lions. Fortunately, we never told Prince of our belief that he is the world's only Tibetan Sheepdog. So, there's no need to trouble him with what a re-reading of *The Road Past Mandalay* has revealed. But now, we are wondering if the time has come to tell him he's adopted?

©2016. 1834

MURDERED SLEEP: IS MACBETH TO BLAME?

Shakespeare claimed "Macbeth does murder sleep." But wait. Maybe Macbeth is not entirely to blame for killing off the benefits of sleep which Shakespeare extolled as follows: *"...Sleep that knits up the raveled sleeve of care. The death of each day's life, sore labor's bath, balm of hurt minds, great nature's second course. Chief nourisher in life's feast..."*

Okay. Macbeth is long dead. So what is making it so difficult for so many 21st Century people to get a "good" night's sleep? In his fascinating history of sleep, *"Wild Nights: How Taming Sleep Created Our Restless World,"* (2017) Emory University Professor Benjamin Reiss says pre-Industrial Age peoples slept a lot differently and maybe even better than we denizens of the 21st Century who have been taught that our best chances for a good eight hours of sleep are found in private, secluded, dark, quiet, properly-mattressed, relatively cool bedrooms, with children exiled to their own room or rooms.

Prior to the Industrial Revolution, men, women and children slept together in ways far different than we moderns. Pre-modern villagers tended to sleep in groups, usually related, but not necessarily. They did so for safety and sometimes to keep each other warm. Instead of the straight eight hours of sleep we are taught to seek, the rustics would sleep for a few hours then wake up for an hour or so of sleepy conversation. Then, back to sleep until the cock crows at dawn. In other words, "segmented sleep."

As darkness fell in the jungles of Vietnam and Cambodia, we became very sleepy -- circadian rhythms at work -- and, unless on watch, we slept well until just before first light, when the enemy were most likely to attack our night-defensive position. Soldiers in two-man foxholes used a form of segmented sleep in that they took turns sleeping, the system enforced by periodic visits from non-commissioned officers and lieutenants, crawling their rounds. Our company headquarters was in the center of the perimeter where the only sound was the almost inaudible rushing noise coming from the radios that connected us to higher headquarters and to our beloved direct-support artillery battery, to the on-call helicopter gunships, and, if need be, to medivac helicopters.

We had no night-time entertainment, save my recitations from what I could remember from the poems of Rudyard Kipling and Robert Service. If that did not put my headquarters troops to sleep, nothing would. To this day, I cannot recite "Gunga Din" clear through without putting myself to sleep. In many ways, we soldiers were like the ancients of yesteryear: a circle of unrelated males practicing segmented sleep for mutual safety. Looking back, the best sleep I can ever recall was on the lumpy jungle floor covered only by a poncho liner.

The mills and factories of the Industrial Revolution depended on workers showing up on time and staying awake through shifts of ten hours or more. No time for napping. Therefore, we can "thank" industrialization and mechanization for where the "civilized" world finds itself today with our ubiquitous laptops, smart phones, caffeine-laced lattes, 24-hour cable TV news and weather. In other words, all the things that keep us from getting a good night's sleep.

©2017. 1895

THE PHUOC VINH FLYING CLUB

Those who remember the TV series *M*A*S*H will recall the zany antics engaged in by the medics to keep themselves sane in the midst of the Korean War insanity. Vietnam was no different.

From 1968 to 1971, the headquarters of the 1st Air Cavalry Division was located near Phuoc Vinh, where this writer spent the latter six months of 1969 as the division's G-3 operations officer. Staying on top of the division's far-flung operations was one of those virtually sleepless 24/7 jobs that can drive you nuts.

To keep ourselves sane, this then Army major, aided by brilliant Army captains "Skip" Taylor, and Bill Lacey, floated rumors about the existence of Phuoc Vinh University, a degree-granting college supposedly run by the USO. Preposterous as it sounds, some were willing to believe that college credits might be available in the middle of a war zone.

A Vietnamese tailor was just outside our barb-wired compound. We got the Vietnamese tailor to print "Phuoc U!" T-shirts. Supply struggled to keep up with demand. We boosted the local economy!

But our zaniest creation was the Phuoc Vinh Flying Club. We felt the usual rumor mill would be insufficient. So, we decided to slip the notice of the organizational meeting of the Phuoc Vinh Flying Club into the Unofficial Section of the division's Daily Bulletin, a division-wide publication.

Mind you, despite the division's over 450 helicopters, there was no way that any of our helicopters could be spared to form an off-duty flying club. But then, a few people had fallen for "Phuoc U!"

The mimeograph stencil (does anyone remember mimeograph?) for the Daily Bulletin was typed each evening in a tropical building right next to the Division Tactical Operations Center, the DTOC. Each night, the clerk-typist for the Daily Bulletin would leave the stencil for the next day's Daily Bulletin in his typewriter, just in case the morning brought the need to add an item at the bottom of the stencil. That done, the clerk would padlock the door and hit the sack.

Noting we had an identical padlock on hand, I had one of my captains switch locks. When the clerk locked up that night, he unwittingly locked up with our lock. In the wee hours, we typed this addition to the Unofficial Section of the Daily Bulletin: *'The organizational meeting of the Phuoc Vinh Flying Club will be held at 1900 hours, on 20 November, 1969, at the USO Center. Soldiers wanting to learn to fly should report 15 minutes early with their health records in hand.''* That done, we switched the lock and stole back into the DTOC.

About 0800 hours the next morning, when the division chief-of-staff read his copy of the Daily Bulletin, a 200-decibel bellow erupted from his tent. He ordered the Military Police to find the culprits. Rather than see precious resources wasted, I confessed to my boss, the G-3, who gave me a quiet, but stern, talking to.

Years later, the chief-of-staff, a newly minted Major General, came to speak at the Naval War College. Sitting next to him at lunch, I asked, "Whatever became of the Phuoc Vinh Flying Club?" He said, "You S.O.B. I always suspected that was you!"

©2017.1903

CHAPTER TWO

CULTURAL CONCERNS

STUDY HARD, KEEP ON DANCING UNTIL IT RAINS

Apparently, the current thinking among Madison Avenue advertising executives is that age 14 is about the age when teenagers develop "brand loyalty." Consequently, many TV commercials are designed to appeal to what the copy writers and producers imagine to be the 14-year-old mind. Whether they understand the 14-year-old mind or not remains to be seen; however, that explains why you see so many young people jerking and twerking around on your TV screen as if they have terminal Sydenham's Chorea (AKA St. Vitus' Dance Disease).

Unfortunately, TV commercials designed for 14-year-olds do not provide more mature viewers much in the way of product description or explain why our existence would be improved by purchasing the product depicted in the commercials. Once suspects, David Ogilvy, known as the father of modern advertising, must be rolling over in his grave.

Ogilvy, for those too young to remember, wrote the most famous print advertising copy in automotive history for Rolls Royce which read: "At 60 miles an hour the loudest noise in this new Rolls Royce is the ticking of the electric clock." But did David Ogilvy dream up that Ad copy while having a Madison Avenue three-martini lunch? No way. Ogilvy believed and taught that copy writers must study and learn every detail about the product being advertised. In fact, the most famous line in automotive print advertising history was discovered by Ogilvy in a technical report written by one of the Rolls Royce engineers.

Ogilvy also dug into the chemistry of Dove soap. He discovered Dove, which was languishing on store shelves, contained one-quarter cleansing cream. Ogilvy's caption that "Dove is 1/4 cleansing cream," made Dove the hand-soap market leader for over 30 years. For American Express credit cards, Ogilvy created, "Don't leave home without it!" an admonition that has become imbedded in the American lexicon.

Yet David Ogilvy's greatest contribution was not to advertising, but to management philosophy. Whenever his firm, Ogilvy and Mather, opened a new branch office, the new executive placed in charge found a set of those Russian Matryoshka nesting dolls on his or her desk. When the executive uncovered his or her way down to the smallest doll, there was this personal note from David Ogilvy: *If each of us hires people who are smaller than we are, we shall become a company of dwarfs. But if each of us hires people who are bigger than we are, we shall* become a company of giants." Granted, in today's PC environment, comparing dwarfs unfavorably to giants would not find favor.

Even so, Ogilvy's credo of detailed study and unremitting hard work brings to mind the tale of the Indian tribe that was renowned for the success of its rain dancers who were always in great demand in the drought-parched areas of the American southwest.

When asked about the secret of his tribe's success, the Indian Chief replied, "It's simple. We keep on dancing until it rains." Parents of today's 14-year-olds might be well-advised to get one of those refrigerator door magnets and post this lesson: "Success comes to those who study hard and keep on dancing until it rains."

©2017. 1904

MARTHA STEWART SERVING?

One time this observer happened to watch Martha Stewart on television. The Domestic Diva demonstrated "the" proper way to fold bath towels. We have folded our bath towels the Martha Stewart way ever since.

At her zenith, Martha Stewart was the world's most successful businesswoman. Not bad for a New Jersey girl from a large and relatively poor Polish family. But her father was not poor in enthusiasm. He mentored Martha to a first place in virtually every activity she attempted.

In her youth, she was a stunning New York fashion model whose academic achievements won her scholarships into a prestigious New York finishing school. And, before she founded her media and product-merchandising empire worth millions, she was a highly successful stockbroker earning over $100,000 per year back when female stockbrokers were almost unheard of.

If ever a female achieved the feminist goal of breaking through the "glass ceiling" of corporate America, it was Martha Stewart. If ever there was a female Horatio Alger, it was Martha Stewart.

But, for some reason, Martha Stewart never became the poster girl for the feminist movement in this country. And, despite her generous contributions to the Clintons and other Democrat political candidates, the feminist Left has largely ignored her enormous achievements. Somewhere I read Hillary's staff, much less Hillary, won't return her phone calls in her time of need.

While one might understand how the Clintons might distance themselves when the Domestic Diva is now in deep do-do, she was never embraced by the feminist movement to begin with. Why?

Here's the answer: Martha Stewart broke through the corporate "glass ceiling" so despised by the feminist Left by doing something even more despised by the Feminazis – she raised homemaking to an art form. Even her rather late-in-life divorce failed to win her higher standing with the anti-traditional-values feminist movement.

Martha's not alone. Here are some other accomplished women whom the Feminazis refuse to celebrate: Former British Prime Minister, Margaret Thatcher; former UN Ambassador, Jeanne Kirkpatrick;

former National Endowment for the Humanities Director, Lynne Cheney; and Violeta Chamorro, the woman whose free election displaced the communist dictator of Nicaragua, Daniel Ortega.

Nor will they celebrate the accomplishments of women who have been in power such as: Senator Elizabeth Dole, National Security Adviser, Condoleezza Rice; Labor Secretary, Elaine Chao; or Congresswoman, Barbara Cubin. Why? Because all of the women named above stand for traditional values.

Conversely, the feminists support liberal politicians even when they have track records of harming women. For example, Senator Ted Kennedy who ran his car off a bridge, leaving one of his female staffers to drown. They refuse to condemn the serial sex-predator, Bill Clinton.

But their biggest failure is their silence about the continuation of the 14th Century treatment of Arab women. The liberation of the Afghan women from Taliban oppression was met with even less enthusiasm than they show for Martha Stewart.

Why aren't they railing against the genital mutilation of young Arab women or the forced extraction of the two upper center teeth of some Arab women so they can pit dates with their teeth more effectively?

Why? Because the feminist movement in America is part and parcel of the political Left, it will only promote and protect those who march to its anti-traditional-values, pro-abortion drumbeat. Deviate from far-Left orthodoxy and you are dead meat. How sad because there was and still is noble work to be done on behalf of women of all political persuasions and parties.

No, they won't speak up for Martha Stewart, one of the most successful women in world corporate history. Instead, the Feminazis are probably hoping a convicted Martha Stewart will end up in the prison laundry putting a fine patina on those government-issued sheets and making sure her fellow inmates have properly folded towels. To the feminist-Left, that would be exactly what Martha Stewart deserves. *NB: Stewart served a term in prison and successfully resumed her career as America's home-maker. Al Jazeera and Qatar Airlines are major sponsors of her TV cooking school. She teaches mostly Arabic cuisine.*

©2003. 1106

AFTER THE REVOLUTION: THERE'S STILL HOPE

As my high school class prepares for its 50th reunion, I wonder why my generation -- the pre-baby boom generation -- did not experience the counter-culture upheaval that came with the baby boomers?

Of course, we weren't angels. But the only behavior problems I recall came from seven or so fellows who, apparently, weren't there to learn and hoped no one else would either. Yes, there was some underage smoking and drinking. But, by and large, our classmates lived the lives depicted by TV's "Leave it to Beaver."

So, why did the generation coming after ours fall into drugs and alcohol abuse, bizarre sexual behaviors and then attempt to counter in every way possible the Traditional American Values Culture built, fostered and protected by earlier generations?

The answer, for this observer anyway, lies in what I call "The Ten P's": Population, the Pill, Penicillin, Playboy, Poisons, Political Folly, Propaganda, Populism, Pop Culture, and liberal Professors

Population. The baby boom (births between 1946 and 1964) created the largest bubble of late teens and early 20s in American history. If people are going to break the law or become revolutionaries that happens, most often, between ages 17 and 23.

Prior to the advent of The Pill and Penicillin, young people feared unwanted pregnancy and/or catching some sexually transmitted disease. The advent of the Pill and Penicillin formed the physical basis of what became the Sexual Revolution.

Hugh Hefner and his Playboy Philosophy provided the Pop Culture Propaganda designed to promote the Sexual Revolution. The so-called intelligentsia took a similar message from the existentialist teachings of Albert Camus and Jean Paul Sartre. Back then, the only news outlets were the in-liberal-lock-step ABC, CBS and NBC which gave rosy coverage to the opinions of Hefner, Camus, Sartre, and even to the prison population-based and factually-flawed findings of the Kinsey Report.

Professor Timothy Leary, and other academics who thought America could be liberated from conservatism by taking LSD and other mind-altering drugs, provided increased acceptability to hard drug use in general, thereby helping to create the drug demand that put much of Central and South America and Mexico into the drug-supply business.

With these P's in place, we entered into a period of Political Folly that became the catalyst (the excuse) for the advent of the counter-culture movement of 1960s.

The 1960 election of John F. Kennedy gave us a President who was good on tax policy but was virtually clueless on military matters. The humiliation he suffered at the hands of Khrushchev in Vienna, and by letting the Russians get away with the Berlin Wall, prompted Kennedy to seek redemption in Southeast Asia.

His assassination in 1963 led to the even more militarily inept President Lyndon Johnson who committed the folly of not heeding Generals MacArthur and Ridgeway and former President Eisenhower who advised against a long drawn-out land war in Asia. Instead of taking the war to North Vietnam and winning quickly, Johnson allowed the war to drag on and on.

Draft age college boys, who were happy lounging about in their "Animal House" dorms and frat houses taking drugs, enjoying the Sexual Revolution and terrorizing college officials, used the Political Folly of Kennedy and Johnson as a reason to dodge the draft. Eventually, they set off a counter-culture revolution that shook our society to its roots and forced Johnson into political oblivion.

The bitter fruits of the counter-culture revolution are: pervasive use of illegal drugs, record numbers of unwed mothers, rampant pornography, child molestations, failing public schools, an epidemic of sexually-transmitted diseases, and a crude Popular Culture that enrages Muslim fundamentalists around the world and people of conscience everywhere.

But, there's hope. Recent surveys of those born between 1982 and 2002 -- the Millennial Generation -- reveal a strong interest in community and national service, in higher academic standards and in a return to the traditional American values that built the greatest nation on earth. *NB: As usual, the surveys turned out to be in error*

©2003. 1117

KICKING THE "YES, BUT," SYNDROME

Have you ever noticed how the mainstream media (AKA the Sinistra Media) cannot report the news without saying: "Yes, but?" If the economy posts 11 months of positive growth, the Sinistra Media will report: YES, the economy is growing BUT, in the month of December, sales did not live up to expectations.

Or, YES, Coalition forces eliminated the leader of al-Qaeda in Iraq, BUT the death of Al-Zarqawi is not expected to win the War on Terror. Apparently, the rule in newsrooms across the nation is that no good news can go unpunished unless a "balance" of bad news is attached to it. Bad news, however, can be reported without the "balance" of good news.

Here's a variation: Housing figures continued to climb, BUT the experts say the growth in housing inventory will reverse that trend. Of course, the experts are rarely, if ever, named.

Following the dismal economic experience of the Carter years, the Reagan tax cuts brought about a boom rivaling the economic recovery that followed World War II. In fact, the economy produced 98 straight months of economic growth. The Sinistra Media reported the good news as follows: YES, the economy just recorded 98 months of growth, BUT the homeless problem remains.

Another Sinistra Media phenomenon is that the homeless disappear from the news during Democrat Administrations only to resurface in the media during Republican Administrations. When the economy boomed under Reagan, the Sinistra Media labeled it a period of greed and corporate mergers that cost people their jobs. Ironically, the eight Clinton years saw more corporate mergers and downsizing (firings) than at any time in our history. Those facts went largely unreported.

All too often, the "yes, but" phenomenon can be heard in ordinary conversation. One person makes a positive statement; however, for some strange reason, the listener feels compelled to respond with: "Yes, but…and so on." Some authorities feel that "yes, but" is a form of verbal abuse.

One of the typically human purposes of making a positive statement to another human being is often to elicit positive feedback such as a simple "yes." Notice the absence of: But.

Some married men are fond of posing this philosophical question: "If a man is alone in the forest and there is no one there to hear him. Is he still wrong?" While amusing, this highlights an actual problem in human communications.

In his seminal book on social psychology, *Influence: The Psychology of Persuasion,* Dr. Robert B. Cialdini, lists six "weapons of influence." One of those weapons is: "Liking." That is, people are easily persuaded by people they like. People are more likely to buy something if they like the person selling it to them. That was the principle behind the success of the Tupperware™ Party. And, of course, a good way to be liked is to avoid what I'll dub: the Yes, But Syndrome.

Family Practice physicians trying to learn how to get patients to be more forthcoming in reciting their symptoms or past medical histories are taught "mirroring," whereby they subtly match the tilt of the patient's head, how the patient's legs or hands are positioned or other mannerisms. Soon, the patient gets the sense of talking with someone wholly sympathetic to them and their problems. Of course, a lot of this was discovered by Dale Carnegie and is contained in his book: *How to Win Friends and Influence People.*

So, while the Sinistra Media are not likely to cure their cases of Yes, But Syndrome, it is probably something we all need to work on. If you do suffer this syndrome, think about kicking your own But. If someone practices it on you, think about kicking theirs.

©2006. 1268

MINISTRY OF TRUTH: NO ENEMIES, WAR'S OVER

Since November 4, 2008, our language has been undergoing a revolution. The terms we learned following the 9/11 attacks are no longer in vogue. Recently, Barack H. Obama declared that the people who killed Americans on 9/11 and continue to kill Americans are no longer "enemy combatants." Moreover, my journalist colleague, Rich Galen, reports a recent memo from the Office of Management and Budget (OMB) saying there is no "War on Terror." If you want your budget approved by OMB ask, instead, for money to fund an "Overseas Contingency Operation."

This sounds like The Ministry of Truth, one of the four ministries described in George Orwell's novella *Nineteen Eighty-Four*. "Newspeak," was the language decreed by the Ministry of Truth. Spoken in "Newspeak," a negative term such as: "ward-heeler" (a worker for a corrupt political boss) might be transformed into the more positive: "community organizer."

But George Orwell's *Animal Farm* may be more germane to today's political environment than Orwell's *Nineteen Eighty-Four*. Readers may recall that the leader of the barnyard animals in *Animal Farm* was Napoleon, who, like his namesake, Napoleon Bonaparte, was not actually born in the place he came to rule.

The animals even cry, "Napoleon is always right." The animals go on to observe: "No one believes more firmly than Comrade Napoleon that all animals are equal. He would be only too happy to let you make decisions for yourselves. But sometimes you might make the wrong decisions, comrades, and then where should we be?"

According to Barnes & Noble's sparknotes.com, "From the very beginning of Orwell's novella, Napoleon emerges as an utterly corrupt opportunist. Though always present at the early meetings of the new state, Napoleon never makes a single contribution to the revolution—not to the formulation of its ideology, not to the bloody struggle that it necessitates, not to the new society's initial attempts to establish itself. He never shows interest in the strength of the animal farm itself, only in the strength of his power over it."

Orwell goes on to observe: "It had become usual to give Napoleon the credit for every successful achievement and every stroke of good fortune. You would often hear one hen to remark to another, 'Under the guidance of our Leader, Comrade Napoleon, I have laid five eggs in six days; or two cows, enjoying a drink at the pool, would exclaim: Thanks to the leadership of Comrade Napoleon, how excellent this water tastes.'"

Napoleon's chief spinner was Squealer, who always put the best possible spin on Napoleon's pronouncements. If the TelePrompTer had been invented in those days,

Squealer would have polished Napoleon's prose and posted it for Napoleon to read.

Both *Animal Farm* and *Nineteen Eight-Four* are considered to be light, bantering looks at the British society that surrounded George Orwell at the end of World War II. For a worldview that is not so light and bantering, read D. Keith Mano*'s The Bridge*, a novel that presents a world dominated by global environmental fascism. A world where the government ultimately promotes the extinction of the human race by enforced mass suicide, so as to "save" the environment.

For those who are not into reading and prefer movies, check out the movie "Soylent Green" in which the people who opt for government-assisted suicide are fed into a machine that turns them into Soylent Green Wafers. The wafers are used to feed the remaining population -- the ultimate in "green" recycling.

But if all the "Newspeak" coming from Washington these days is too troubling, pick up a copy of Voltaire's *Candide,* the story of a very nice person who thinks everyone is as nice as he is. But after encountering more than his share of mean and evil people, Candide retires to his garden -- the same kind of emotional garden into which the Republican Party seems to be retreating until the 2012 elections.

©**2009. 1416**

HAVE A HAPPY NEW(S) YEAR!

There has been so much breaking news that it is hard to keep up: Tiger still isn't out of the woods. He's in a sex rehab clinic in Mississippi. If all they do is talk about sex, that's seems rather counterintuitive.

Vice President Joe Biden held a conference on how to make government more transparent. It was a closed-door meeting.

One of the inherent flaws of capitalism is a natural tendency toward monopoly via sharp business practices, fair or foul. But even after engineering the demise of its former competitor, *The Rocky Mountain News*, *The Denver Post* will seek bankruptcy protection under Chapter 11. Instead of left-winging its so-called news pages, one wonders if a more "fair and balance" approach might increase readership and revenues.

Interestingly, the "fair and balanced" Fox News Channel is raking in huge advertising revenues to the point that Fox News creator, Roger Ailes, is making a higher annual salary than his media-baron boss, Rupert Murdoch.

As Winston Churchill famously said, "The inherent flaw in capitalism is the unequal distribution of benefits. The inherent flaw in socialism is the equal distribution of misery." The Obamessiahs are determined to convert the USA from a health-care system that satisfies over 83-percent of our population into a socialized-medicine system that will make everyone equally miserable.

The U.N.'s climate-change conference in Copenhagen was hit by a blizzard that extended south to the beaches of the French Riviera. Unfortunately, the U.N. organizers messed up the registration procedure to the point that the global warmers were left standing for hours outside the conference hall in blizzard conditions.

The global warmers could have walked over to the Danish Nationmuseet (national museum) and taken shelter; however, they would have been embarrassed by exhibits extolling the exploits of the Viking explorers during the Medieval Warming Period (800 A.D. and 1300 A.D.) Back then, the planet warmed up to the point that the Vikings were able to explore Iceland, Greenland and the fringes of North America. Oops! All that global warming occurred across five centuries when fossil-fueled human activities were limited to cooking fires and forging swords.

Global warming has had its ups and downs. On the upside, food became abundant. Humankind, other animals and plant life thrived as never before. Wine-making extended northward into the British Isles and Scandinavia. On the downside, fewer farm workers were needed. That began the process of urbanization as the displaced workers sought work in town. Unfortunately, the lush times made it easier for disease-carrying rodents to multiply, setting in train the Bubonic Plague that wiped out almost half of Europe's population.

Because its negative impacts were far worse than the Medieval Warming Period, the recent record low temperatures across Europe and North America suggest more study of the Little Ice Age (circa 1600 A.D. to 1850 A.D.) is in order. Famine and death by hypothermia were rampant. Food prices skyrocketed. In 1780, New Yorkers could ice-walk between Manhattan and Staten Island. Entire Swiss towns were crushed by advancing glaciers. Today, one-third of Florida's citrus crop is gone. Florida has been declared a disaster area.

Quite properly, the Obamessiahs are allowing earthquake-displaced Haitians to remain in the U.S. for the next 18 month. Unfortunately, Haitians already here illegally are included in this amnesty, insuring that untold thousands of Haitians will be here for the next election cycle. In the world of the Association of Community Organizations for Reform Now (ACORN,) there are no illegal aliens. They are undocumented Democrats.

The Pentagon report on the Ft. Hood massacre said nothing about Islamic-jihadist terrorism. The report faulted the superiors of Army Major Nidal Malik Hasan for failing to write down their negative observations of Major Hasan. No mention was made of the fact that the political-correctness police would have ended the careers of any officer who had written down anything negative about Major Hasan. Have a Happy New(s) Year!
©2010. 1458

MUSLIM VICTORY MOSQUE: GLOAT VS. RESPECT

Imam Feisal Abdul Rauf is on a U.S. taxpayer-funded trip through the Middle East to bolster support for the construction of what one might think of as the Muslim Victory Mosque (MVM) planned to be a mere 1,056-feet from where 19 Muslims murdered almost 3,000 innocent Americans during the most deadly attack on the U.S. mainland in history.

Imam Rauf says the purpose of the mosque he proposes to locate at 45 Park Place is to build understanding between Muslims and non-Muslims. If Iman Rauf is sincere about his stated purpose, then he must have received some incredibly stupid advice from some Madison Avenue public-relations firm.

Conceivably, the Imam got the bad advice from; let's say satirically, the PR firm of Schmok and Meerhers. In turn, Schmok and Meerhers must have subbed out the MVM location decision to the Muslim-owned Global Location Occupation Advisory Team (GLOAT). No one else would be cunning enough to pick a location that would cast the long Shadow of Islam across the area where so many office workers, firefighters, police and other emergency workers died on September 11, 2001.

Satire aside, we turn now to some serious trigonometry. During summertime, and just after dawn each day, a 13-story mosque located at 45 Park Place would cast a 2,080-foot-long shadow over Ground Zero and well beyond. Therefore, Imam Rauf's idea is so preposterous that it could not possibly have been conceived by Muslims truly seeking better relations with non-Muslims.

Amazingly, some on the Left contend Israel's Mossad must have planted the idea for the MVM location right next to Ground Zero as a way of fomenting anger toward Muslims. If so, the Mossad succeeded.

Alternatively, some think a Christian or Jewish group planted the idea as a way to get the anti-religion, secular-Left to come out in favor of religion in the public square. Recall, for decades the Left (aided by the ACLU) has tried to get Christmas and Hanukkah banned from public places and tried (with some success) to get any kind of religious expressions banned from courtrooms and other public buildings. Prime example: the ban on prayer in public schools.

Suddenly, the anti-religion, secular-Left is rushing to defend the mosque as a vivid and badly-needed expression of tolerance toward religion in public places. If the religious community did, indeed, plant the MVM idea in the head of Imam Rauf, then light up the score board for the Judeo-Christians.

The secular Left would be well advised to read Pulitzer Prize winner Daniel Boorstin's *"The Lost World of Thomas Jefferson"* and discover that Jefferson, the co-founder of the Democrat Party, was so deeply religious that he saw God, the Creator, at work in every animal, plant, vegetable, mineral, star and planet. Today, that is called: Intelligent Design.

Perhaps, Imam Rauf's real purpose is to divide the American people between the anti-religious, secular Leftists (who want the MVM built right next to Ground Zero) and the vast majority of Americans who have no problem with, yet another, New York City mosque; provided, it does not overshadow Ground Zero, literally and figuratively.

If discord among Americans is Imam Rauf's true purpose, then he certainly "set the cat among the pigeons." One way to quiet the pigeons would be to ignore the location recommendation made by GLOAT (we are back to satire) and accept the recommendation of the Relocation for Empathy, Sensitivity, Patriotism, Emotion, and Condolence Team (RESPECT).

RESPECT would place the proposed mosque just inside the southern boundary of the 14.9-acre Carl Schurz Park, which is just across the street from Mayor Bloomberg's Gracie Mansion. That way, the Shadow of Islam would fall on Mayor Bloomberg and not on Ground Zero. Between GLOAT and RESPECT, one suspects many Americans would favor RESPECT.

© 2010. 1491

ON WISCONSIN: COMPARING MADISON AND CAIRO

The behavior of the union-led school administrators and teachers of Wisconsin around their Capitol in Madison reminds one of Germany in the early 1930s or of Cairo in early 2011. According to the *Wall Street Journal*, the sick-out "strikers" pay nothing for their pension costs and only 6% for health-care benefits. Asked to contribute 6% toward their pensions and an additional 6% for their health-care, the teachers turned tempestuous.

Wisconsin faces a $3.5 billion-dollar budget gap. The governor the people of Wisconsin just elected has no choice but to demand that all government employees pony up their fair share to close the budget gap.

That said, this writer tends to be pro-teacher because my sainted Mother taught for decades in the public schools. The pay was meager, the hours were long. She spent her evenings and part of her weekends preparing for classes or studying for an advanced degree that would make her better able to serve her students. Or, she would be talking with parents about how to help their children learn.

When she was teaching 5th and 6th grade, she discovered a young man whom everyone had written off as dull and uncoordinated. At a time when most people had never even heard of dyslexia, she found ways to help him overcome his learning disability. He went on to be valedictorian of his class in another school in Oklahoma. He got so good at basketball that he was recruited by the legendary basketball coach, Henry Iba. Eventually, in another state, he founded a successful chain of outdoor outfitters.

My Mother often said federal aid to education would be the death of teaching the 3-Rs. She said, "If you take Caesar's coin, then Caesar tells you what to do. School policies will be set by bureaucrats in Washington, D.C."

In those days, there were few school administrators and they did double duty as classroom teachers. Each school had a principal and a secretary. The overall system had a superintendent and a secretary. That was it. Outside the 3-Rs, we had chorus, band, and sports led by teachers who, for the most part, volunteered their time to support after-school activities.

Granted, one's memories of those Days of Glory may be less than precise. The great English historian, Sir Lewis Namier, wrote, "One would expect people to remember the past and to imagine the future, but, in fact, when discoursing or writing about history, they imagine it in terms of their own experience. So, they imagine the past and remember the future."

Therein lies the problem with an imagined past. It forms a shaky foundation for predicting the future. For example, the mainstream media and the Obama Administration imagine what they want to hear from the Middle East: Arabs chanting about a yearning for Jeffersonian democracy. Not so.

Yes, the people on the Arab streets would like more food, better transportation, better sanitation, better medical care, and less government corruption. But they are not chanting for freedom of speech for all, for tolerance toward all religions, for women's rights, for doing away with marrying old men to nine-year-old girls, for doing away with honor killings, for stopping the routine mutilation of female genitalia. No way.

Our form of Jeffersonian Democracy would not allow them to continue their barbaric practices with regard to women and to continue to persecute non-Muslims. So, in addition to wanting better food, transportation, sanitation, medical care and less corruption, their basic demand is for a semi-police state that prevents them from slitting each other's throats. Therefore, watch for them to "legitimize" a junta of military officers whose primary function will be to stifle internal violence and, now and then, wage war on Israel.

In that context, the Wisconsin teachers look rather pathetic.

©2011. 1516

HOOKERGATE: BLAME BUSH

Given what his advance "party" in Cartagena, Columbia was doing, Mr. Obama should have skipped his speech at Hooker's Point, Florida, on April 13, 2012. Inevitably, "Hookergate" is now part of the political lexicon.

According to the Old Testament, spying is the world's oldest profession. See: Joshua 2:1 [NIV]. When Joshua sent two agents to gain intelligence about Jericho, the agents contacted Rahab, who was practicing the world's second oldest profession which to this day is the profession of at least 21 hookers in Cartagena, Columbia.

Apparently, Mr. Obama's job-stimulus plan extended all the way to Cartagena where your tax dollars created temporary employment for 21 Columbian women. Some of the Secret Service agents said they did not realize the women for whom they were providing temporary employment were prostitutes. They must have skipped the class on facial- and body-language recognition.

Eleven Secret Service agents and 11 military personnel are under investigation, some dismissed already. Everyone lost their security clearance. The alleged military miscreants include: five Green Berets, two bomb experts, two dog handlers, one sailor, and one airman.

Military apologists suggest the troops were under stress. Hello. Bomb disposers are always under stress. Maybe the dog handlers worried because Mr. Obama says he used to eat dogs. Probably least stressed were the crafty, savior-faire Green Berets who typically have: a divorce, a Randall Knife, a Rolex, a Kimber .45, a star-sapphire ring, and are skilled at working "undercover." As for Hookergate, Chairman of the Joint Chiefs, General Martin Dempsey, said he was embarrassed because military personnel took the spotlight off of Mr. Obama's trip to Cartagena.

When the demand by Cartagena entrepreneur, Dania Suarez, for $800 was negotiated down to $225, late-night TV comedians suggested the Secret Service agent in question should be put in charge of our trade deficit. Coming on top of the $823,000 party thrown by GSA officials in Las Vegas, Hookergate prompted *The Financial Times* to editorialize: "The daily parade of details of incompetence and impropriety among Washington agencies accentuates the findings of a Gallup poll last year which found an alarming loss of public faith in U.S. government institutions."

Recently, Peggy Noonan, writing in *The Wall Street Journal,* noted a decline in the American character. For sure, things have changed. During the Reagan Administration, Wonder Wife and I had three occasions to work closely with the Secret Service and the Reagan-Bush White House when then Vice President Bush twice visited

Lincoln, Nebraska, and once when President Reagan made a speech in Omaha.

The Secret Service agents and the political Advance Men we worked with were serious, sober-minded individuals who were all-business. The Secret Service agents were no fun at all. For one thing, they don't have to be buddies with everyone.

Occasionally, the professional responsibilities of the Secret Service and those of the political Advance Men were in conflict; however, the Secret Service usually prevailed. The political Advance Men want maximum safe exposure of the President and the Vice President to the people. The Secret Service agents want the President and the Vice President to have minimum exposure to the masses. If they had not been so serious, some of the debates we witnessed were almost comical.

Today, when things go wrong, Mr. Obama often points his finger at former President G.W. Bush. Hookergate should be no exception. In the wake of 9/11, the U.S. Secret Service was transferred from the Treasury Department to the newly-created Department of Homeland Security -- where it obviously suffers from a lack of adult supervision. Blame Bush.
©2012. 1620

AMERICAN WORK ETHIC: NOT DEAD YET

In 1904, the world-renowned German sociologist, Max Weber, toured America. Herr Weber found a vibrant people feverously engaged in purposeful, capitalistic, economic activity which Weber characterized as the: Protestant Work Ethic. Actually, the American Work Ethic would have been a better choice of words because Americans of all religions were carrying out their desire to better themselves and their families, resulting in the world's most successful representative democracy and the greatest nation on earth.

But for some Americans who suffered through the Great Depression of the 1930s, World War II, and the Cold War, there is the feeling that the young people of today have lost the American Work Ethic. That too many of them fit the stereotype of a "lost generation," smoking dope, speaking with vulgar language, defacing their bodies, relying on welfare, and chilling out.

Having just spent a week working literally elbow-to-elbow with a movie production company that was using our sailboat as its floating stage property, this commentator-sailor can attest that the American Work Ethic is alive and well. Not since retiring from the military has this observer seen a group of young people so willing to work 12-to-14-hour-days while applying the most meticulous standards of professionalism to their craft. And that does not count the evening hours spent reviewing the day's footage for any errors of framing, lighting, sound, dialogue, and continuity.

On Day One of the filming, so much high-tech electronic gear was installed below deck that our boat's cabin looked like the control room for the launch of a space shot. As for people, Steerage Class on the *Titanic* was probably less crowded.

Topside were the three actors, the writer/director/co-producer, the director of photography and his two assistants, a sound man with a boom microphone, an electronics technician, and yours truly. Alongside was a big pontoon boat carrying a huge light reflector, an assistant producer, a make-up artist, caterers, gaffers, and grips. A rubber dingy used as a messenger boat was alongside as well. From the shoreline, our movie-making flotilla must have looked like a tiny version of the Spanish Armada.

Despite the oxygen-depleted high altitude, the skin-blistering UV rays, and the gusty winds that produced gut-wrenching waves, the crew of 25 mostly-young Americans worked without complaint and unending determination to each do their part at the highest level of movie-making professionalism. Again, other than today's military, this observer was unaware such hard-working young Americans even existed.

The actors for "Teddy Boy," who spent most of their time waiting for the camera, the lighting, and the sound elements to be in place, used their "down-time" to do calisthenics and to rehearse the lines they delivered without any prompting. When called on to dive into 50-degree lake water, the actors did so without complaint.

So, at a time in our nation's history when some doubt that America can remain an exceptionally strong and vibrant nation, it is comforting to know that a company of college-age film students, along with only slightly older actors, directors, and producers are working long, hard hours to perfect their craft with a dedication that would make Herr Max Weber very, very proud.

©2012. 1627

ANNUAL CONFLICT: ATHEISTS VS. BELIEVERS

You can set your calendar by the annual attempts by the adherents of the Atheist Religion to ban any manifestation of Christmas and Chanukah from public view. To front for their disdain for Christianity and Chanukah, in particular, and religion, in general, they use the American Civil Liberties Union (ACLU) which brings lawsuits against units of local government, trying to force them to abandon the centuries-old practices of religious displays during the Christmas and Chanukah seasons.

But why are the Atheists such zealots? What is it that drives the adherents of one religion (believe me, Atheism meets all the traditional theological tests to be classed as a religion) to want to punish the adherents of a different religion by banishing Christian and Jewish icons from public view?

One theory is that the Atheists have this way-down-deep suspicion that they might be missing the boat with regard to Salvation. What if the Atheists are wrong in their devotion to the idea that there is no life after death? What if those who believe in a Supreme Being and believe in a life after death are correct? Ouch!

Maybe the Atheists reason that if they, the Atheists, are going to miss the boat to Salvation, then they must see to it that the rest of humankind misses the boat to Salvation as well. Then, thinking again, they might say there is no Salvation to begin with so there is no boat to be missed. That is certainly the constitutional right of the Atheist Religionists to believe as they do. But every American has the same constitutional right, if he or she so chooses, to believe in a life after death and the idea that living on this earth in certain ways might enhance one's chances of Salvation and offer a shot at experiencing an afterlife in the Forever.

Going around the Internet again this Christmas season, is a youtube.com video of one of those flash mobs cleverly designed to spring up in the middle of a crowded department store, food court, or mall, bringing gorgeous *a cappella* Christmas music to the startled shoppers. If you are having trouble getting into the Christmas Spirit, watching this particular video should fix that problem. While the video is so meaningful to Christians that many are moved to tears of joy, just imagine if you were an Atheist caught in the middle of a shopping mall surrounded by Christians singing in joyful praise of the Christ Child. Man, being suddenly surrounded by joyful people must really be disorienting.

Indeed, when you look at the soaring cathedrals found throughout Christendom that seem to pull the human spirit upward toward the heavens, and when you hear the glorious music performed over the centuries by Christian choirs and congregations, you kinda feel sorry for the

Atheists whose only liturgy is the law suit and whose music seems to be limited to gangsta/acid rock. That alone, proves that the Devil does not have the best tunes.

Merry Christmas and Happy Chanukah!

©2012. 1655

WEAPONS CONTROL: YE OLDE HISTORIE

In Olden Tymes, law-enforcement officers (LEOs) kept the Peace with bows and arrows, swords, and knives. For personal and home defense, the honest, common Folke had the same kinds of weapons. That worked well until someone invented the crossbow and the crossbow arrow; technically, the cross-bow Bolt.

Unfortunately, some Villains obtained crossbows and the LEOs and ordinary Folke found themselves out-Bolted. The Court Fools' Union -- often shortened to F.U. -- demanded the banning of crossbows. The honest, common Folke responded with sayings such as: "When crossbows are banned, only the Villains will have crossbows."

Grudgingly admitting the logic of the honest, common Folke, the Fools' Union demanded a ban on high-capacity cross-Bolt Quivers. They said no Quiver should contain more than five cross-bow Bolts.

Fortunately, some wise Princes saw this circular debate was going nowhere. So, they invented the Castle. Once inside the Castle, you were safe from the Villains outside. In fact, you were protected inside by armed Knyghts. The Knyghts posted signs that read: "Ye who enter here with intent to harm our children will be shot with crossbow Bolts."

While that kept the children safe inside, it did not protect the honest, common Folke on the Commons outside the Castle from ye olde Villains who were insane from dancing inside the tangled forests of their Goth-infested minds.

So, the honest, common Folke put up signs that read: "Register the Insane. Not Crossbows." The Fools' Union and the American Civil Liberties Union (ACLU) objected.

Sometimes, the younger Knyghts cast lustful eyes on the fair Maidens. To fix that problem, the wise Princes invented the Code of Chivalrie which caused the Knyghts to slay would-be rapists with their unregistered Lances.

One day, a Towne Crier maliciously, albeit lawfully, cried out the Names and Castles of the Crossbow Owners. Actually, the wiser Crossbow Owners were delighted because the malicious Towne Crier had tripped over ye olde Writ of Consequences Unintended. Zounds! Now the Villains knew which Folke and which Castles to avoid. Ergo: the Villains would likely commit their raging, insane violence away from the Crossbow Owners. The Crossbow Owners put up signs on their Castles that read: "No Raging Allowed" -- often shortened to NRA.

At the same time, some of the Folke who were living without the protection of crossbows were verily upset. Thanks to the Towne Crier, the Villains knew who amongst the common Folke were unprotected. Soone, there developed a blacke market in both real and faux

NRA signs. In terms of deterrence, the NRA signs were almost as good as possessing a crossbow.

Meanwhile, the Villains held a Rallye to celebrate their victory over the common Folke who had no protection except for the pedestrian Sheriff of Nottingham. (Robin Hood stole his horse.) To maximize their advantage, the Villains rode to New York, Chicago, and San Francisco where the Towne Princes -- whilst surrounding themselves with armed Knyghts -- had taken away the crossbows of the honest, common Folke.

When the honest, common Folke saw the hypocrisy of the Princes of New York City, Chicago, and San Francisco, they forced King John to sign the *Magna Carta* which read, in part: "...the right of the common Folke to keep and bear crossbows shall not be infringed." Now, Ye knoweth the Reste of the Storie.

©2013. 1658

WEAPONS CONTROL: YE OLDE HISTORIE, PARTE II

In Olden Tymes, Good King John was overthrown by Baron Hussein the Omnipotent -- often shortened to BHO -- who trashed the *Magna Carta* and the provision that "the right of the common Folke to keep and bear crossbows shall not be infringed." In fact, the Baron appointed his Court Jester to lead the Court Fools' Union -- often shortened to F.U. -- in an attempt to get the honest, common Folke to turn in their crossbows. The attempt was countered by the Crossbow Owners who met with the Court Jester. But the Jester's only response was the same as the Court Fools' Union. In other words, F.U.

The Baron, the Jester, and the F.U. ignored a study by the Kingdom's Bureau of Investigation (KBI) that the leading killers of the honest, common Folke were: medical malpractice (bleeding), blunt-force instruments such as hammers, edged-instrument such as knives, ale abuse, and drug abuse (herb smoking). Crossbow homicides were at the very bottom of the KBI list.

Meanwhile, the Towne Crier, who hath cried out all the Names and Castles of the Crossbow Owners, hath so displeaseth both crossbow owners and non-crossbow owners to the pointe that the Towne Crier had to hire a bunch of armed Knyghts to protect his Premises. The Amalgamated Association of Retired Perpetrators (AARP) warneth that the Towne Crier hath also made targets of the Crossbow Owners because stolen crossbows were now in high demand and fetching high prices on the blacke market.

With the exception of the armed Castles where the children were now safe from the ragingly insane, nothing meaningful had been done Kingdom-wide to protect the children from the ragingly insane. Verily, the armed Castles had their No Raging Allowed (NRA) signs posted everywhere. But that only protected the NRA Castles. The ragingly insane were still free to roam about looking for Crossbow Free Zones where they could kill innocent children without feare of interference from the honest, common Folke armed with crossbows.

Ironically, the actions of BHO and his Jester increased the demand for crossbows, crossbow bolts, and high-capacity, crossbow-bolt Quivers. Sales of the NRA signs went through the roof.

So, the Sheriff of Nottingham and the other Sheriffs were ordered by the Baron and his Court Jester to collect all the crossbows in the Kingdom. But the Sheriffs saw the Crossbow Owners as helpful in their war against the Villains who would harm the innocent children and the Common Folke as well. So, the Sheriffs, as the most powerful officials in their Shires, refused to do so. Some of the Shires even passed laws forbidding the Baron's men-at-arms from entering their Shires for the purpose of crossbow and high-capacity, crossbow-bolt Quiver confiscation.

For his part, the Baron had his men in Parliament introduce legislation that would make the Baron Ruler-for-Life. As expected, this legislation was endorsed by the AARP, the ACLU, and F.U.

To resolve the crossbow impasse, the warring parties asked a neutral group of academics in Texas at the Sam Houston Institute of Technology -- which is never abbreviated -- to mediate. So, in the end, the entire controversy was turned to, well... you know.

©2013. 1659

RELIGIOUS SYMBOLS: TWAS THE NIGHT *AFTER* CHRISTMAS

Wonder Wife in her kerchief, and I in my cap, had just settled our brains for a long winter's nap when I found myself walking into our town's public square where all the major religions had their symbols on display. There was the Nativity Scene. Close by, was a Menorah representing Judaism. The Crescent of Islam was on display. The seven lighted candles representing Kwanzaa, the African-American holiday, were blazing as well.

About 75-percent of the people were admiring the Nativity Scene. Maybe two-percent were looking at the Menorah. Fewer than two percent were staring at the Crescent of Islam and some people of color were gathered around the seven candles of Kwanzaa. Everyone seemed happy. Well, except for this one lady. She was looking daggers at everyone.

She waved a poster that said in bold letters: "Down with all religions! Get them out of public places!" Except for her hate-filled face, she could have been rather attractive. So, I asked her name. She said, "Polly Amory."

"Season's greetings, Polly," I said, my smiling face displaying good will, even to the angry Miss Amory. "It is the season to be jolly!"

"Not when you are a Secular Progressive Atheist!" said Polly, aiming a one-fingered salute at a startled passerby.

"Look, Polly, the First Amendment gives you the right to practice your Atheist Religion just as it does for all the religions displaying their symbols here on the public square. Surely, you have a symbol other than your middle finger?"

"Atheism is not a religion!" she retorted.

"But surely, you believe in something. You would not be standing out here in the freezing cold unless you have a set of firmly held beliefs."

"Yes, I believe people should not judge each other. Your Holy Scripture in Matthew 7:1 (KJV) says, 'Judge not, lest Ye be judged.'"

"Polly, you seem to be a New Testament scholar. If you are an Atheist, why bother?"

"You must know your enemy. All you fools gawking at your religious symbols are my enemy."

"Oh my! What have we done to make us your enemy?"

"All religions make judgments as to how people are supposed to behave. We want to live as we please. For example, do whatever we want to do. Have sex whenever, wherever, with whomever, or even with whatever we please."

"Polly Amory, perhaps, you are waging a war against 'judgment.' Not a war against religion."

"Religion and judgment are two sides of the same coin!" cried Polly, her unsmiling face sullen with sorrow.

"Polly, you are entitled to your opinion. But aren't these happy, smiling folks here in the public square entitled to their religious beliefs?"

"Karl Marx said, 'Religion is the opiate of the masses.' If people are doped up on religion, they can't focus on Marxist Doctrine. We cannot tolerate competing ideologies!"

"So now, you are against both judgment *and* competition. Frankly, young lady, your annual protests against religion are rather amusing. I know it is un-Christian of me; however, I can't help my feelings of *Schadenfreude.*"

"What's that?"

"Well, if you are so smart, you could look it up."

[*Schadenfreude*: A feeling of enjoyment that comes from seeing or hearing about the troubles of other people.]
©2013. 1710

MINISTRY OF TRUTH: SCHMOK & MEERHERS EMPLOYED

Long-time readers may recall the advertising/public-relations and political-consulting firm of Schmok & Meerhers which has just been awarded a no-bid contract by the Ministry of Truth (formerly known as the Federal Communications Commission (FCC)) to conduct a survey of how the nation's television and radio stations and newsrooms decide which news stories to cover and which news stories to ignore.

As seasoned political operatives, Mr. Ho Lee Schmok and his partner Mr. Erich Maria Meerhers understand their real mission is to identify those media outlets that are critical of the current Administration and recommend to the Ministry of Truth that their FCC licenses be revoked.

Also, long-time readers may notice that both partners, in order to better compete for federal contracts that favor "minority-owned" and "gender-sensitive" businesses, have changed their first names.

"Now that we have this $900,000 no-bid contract from the Ministry of Truth, what's our next step?" asked Ho Lee Schmok of Erich Maria Meerhers.

"We look into the personal backgrounds of all the reporters, commentators, news anchors, TV producers, and newspaper editors to see if they are registered Republicans or Democrats," responded Meerhers.

"I agree," said Schmok. "If we can figure out where they have been politically, we can determine which ones are more likely to be critical of the current Administration and recommend FCC license revocation."

"What about that comedian who makes fun of the current Administration?" asked Meerhers? "I'll bet we can get him replaced by someone favored by the White House. There's the comedian who likes to have the First Lady and the Vice President as guests."

"Right. We'll get him hired. I don't know about the First Lady, but every time the Vice President opens his mouth, people can't stop laughing."

"Look, Ho Lee, I don't mean to stare the gift horse in the mouth; however, I don't understand why the Ministry of Truth would spend $900,000 on this survey when there are so many outfits on both sides of the political aisle that gather media-bias data for free."

"You're correct. On the Left, there are: Media Matters (MM), the Center for Media and Democracy

(CMD), and Fairness and Accuracy in Reporting (FAIR). On the Right there are: the Media Research Center (MRC) and the American Center for Law and Justice (ACLJ) and, near the Center, there is Accuracy in Media (AIM)."

"Those outfits will save us a lot of time and trouble," said Meerhers. "Since our company has never done this type of survey before, we'll just plagiarize some of their findings and work them into our report."

"That's a good idea. But let's also touch base with the IRS. The IRS has a lot of experience targeting and denying tax benefits to groups that oppose Administration policies. Also, they force those groups to spend lots of money on tax lawyers. It's brilliant."

"What about films? Not that Hollywood makes anti-Administration movies."

"Right. But there are independent film makers like that guy who made '2016: Obama's America.' I'm told the IRS, the FCC, and the FBI will silence him."

"Okay. Let's get going. Who's our first target?" asked Erich Maria Meerhers.

"Fox News Channel," said Ho Lee Schmok, heading out the door.

©2014. 1718

SATIRE: THE WASHINGTON WARRIORS?

In the Virginia U.S. Senate race, the GOP contender wants the Washington Redskins to retain their name. The Democrat incumbent refuses to take a stand. Recently, the

Redskins defeated the Dallas Cowboys whose name, by the way, ignores the many contributions made by women in the winning of the West. Maybe they should be the Dallas Cowpersons? Also, those scantily clad cheerleaders are probably offensive to Muslims.

After Clarence Page of *The Chicago Tribune* wrote a column urging the Washington Redskins to change their name, Mr. Larry McGrorty responded to Mr. Page with a satirical email which has been edited here for brevity and for good taste:

"Dear Mr. Page:

"...I am highly insulted by the racially charged name of the Washington Redskins. One might argue that to name a professional football team after Native Americans would exalt them as fine warriors, but nay, nay. We must be careful not to offend, and in the spirit of political correctness and courtesy, we must move forward.

"Let's ditch the Kansas City Chiefs, the Atlanta Braves and the Cleveland Indians. If your shorts are in a wad because of the reference the name Redskins makes to skin color, then we need to get rid of the Cleveland Browns.

"The Carolina Panthers obviously were named to keep the memory of militant Blacks from the 60's alive. Gone. It's offensive to us white folk.

"The New York Yankees offend the Southern population. Do you see a team named for the Confederacy? No! There is no room for any reference to that tragic war that cost this country so many young men's lives.

"I am also offended by the blatant references to the Catholic religion among our sports team names. Totally inappropriate to have the New Orleans Saints, the Los Angeles Angels or the San Diego Padres.

"Then there are the team names that glorify criminals who raped and pillaged. We are talking about the horrible Oakland Raiders, the Minnesota Vikings, the Tampa Bay Buccaneers and the Pittsburgh Pirates!

"Now, let us address those teams that clearly send the wrong message to our children. The San Diego Chargers promote irresponsible fighting or even spending habits. Wrong message to our children.

"The New York Giants and the San Francisco Giants promote obesity, a growing childhood epidemic. Wrong message to our children.

"The Cincinnati Reds promote downers/barbiturates. Wrong message to our children. The Milwaukee Brewers. Well, that goes without saying. Wrong message to our children.

"So, there you go. We need to support any legislation that comes out to rectify this travesty, because the government will likely become involved with this issue, as they should. Just the kind of thing the do-nothing Congress loves.

"As a diehard Oregon State fan, my wife and I, with all of this in mind, suggest it might also make some sense to change the name of the Oregon State women's athletic teams..."

As the mid-term elections suggest, the truly offensive part of the NFL team name is "Washington," not Redskins.

But if the Redskins have to go, how about: The Washington Warriors? Not only is that alliterative, the Warriors have always been this fan's favorite team.

NB: The Oregon State women's teams are called: the Beavers.

©2014. 1754

LIFE IN THE PEOPLE'S REPUBLIK OF AMERIKA

An allegory: Seth and Sarah decided to marry; however, they needed State permission. Only the portrait of the U.N. Secretary General adorned the Office of the Justice of the Peace who checked their ID cards, asked them to verify that they possessed no fire arms, and handed them their Certificate of Marriage.

A Gay couple was in line behind them. One of the Gays thought Seth and Sarah looked Jewish; however, that would be Lookism, the forbidden practice of cataloging people by how they look. The other Gay wanted to wish Seth and Sarah "Mazel Tov!" but held his tongue for the same PC reasons.

Seth and Sarah headed for their Manhattan State-owned apartment. Due to the rotten economy, they had wanted to move in with Sarah's parents in the Hamptons; however, that home was shut down by the State because its many fossil-fueled electrical appliances were considered anti-environment.

They had no wedding cake. The Muslim bakeries would not bake baklava cakes for Gay or Jewish weddings. The Christian bakeries would not bake red-velvet wedding cakes for Gays. The Atheist bakeries would not bake angel-food cakes for people of religious faith. The Agnostic bakeries did not know what to bake. As a consequence, there were no more store-bought wedding cakes.

Seth and Sarah had hoped for a traditional family celebration; however, to dance the Horah and clap hands to Hava Nagila were considered offensive to the growing Muslim population. In fact, everything was now forbidden except that which had been expressly permitted by the new U.N.-controlled government. There was no longer any joy in what the Rev. Jesse Jackson had once described as "Hymie Town."

Due to the Obama/Jarrett Plan, the Iranians had become a nuclear power, although, like the Israelis, the Mullahs denied it while, at the same time, letting the Israeli population know that Tel Aviv could be wiped out in a New-York-minute.

In response to Iran, the Saudis and the Gulf State Arabs armed themselves with enough nukes to incinerate the world. Israel's future was so much in doubt that emigration by Jews into Israel had stopped. Israelis with children to raise were leaving for safer lands. Investment capital was flowing out. Israel's Arab population would soon outnumber the ethnic Jews and the Knesset would come under Islamic control.

Before leaving to get their marriage certificate, Seth had carefully shut down his desktop computer. Yet it had mysteriously turned itself on and words were being typed by somebody from far away. Seth thought: *Wow, this is like what happened to Sheryl Attkisson, that investigative reporter who tried to investigate Fast and Furious, the IRS, and Benghazi.*

The computer screen read: *"People of your faith are no longer authorized to practice a long list of professions which you are directed to read when you report to your local government headquarters. There, you must pick up distinctive arm bands to wear when you and your new wife are in public. This is a public-service announcement provided by your political party. Thank you for your previous donations. Have a nice day."*

Sarah invited Seth into the kitchen where she had cobbled together a White House-approved wedding cake. It was made of kale and tofu. No icing.

©2015. 1777

THE WAR ON SYMBOLS

There's lots of talk about removing symbols that offend one activist group or another. Just to name a few symbols: Confederate Flags, Christian Crosses, the Ten Commandments, Swastikas, Hanukkah Menorahs, Christmas Manger Scenes, and Wedding cakes. Well, folks who grew up in Indian Territory (now Oklahoma) have many good reasons to be offended by President Andrew

Jackson; so, while we are banishing symbols, let's remove Andrew Jackson from the face of the $20 dollar bill. Here's why:

In 1816, General Andrew Jackson led the efforts to exterminate the Seminole Indians of Florida. Memo to the National Association for the Advancement of Colored People (NAACP): The Seminoles were a mix of Native Americans and African-Americans. Reverends Al Sharpton, Jesse Jackson, and Wright, pay attention.

Most of the Seminoles were killed in battle during the course of three Seminole Indian Wars that raged intermittently between 1816 and 1858. The few Seminoles who were not killed outright by U.S. troops led by General Jackson were placed in concentration camps in central Florida.

Memo to the British: On December 24, 1814, you signed The Treaty of Ghent, signifying your defeat by the United States in the War of 1812. But, to add insult to injury, two weeks after you had already surrendered, General Jackson, at the Battle of New Orleans, put your Royal Army to ignominious flight: *"Yeah, they ran through the briars. And they ran through the brambles. And they ran through the bushes, where the rabbit couldn't go. They ran so fast that the hounds couldn't catch 'em, on down the Mississippi to the Gulf of Mexico..."* One suspects many Britons would be jolly-well pleased to see Jackson banished from the American's $20 dollar bill.

In 1830, President Andrew Jackson pushed the Indian Removal Act through Congress. Members of the Five Civilized Tribes, the: Cherokees, Chickasaw, Choctaw,

Creek, and the few remaining Seminoles were forced by President Jackson onto the infamous Trail of Tears to Indian Territory, which is modern-day Oklahoma. Along the Trail of Tears over 4,000 Cherokees perished. During Jackson's eight years as president, over 45,000 Native Americans were forced to give up their lands to white settlers and walk the over 2,200 miles to Oklahoma.

Along the Trail of Tears, the Native Americans were sometimes packed into hastily constructed concentration camps where many died of communicable diseases. The exposure, diseases, and starvation experienced by the Native Americans along the Trail of Tears puts one in mind of 1915 when the Turks marched 1.5 million Armenians to death or 1942 when the Japanese conducted the Bataan Death March that killed almost 10,000 Filipinos and 650 Americans. Memo to the American Indian Movement (AIM): Andrew Jackson was not your friend.

Now, in place of President Jackson on the $20 dollar bill, imagine a photograph of Caitlin Jenner. In one stroke, our currency would be rid of Jackson, the racist, genocidal, Indian-killer, Anglophobe and, at the same time, honor a person who would please the Lesbian, Gay, Bi-Sexual, Transgender (LGBT) Coalition and five members of the U.S. Supreme Court.

Memo to Andrew Jackson supporters: President Jackson would not be banished entirely. As co-founder of the Democratic Party, he will still be celebrated at the annual Jefferson-Jackson Day Dinners.

©2015. 1788

REBELLION: BLOWING IN THE SAGEBRUSH?

Almost 20 years ago, Wonder Wife and I were on horseback on the King Ranch northwest of Granby, Colorado. Between our horses rode the legendary western singer, Michael Martin Murphey. As we rode along, the bizjet-owning Murphey suggested our local airport would attract more traffic by having its own web pages plus an automated weather observation system, an AWOS. Not long after, www.granbyairport.com was created. And, if you dial 970.887.1803, anyone with a landline or a cell phone can hear the automated weather broadcast from Granby/Grand County Airport -- Emily Warner Field.

Yet the larger importance of our conversation had to do with the lyrics of Murphey's hit single "Rangeland Rebel." We did not understand it at the time; however, Michael Martin Murphey was foretelling what we witnessed last week when we saw long lines of voters waiting, in some cases, for as many as three hours to cast their votes in the Republican and Democratic caucuses and primary elections. And not just anywhere. But in sagebrush-covered western states spreading from the Canadian to the Mexican border.

We may be witnessing the rebirth of the Sagebrush Rebellion, the tide that swamped Jimmy Carter and lifted Ronald Reagan into the White House. Why? Because people on both sides of the political aisle and independents are fed up! Fed up with throwing away American lives without victory. Fed up with America's loss of stature in the world. Fed up with economic policies that punish small businesses, salaried workers, and seniors on fixed incomes. Fed up with a fantasy health-care scheme. Fed up with a Republican-Democrat coalition in Washington that seems tone deaf to the concerns of work-a-day Americans.

A few verses from "Rangeland Rebel" illustrate the frustrations we saw welling up last week out of the Rocky Mountains.

"...Now gather 'round cowboys.
Saddle up a good horse.
And ride for your land,
Or it'll be a golf course.
Before they tear down the mountains,
And cover the trails,
You won't find the bean counters,
When the banks start to fail.

"In a high rise in Denver, there's a CEO.
Can't wait for the winter.
Take your water for snow.
He'll charge you for water.
He'll charge you for air.
Cheat his own son and daughter,
For his insider share.

"You might wake up one morning
And get a big shock.
To see the name 'Ted and Jane' on your neighbor's mailbox.
But it ain't Ted and Jane's fault.

It's the ones who sell out.
Put the money in the bank vault,
Before they get the hell out..."

With Murphey's permission, we sprinkled those verses through *The Grand Conspiracy* by William Penn, our novel about how the waters of the Rocky Mountains were "stolen" to accelerate urban sprawl along Colorado's Front Range.

Now, fast forward to 2016: Ironically, today's front-running candidates, both Democrat and Republican, are distrusted by 65-percent of the American people. That runs counter to the spirit of the Sagebrush Rebellion that calling for America to saddle up an honest, straight-shooter president who will ride in support of the Constitution and the Bill of Rights. Come November, pray America elects a true Rangeland Rebel.

©2016. 1829

DO ALL LIVES MATTER?

Depending on one's value system, it can be said that some lives can be judged to be of more value than others. Mother Theresa comes to mind. So, if you can find a place where ambient urban light does not blot out the Milky Way, lie out under the stars and planets some cloudless night and contemplate how we humans fit into the infinite Universe.

While lying there, try to realize that if it were not for the Law of Gravity (which, despite some liberal claims,

President-Elect Trump does not intend to have repealed), each of us would be hurled out into space. After all, we are traveling around the Sun at 67,000 miles-per-hour and the Earth is rotating at 1,040 miles-per-hour. No telling how far centrifugal force would fling humankind out into space. (Probably, depends on body mass.) Ergo: we can thank our Creator for the Law of Gravity and Isaac Newton and Albert Einstein for explaining Gravity to us. But, lest those three fail us, it might be a good idea to keep our seat belts fastened at all times.

So, realizing we are the tiniest imaginable specks in a Universe so large that it is beyond imagination, we come to the question: Do some human lives matter more than some other human lives? And, if so, to whom?

Human nature being what it is, we can posit that most humans would like to amount to something, to be lauded by their peers for their accomplishments. Granted, we are not all born physically or mentally equal nor are we all nurtured by loving, well-educated parents. So, if life were played out on an Olympic running track, the starting blocks would be staggered way back around the track.

Inexplicably, some, whose starting blocks were at the very front, stumble and fall. Others, whose circumstances placed them well behind the others, somehow manage to struggle forward and be first across the finish line. Countless books on leadership and management are written trying to explain why some people succeed and why some people fail.

But success or failure, like beauty or ugliness, is in the eyes of the beholders. Consider the genetic scientist whose minor discovery does not garner acclaim but one day leads to the prevention of cancer. Consider as well the scientist whose string of failures points the way for other scientists to go in more promising directions. Both lives matter. Or, to quote the poet, John Milton: "...They also serve who only stand and wait."

But it gives one pause to see so many of today's millennial-snowflake, youth shuffling along, eyes downcast, thinking their tattered jeans, scruffy facial hair, tattoos, and body piercings count for something, while their ear buds blot out any chance of hearing the kind of still, small, inner-voice that must have spoken to a Mother Theresa, a George Washington Carver, a Thomas Edison, or to a Jonas Salk. President Ronald Reagan often spoke about the optimist who looked at a pile of manure and said, "There's got to be a pony in there somewhere." So, we end the tumultuous year 2016 with the certainty that all lives matter and with hope for a better 2017 to come.

©2016. 1869

E PLURIBUS UNUM? STILL NOT THERE

Whenever the Martin Luther King, Jr. national holiday comes around, this writer's thoughts go back to the late 1960s when some of us thought our marching footsteps would stomp Jim Crow into dust. Well, yes and no. While we have witnessed the rise of a class of African-American professionals, we have also witnessed the rise of a class of professional African-Americans. The former are exemplified by Professors Thomas Sowell and Walter Williams, Dr. Ben Carson; the writer, Shelby Steele; and by U.S. Supreme Court Justice, Clarence Thomas, just to mention a few. The latter are exemplified by the Revs. Jesse Jackson, Jeremiah Wright, Al Sharpton, and Louis Farrahkan, to mention far too many.

Unfortunately, there remains an African-American underclass which, unlike the upwardly mobile Jewish experience in America, resists assimilation into the mainstream culture and even has its own manner of speaking which is called: Ebonics, defined as: "American black English regarded as a language in its own right rather than as a dialect of standard English."

Writing in the January, 2015, issue of *Imprimis*, Jason L. Riley of *The Wall Street Journal*, recounts a visit to the Buffalo, NY, neighborhood where he grew up: "I was visiting my older sister shortly after I had begun working at *The Wall Street Journal*, and I was chatting with her daughter, my niece, who was maybe in the second grade at the time. I was asking her about school, her favorite subjects, that sort of thing, when she stopped me and said, 'Uncle Jason, why you talk white?' Then she turned to her little friend who was there and said, 'Don't my uncle sound white? Why he tryin' to sound so smart?'

"... I couldn't help thinking: Here were two young black girls, seven or eight years old, already linking speech patterns to race and intelligence. They already had a rather sophisticated awareness that, as blacks, white-sounding speech was not only to be avoided in their own speech but mocked in the speech of others.

"... My siblings, along with countless other black friends and relatives, teased me the same way when I was growing up. And other black professionals have told similar stories. What I had forgotten is just how early these attitudes take hold—how soon this counterproductive thinking and behavior begins..."

Mr. Riley's niece has a choice: She can remain in her current culture or she can choose to follow her uncle into the dominant mainstream culture. Her decision will likely be decided on the basis of which culture offers her the greater value. And that bring us to the late Robert Ruark's 1955 bestseller: *Something of Value* in which Ruark contended that the only way for the British colonials to get the insurgent Kikuyu tribe to end its rebellion was to offer them admission and status within the then existing British colonial culture.

But *E Pluribus Unum* was not the British settlers' cup-of-tea. So, by 1963, the British found themselves second-class citizens in a Kikuyu-ruled Republic of Kenya.

In this country, a recent Rasmussen Poll finds race relations have grown worse over the previous eight years. Pray, in the years to come, that jobs, good jobs, will provide that missing "something of value."

©2017. 1873

THOUGHT CONTROL AND THE MSM

Ever wonder what some of TV's on-air personalities talk about among themselves when they think they are not on the air? James O'Keefe's Project Veritas is in the process of making public over 100 hours of audio "out-takes" from CNN. But you won't have to listen to all 119 hours of audio to determine if CNN is a fair and balanced news source or not. Hint: Not.

But CNN is not the only member of the myth-stream media (MSM) making news. Recently, MSNBC's Mika Brezezinski, the co-host of MSNBC's "Morning Joe," said, "[Trump] is trying to undermine the media and trying to make up his own facts. And it could be that while unemployment and the economy worsens, he could have undermined the messaging so much that he can actually control exactly what people think. And that, that is our job."

Ms. Brezezinski's conception of the role of the media brings to mind the "Ministry of Truth," as conceived by George Orwell in his classic novel "1984." For those who never read "1984," or lost their copy of Cliff's Notes or Spark Notes, the novel's hero, Winston, labors in the Ministry of Truth re-writing history to make history politically correct. Although published in 1949, "1984" predicted the rise of the Politically Correct (PC) movement in this country in the 1960s.

In "1984," The Ministry of Truth is busily engaged in creating a language known as "Newspeak." Certain words deemed politically incorrect are deleted from the

"Newspeak" dictionary. The definitions of other words are changed to be more politically correct. For example: "Freedom," in the sense of freedom-of-thought is banned. But "free," as in a "free coupon" for groceries, is okay.

But Orwell's greatest contribution to today's political situation is "Doublethink," which means the ability of keeping two totally contradictory thoughts in mind at the same time and being wholly accepting of both of them. For example: Virtually all college faculty and staff say they support "free speech." But if students invite a conservative speaker on campus, the conservative speaker is either banned from speaking at all or shouted down by liberal faculty, staff, and students. In urban areas, we are seeing riots in opposition to the Trump Administration's supposed "totalitarianism." But the rioters are using violence reminiscent of Hitler's Brown Shirts. Another classic example of "Doublethink."

The deplorable, dumbed-down state of public education in certain urban areas brings to mind Aldous Huxley's "Brave New World," published in 1932. The novel begins at the state-run hatchery where human embryos are injected with chemicals designed to produce humans in five classes in descending order of mental and physical abilities: Alpha, Beta, Gamma, Delta, and Epsilon. The Alphas are programmed to be leaders. Epsilons are programmed to be morons. None of the classes are capable of forming rebellious thoughts.

If, at this point, your mind reflects back on Ms. Brzezinski's idea that the role of today's media is "to tell you exactly what to think," you might want to revisit

"1984," "Brave New World," and, while you are at it, Orwell's "Animal Farm" (1945). Although British, both Huxley and Orwell were amazingly prescient about what is happening in today's America.

©2017. 1878

THE NIGHTMARE OF THE LIVING ALGORITHMS

In Miss Tarpley's ninth-grade algebra class, this survivor does not recall Miss Tarpley using the word "algorithm." In fact, and until recently, I thought Algorithms referred to a rock band led by a former U.S. vice president.

For sure, Miss Tarpley taught us about equations which she insisted be kept in balance and even expanded. But once you started expanding equations, they, like zombies, would take on a "life" of their own, running clear off the chalk board, across the wall, and end up out in the hall at an enormous expense of caulk which someone who threw spit balls in class had to stay after school and clean up.

Today, those of us who use Internet search engines and news-gathering websites face a threat much greater than Miss Tarpley's algebraic equations. With almost every stroke we make on our computer keyboards, we attract the attention of one or more or even hundreds of algorithms lying in wait to record our interests, our likes, and our dislikes.

Let's say you buy a circular saw on Amazon.com. Almost immediately, you will be informed about accessories to go with your saw. You will also be reminded of your previous searches for other items. That is a rather benign and even helpful use of algorithms.

But what if you are a writer of espionage novels and you do Internet research using words related to that particular genre? Certain key terms, such as bomb-making, are of interest to those whose job it is to protect us from the Islamic terrorists and others. Searching certain words could lead to an unpleasant visit from the FBI. On a lighter note, consider the joke about the man who dialed a suicide hot line and was transferred by an algorithm to a call center in Pakistan. After explaining his intention to take his own life, the guy in Pakistan got excited and asked, "Can you drive a truck?"

Seriously, some packages of algorithms can be used to predict future events such as when and where crimes are likely to occur in urban areas. A package of algorithms called: Criminal Reduction Utilizing Statistical History (CRUSH) combines crime statistics with outside temperature/humidity and housing area maps to identify crime "hot spots."

On August 4, 2005, the Memphis police, directed by CRUSH, deployed in certain areas over a three-day period, making 1,200 arrests, and achieving a 25-percent reduction in crime. According to University of Memphis Professor Richard Janikowski, "It is putting the right people in the right places on the right day at the right time." But not everyone is a fan of CRUSH; in particular, the American Civil Liberties Union (ACLU).

By the way, some algorithms talk to each other. So, do not be surprised after you have expressed an interest in something or subject on one website when the next website you visit confronts you with advertisements related to your visit at the previous website. And be aware those devices such as Amazon's Alexa are always recording what you say to "her." Finally, if you are reading this column on-line at: www.central-view.com, some algorithm may have brought this column to your attention. Some algorithms are more discerning than others.

© 2017. 1900

OBAMACARE: THE LOVABLE SHMOO

In 1948 cartoonist Al Capp invented the Shmoo, a lovable creature that produced bottles of Grade A milk, cage-free eggs, and would even convert itself into filet mignon for grilling after which a Shmoo's owner could use its charred whiskers for toothpicks.

For some, but not all, ObamaCare is a Shmoo: a government-mandated health-insurance scheme which is openly adored by the Democrats who created ObamaCare without a single Republican vote. ObamaCare is secretly beloved by certain Republican members of Congress who claim they want to repeal and replace ObamaCare but will not cast meaningful votes to do so.

Republicans have taken in tons of money from donors who want to see the end of ObamaCare. Democrats have raised tons of money from donors who want to see ObamaCare protected. A bi-partisan Shmoo.

Members of Congress and staff do not participate in "true" ObamaCare as ordinary citizens must. President Obama had Congress declared a "small business," clearing the way for Congress and staff to enjoy Gold-level health insurance with 72-percent of their premiums subsidized by you and me. Plus, they have free or low-cost care from congressional medics and free outpatient care at D.C.-area military medical facilities. Super Shmoos.

Young adults under age 26 can remain under their parent's health-insurance coverage. A Shmoo for Millennials. ObamaCare provides a Shmoo for employers who do not want to offer health-insurance to their workers: By cutting the full-time workforce to below 50 employees or by moving to less than 30-hours-per-week part-time jobs, ObamaCare lets employers off Scot-free. Although these personnel reductions might make employers richer in the short run, in the long run, the reduction in the workforce stagnates economic growth. A counterproductive Shmoo.

Hospital emergency rooms, which had been treating the uninsured for "free" and passing those costs onto paying patients, are enjoying the $714 billion President Obama took away from Medicare. Money being fungible, those billions are made available to emergency rooms via the tax-payer-funded welfare program for the indigent called: Medicaid. Teaching Hospitals enjoy their total tax exemption which is protected under ObamaCare. Certain industries, trade unions and associations within the Obama donor/voting bloc support ObamaCare because, via executive orders, President Obama exempted them from ObamaCare mandates. Super Shmoos.

Still, not everyone wanted to buy ObamaCare insurance. Seventy-three percent of those who bought ObamaCare insurance only did so to avoid paying what Chief Justice Roberts calls a "tax." Those who refused to buy health insurance paid over $3 billion dollars in "taxes." A Shmoo for the U.S. Treasury.

Initially, insurance companies liked the idea that some 20 million young, unlikely-to-get-sick uninsured would be forced to buy health insurance or pay the "tax." But the pre-existing condition provision is forcing some insurers to stop providing any kind of coverage.

As radio commentator Mark Steyn suggests, ObamaCare's provision for pre-existing medical conditions could be used as a model to also wreck the home-insurance industry. Just imagine fire or a tornado totally destroys your home. Then, and only then, do you sign up for home insurance. Just like ObamaCare, the home-insurance industry would have to raise premiums and deductibles to unaffordable heights or go out of business.

Tip for President Trump: Use your pen to put Congress and staff under "actual" ObamaCare and let's see what happens.

©2017. 1901

CHAPTER THREE

GEOPOLITICAL

THE FRENCH MILITARY: AN UNFAIR JOKE?

The recent antics of French President Jacques Chirac have given rise to yet another round of jokes about the French military. Actually, this is somewhat unfair because the problem is, and always has been, with their civilian masters who are weak yet seek a place in world affairs no longer warranted by France's position in the post-colonial world.

If you have ever spent any time traveling around France, you know it is mostly one huge farm surrounding one major city called: Paris. The farmers are more interested in government subsidies than world affairs, and their elected representatives reflect that view. The population of Paris is now more devout Muslim than practicing Catholic. In fact, there are parts of Paris where the French equivalent of our Secret Service won't allow President Chirac to visit.

Until recently, Wonder Wife and this observer were planning to spend a week cruising through the canals of

Burgundy on one of those barges the French have fancied up to serve as luxury tourist accommodations. I was even fond of telling the joke about how sailing through Burgundy stains the bottoms of the barges. But only on the left side. It's called: (get ready) Port Wine Stain.

However, given the recent ungrateful behavior of the French, Germans, and Belgians, we won't be spending any money in those countries. Instead, we will probably take a barge trip through the canals of true allies Scotland or Ireland or England. I even wrote our Congressional delegation urging legislation saying we won't accept any more *Merde du Chirac, 2003.*

One of the many jokes about France asks: "How many Frenchmen does it take to defend Paris? No one knows. It's never been tried." Actually, the French did defend Paris when it was under siege by the Germans during the Franco-Prussian War of 1870-71. But their most aggressive action was to launch dozens of hot air balloons to observe the Prussian artillery positions and to drift balloons toward the West containing urgent appeals for other nations to come to their rescue. The French, of course, surrendered before Paris suffered much damage. But, as you can tell from the recent speeches of French President Chirac (Saddam's long-time friend and business partner) they still produce hot air.

Ironically, in the peasant uprising after the French surrender, the French Army killed over 20,000 French citizens; proving the French, like Saddam Hussein, are more adept at killing their own people than their enemies.

More jokes: "Why are French streets tree-lined? So the Germans can march in the shade. What do you call 100,000 Frenchmen with their hands up? The Army. FOR SALE: French military rifles. Never fired, only thrown down once."

Actually, this observer has some respect for some parts of the French military. When I commanded an airborne battalion in West Germany, we had an informal arrangement with the French Special Forces and the French Foreign Legion stationed just inside West Germany in the town of Langenargen. After doing some parachute jumps with the French, I came to admire the French "paras," as they like to be called. Later, when I commanded an armored cavalry squadron at the Fulda Gap, we continued our relationship. The first language of many Legionnaires is German, not French. Since my German is better than my French, this made for an easy relationship.

Ironically, France's only successful fighting force is staffed by Legionnaires who, by law, cannot be French by birth. The web pages for the French Embassy in Washington, D.C. say this about *La Legion Etrangere Francaise*: "Foreign by birth, the Legionnaires have become Frenchmen by the blood they have spilled." The French Embassy goes on to point out that 902 officers, 3,176 non-commissioned officers and over 30,000 other ranks have died as Legionnaires fighting for France.

Reluctantly, the French admit the Legion's biggest problems are petty theft and desertion. But the larger question is about a nation whose best fighting force is mostly made up of mercenaries who cannot be born in the country they serve.

©**2003. 1091**

This article appeared in the June 30, 2004, issue of USA Today

'HEARTLAND' STRATEGY IN IRAQ: RIGHT IDEA, IF DONE THE RIGHT WAY

Some critics like to say American foreign policy is discernible only in retrospect. Even so, such opinion could be taken as a left-handed compliment for a nation that has done rather well in defending itself and its allies in the previous century, and now, at the beginning of the 21st Century as well.

While it may be too early to put a name to the Grand Strategy we are employing with regard to Iraq, just "being there" suggests we may someday look back and find that we have been employing the Heartland Theory as put forth in 1904 by Sir Halford John Mackinder – one of the great strategists of the 20th Century.

Here's how the Heartland Theory would apply to Iraq: Get a globe and put your finger on Iraq. Notice how your finger is resting right in the middle, the "heartland," of the Middle East, halfway between Egypt and Pakistan. In 1904, British geographer Sir Halford John Mackinder placed his finger on Eastern Europe and declared that to be the "pivot area" or "heartland" of Europe. Sir Halford declared: "Who commands Eastern Europe commands the heartland; who rules the heartland commands the world-island, and who rules the world-island commands the world." (By world-island, he meant the Euro-Asian-African landmass.)

Did anyone buy the Heartland Theory? Yes. Napoleon understood it even before Mackinder was born. That is why he attacked Czarist Russia. Moreover, Kaiser Wilhelm II, Adolph Hitler, Josef Stalin and three generations of the world's foremost military strategists embraced it as gospel and acted upon it.

German Kaiser Wilhelm II formed the Central Powers with Austria. Hitler attacked European Russia, and Stalin knew the loss of European Russia would put Hitler in charge of his industrial heartland. Bye, bye communist-fascism. Hello, Nazi fascism.

Even now, the U.S. is moving NATO into the heart of Mackinder's Heartland with the addition to its ranks of Bulgaria, the Czech Republic, Estonia, Hungary, Latvia, Lithuania, Poland, Romania, Slovakia and Slovenia.

Just being there is enough.

The essential element in the Heartland Theory is simply "being there." Properly applied, being there means Iraqi oil revenue cannot go to al-Qaeda. Being there means the Iraqis can choose whatever government they want as long as it does not support terrorism. Being there means interdicting the radical Islamists' lines of communication that run across the Middle East from Cairo to Islamabad.

But being there need not include the imposition of a Pax Americana on Iraq's cities. The inevitable collateral damage of urban warfare creates a no-win situation in a news media world dominated by the hostile Al-Jazeera TV network and by a Western media that daily prove the dictum: Bad news will travel around the world before good news can tie its shoelaces.

George Friedman, who runs a private intelligence service, suggests the U.S.-led coalition can still be there while, at the same time, withdrawing our troops from Iraqi cities. By occupying a series of desert outposts, we retain the strategic advantage of being in the heartland of the Middle East. If al-Qaeda or the Iraqi insurgents want to fight our troops, they must expose themselves in the open desert, where their rusting, bomb-laden pickups are no match for our Abrams Tanks and Bradley Fighting Vehicles. Our casualties would plummet. Theirs would skyrocket.

But even as it becomes increasingly clear that our troops are being withdrawn from Iraq's troubled cities, the current debate as to the wisdom of being there in the first place rages on. One way for the administration to answer its critics would be to explain the invasion of Iraq and our continued presence there in terms of the Heartland Theory. While that explanation might make a great deal of sense to armchair strategists and war college graduates, it could be a difficult sell to a pop culture that cast more votes for the American Idol than were cast in the most recent presidential election..

At the other end of the "explain why we are there" spectrum, former Clinton political adviser Dick Morris says President Bush needs to tell America's soccer moms that if we do not kill the bad guys over there, they are going to come over here and kill their kids. Hopefully, it will not take more beheadings and 9/11s before that lesson soaks in.

Meanwhile, the inescapable geographic truth is that we have now occupied the heartland of the Middle East. If Sir Halford John Mackinder's Heartland Theory is correct, our mere presence there will have a major impact on the outcome of the War on Terror. But maintaining public support for our continued presence will require military tactics that reduce our casualties to more acceptable and sustainable levels. If that can be achieved, then the armchair strategists and the soccer moms may create the common ground of broad public support that will be essential to our continued and successful occupation of the heartland of the Middle East.
©2004.

PRESIDENT REAGAN AND THE STRATEGY OF THE INDIRECT APPROACH

Trying to explain Ronald Reagan's love of free-market capitalism and his abhorrence of communism will, no doubt, provide employment for pundits and psycho-babblers for time immemorial. Economics is called the dismal science. Inexplicably, it was Reagan's major in college. Later, he became a disciple of free-market economists such as: Joseph Schumpeter, Friedrich von Hayek, Ludwig von Mises, Milton Friedman, Arthur Laffer and Congressman Jack Kemp.

Reagan's abhorrence of communism is much easier to explain. As a board member for the Screen Actors Guild (SAG), he found himself in a power struggle with labor organizer, Herb Sorrel, a card-carrying member of the Communist Party USA (CPUSA). Sorrel believed in Lenin's dictum: "Of all the arts, the cinema is the most important." Sorrel had been ordered by the CPUSA to capture Hollywood's labor unions for the purpose of turning the movie industry into an even greater propaganda organ of the Soviet Union.

Sorrel engineered a strike. Reagan led the fight against the strike, and broke it. Sorrel had acid thrown in one actor's face, and sent word Reagan was next. Reagan armed himself with a revolver, and hired guards to protect his wife and children.

Unfortunately, he got no support from his wife actress Jane Wyman. While Reagan was fighting the communists, she began an affair with the pacifist actor, Lew Ayres, and then sued Reagan for divorce. Having your life threatened by communists and then losing your wife to a pro-communist, conscientious objector, tends to harden one's attitude.

All this may explain Reagan's response when his future National Security Advisor, Dr. Richard V. Allen, asked Reagan to outline his approach to the Soviet Union. Reagan said, "We win. They lose." Fortunately, as

President Reagan understood the USSR's advantage in nuclear weapons and missiles. So, he opted for "the indirect approach."

Ronald Reagan was an avid reader of books on foreign affairs, strategy and tactics. Presumably, he read: *Strategy: The Indirect Approach* by Sir Basil Liddell-Hart. But, if not a reader of Sir Basil, Reagan was certainly a practitioner of the indirect approach.

For some recent examples of the indirect approach, look no further than Gulf War I and Operation Iraqi Freedom. Both Generals Norman Schwarzkopf and Tommy Franks gave Saddam Hussein the idea that they were going to follow a certain major axis of attack and then did almost exactly the opposite. In both wars, Generals Schwarzkopf and Franks adhered to Liddell-Hart's dictum: "The desired effect [is] to render enemy forces ineffective without a decisive battle."

So what was President Reagan's indirect approach to: "We win. They lose"? First, to increase our defense budget from four percent of our gross national product to seven percent in an arms race during which the Soviets would have to dedicate one third of their economy just to keep up. Second, begin the Strategic Defense Initiative designed to render the Soviet nuclear arsenal of no use. Third, conspire with the Saudis to drop the price of oil from $40 to $9 dollars per barrel, thereby, luring most of the USSR's oil customers away from the notoriously inefficient Soviet oil industry and robbing the Soviets of the income needed to stay in the arms race. Fourth, wage a personal diplomacy campaign designed to convince Soviet Premier,

Mikhail Gorbachev, of our peaceful intentions. Poor Gorbachev, who had inherited 70 years of Soviet economic failure, had no choice but to watch the Soviet system end "with a whimper instead of a bang."

Thus, the elites in academe and in our left-leaning media who thought President Reagan was an "amiable dunce," were caught with Quiche Lorraine all over their faces when President Ronald Reagan brought the Soviet Union to its knees and made the world a safer place, not just for us, but for all of humankind. The late Sir Basil Liddell-Hart would have been proud.

©2004. 1162

SECRET MESSAGE FROM ABU MUSAB AL-ZARQAWI (TRANSLATED):

"Dear Brethren and Fellow Jihadists: May the blessings of Osama fall upon you like the nuclear/chemical/biological rains we plan for the Americans and the Jews.

"I have both bad news and good news. The bad news is: In Iraq, the infidel Americans and British have killed over 55,000 of our comrades. Moreover, millions of Iraqis (who have yet to grasp our vision of a world devoid of Christians and Jews), have flocked to their polling places to adopt a written Constitution that allows the dreaded Kurds and the feckless Shiites and even the Sunnis to vote. Even worse, women are allowed to vote. I spit upon that idea.

"The allied forces have become extremely difficult targets, forcing us to attack 'soft' targets. While the death of women and children is regrettable, we now own Spain and we are working on France. Unfortunately, the British are like bulldogs.

"Good news: While you know we cannot defeat the United States by force of either conventional or unconventional arms, I can report great progress in getting some prominent U.S. elected officials to espouse the idea that withdrawal to a Fortress America will end our attacks. Right.

"I am especially pleased with Senators Harry Reid and Edward Kennedy and Congresswoman (I can't believe the Americans permit women to hold such high office) Nancy Pelosi. In fact, we are so grateful to Senator Kennedy that our facility for training Jihadist swimmers will be named in his honor.

"We are grateful to a number of RINOS (no brethren I have not forgotten how to spell rhinoceros). I allude to those Republicans In Name Only whose personal political ambitions lead them to abandon their party principles so they can gain exposure on the liberal-media-run television programs. Thank Osama, we have al Jazeera and do not have to beg for air time.

"But if you are captured and are taken to some secret location used by the CIA beware: An operative of the CIA may actually slap you across the face with a hand that most likely has been used to ladle morsels of pork into the mouth of your captor. I have reports that the CIA will throw buckets of cold water upon their captives instead of allowing them to have the long, hot showers the Marines inflict upon their detainees in tropical Guantanamo Bay. Even worse, and I know this violates the Geneva Convention and can only be authorized at the highest levels of the CIA, your captured brethren are forced to go without sleep while listening 24/7 to the rapper Eminem's 'Slim Shady' CD – a clear violation of the U.S. Constitution's 8th Amendment prohibition against 'cruel and unusual' punishment.

"By contrast, we do not engage in such long, drawn-out tortures of the infidels who fall into our hands. Using techniques handed down from the time of Suleiman the Magnificent, we quickly end their suffering and the concerns of their loved ones by showing their severed heads on al Jazeera TV.

"I know most of you don't have refrigerators or those yellow, sticky notes to do as some of our 'useful idiots' in America are doing: They post the number: 2,986. That is how many infidels we killed on 9/11. When you kill 2,986 Americans in Iraq, they will trumpet your accomplishments, saying the so-called War on Terror is in vain. Let that inspire you to kill even more Americans so the magic number of 2,986 can be reached even more quickly.

"Meanwhile, my brothers, do not lose heart. I guarantee you that what we cannot win on the battlefield we can win on the TV screens and the newspapers of America. You can count on some of their politicians to 'cut and run' for the reporters who share their point of view. May Osama be with you.

-- *Abu Musab al-Zarqawi*, HMFIC (untranslatable)
PS
Do not forget about those 72 virgins."
©2005. 1238

THE NATIONAL SECURITY AGENCY EAVESDROPS ON OSAMA AND ABDUL...

Imagine this telephone conversation:

"Greetings Abdul. This is Osama. Do you have that nuclear weapon in position?"

"Well, I did. But one of those Nuclear Emergency Support Team (NEST) vehicles was sniffing around and we had to move it away from the D.C. area. Also, maybe we shouldn't be discussing such things on the telephone. According to the *New York Times*, the National Security Agency (NSA) is monitoring international telephone calls between people the NSA, the CIA and the FBI think are terrorists."

"That's old news Abdul. The Americans have been running their ESCHELON and CARNIVORE telephone monitoring program since 1978 and President Carter. But don't worry about this conversation. By the time the Americans get a warrant from their Foreign Intelligence Surveillance Act (FISA) Court, we will have signed off and changed our locations. Besides, the Americans already think we have an atomic bomb in place. They just can't find it. Besides, if you are arrested, they can't use these conversations in court against you. But don't let your men visit anymore porno web sites. NSA can detect it, and that gives our movement a bad name."

"Yes, Osama. But that's a minor issue compared to moving that cursed nuclear weapon around to keep those NEST teams from finding it."

"Patience, Abdul, patience. Just keep moving it from private residence to private residence and the Americans won't be able to get search warrants fast enough to keep up. The ACLU will keep that Bush infidel tied up in court. Trust me on this. I've studied the Americans. When the going gets tough, some of them cut and run for the tall grass."

"Okay, Osama, but what do I do now?"

"When you get that bomb back in position, give me a call and I'll let you know when it's time to detonate. But I can't allow you to destroy Washington right now because the Americans might decide to get serious about their so-called War on Terror. What are you reading and hearing from the American media?"

"The regular American people are still supporting their troops in the field and seeking our defeat; however, the American media and the elite politicians are making inroads against the war. But if the Americans kill you, I fear for our jihad against them."

"Abdul, my son, that's why you and your nuclear weapon are there. If we can't win our battle for Capitol Hill and our forces are defeated in the field, that's when you'll receive the order to use your bomb. While I'm in Paradise enjoying the 72 virgins, I can look down on Washington and see the mushroom cloud rising above it."

"May Allah protect you, Osama. But we may be able to take Capitol Hill. If you can recruit enough suicide bombers and keep this war going long enough, I think the cut-and-runners might hand us the victory we aren't winning in the field."

"That's called snatching defeat from the jaws of victory. The Americans are good at that."

"Oops, Osama, I've got to hang up! Someone is ringing my door bell and there's a strange looking van parked at the curb. Got to run! Bye."

For those of you in Rush Limbaugh's Rio Linda, the foregoing was not real. Sort of *satire noir*, as the French might say. But speaking of Rush, your faithful observer is beginning to think Limbaugh is correct when he says it will take two or three more 9/11s before America wakes up to the fact that we are in a war to the death. We didn't seek it. But we have no choice but to win it.

As always, the first column of the New Year will carry some predictions, to include the one I fear most: Iran's nuclear weapons capability will grow to the point that it provokes a preemptive strike by the Israeli Defense Force. The consequences of that are almost beyond imagination. *NB: Fear unrealized, yet.*

©2005. 1243

NB: This next piece was published in USA Today's Forum Section in September, 2006.

IRAQ AND AFGHANISTAN AT "THE END OF THE BEGINNING."

Amidst the election-year rancor over how best to defend ourselves against Islamic fascist attack, some historical perspective with regard to Afghanistan and Iraq might add a touch of civility to what has become a vulgar, partisan brawl.

Historically, Afghanistan is a collection of wild tribes led by fierce warlords. A strong central government able to call the shots in every province has never been the case and probably never will be. Today, our vital interests are well served by an Afghanistan no longer under the control of the Taliban and al Qaeda. As a result of our defeat of the Taliban, women enjoy vastly improved treatment.

Moreover, persuading NATO, an alliance formed to defend Western Europe from Soviet invasion, to extend itself half way around the world to Afghanistan is a stunning diplomatic accomplishment. At least for now, our mission in Afghanistan is a success.

Iraq, however, has proven more difficult. The underlying reason is because Iraq, unlike Afghanistan, was not created on the basis of tribal or religious groupings. Iraq is an artificial construct formed in the minds of British intelligence agent, Gertrude Bell, T.E. Lawrence (Lawrence of Arabia), and Winston Churchill.

Miss Bell, the outrageously wealthy aficionado of all things Arab, lived in Baghdad for many years and had a personal relationship with many of the movers and sheiks of the Middle East. Fluent in Arabic, Turkish and Persian, she was, both before and after World War I, Great Britain's best agent-in-place.

Even before the outbreak of World War I, Churchill, then First Lord of the Admiralty, had been convinced by First Sea Lord, Admiral Sir John "Jackie" Fisher, that conversion of the Royal Navy from coal to oil would allow British warships to sail faster, to have greater range, and to be refueled at sea. Moreover, the sailors would be spared the physical exhaustion of taking on coal. But the conversion from coal to oil was not popular with England's coal barons because, as the great English geographer, Sir Halford John Mackinder, put it, "England is a lump of coal surrounded by fish."

Nevertheless, in 1921, Churchill, by that time Colonial Secretary, convened a conference in Cairo for the purpose of reducing the human and monetary costs of maintaining Great Britain's access to the oil of the Middle East. Skillfully playing off one sheik or dynastic pretender against the other, Churchill, Bell and Lawrence cobbled together a territorial compromise based on oil rather than religious or tribal preferences. And, like the proverbial committee charged with designing the horse, the Cairo Conference produced the geographical camel we know as Iraq.

By divvying up the oil lands between the powerful sheiks, Churchill, Bell and Lawrence were able to secure

Great Britain's continued access to oil by diplomatic maneuver, rather than by the blood of her soldiers. What Churchill, Bell and Lawrence achieved at the 1921 Cairo Conference lasted until 1958 when an internal coup toppled the Arab dynasty they had installed in Baghdad. As international arrangements go, 37 years is a long time.

Today, in northern Iraq, the relatively united and peaceful Kurds provide a vision of what the Sunnis and Shiites could achieve provided, of course, that they substitute cooperation for bloody sectarian conflict. But, failing that, the teachings of Nicollo Machiavelli would suggest that we get our forces out of the Sunni-Shia-combat-in-cities crossfire and place them where they can better protect the vital interest of the industrialized West which, of course, is the oil of the region. Meanwhile, we should provide overt support to what is, in essence, a peaceful, *de facto* Kurdistan, and hold it up as the model for a regionalized, federal democracy for Iraq.

While you can lead a horse (or camel) to water, sometimes the problem is getting it to drink. But if we focus our military presence on insuring that the peoples of Iraq profit from the flow of oil to the industrialized world, we may begin to see a rudimentary democracy that is strong enough militarily to stand up for itself while not so strong as to provoke preemptive aggression by Iran.

Meanwhile, our domestic challenge is to retain the political will to neither cut-and-run, nor even cut-and-walk, from our vital interests in Iraq, the Persian Gulf and the Arabian Peninsula.

November's congressional elections will indicate our willingness or unwillingness to exhibit the bulldog determination of Sir Winston Churchill when he said of the first British victory of World War II at El Alamein, *"This is not the end. It is not even the beginning of the end. But it is, perhaps, the end of the beginning."*

But, for Americans habituated to conflict resolution within the span of a 60-minute TV drama or even a football game, the "end of the beginning," may not have arrived quickly enough.

NB: President Obama removed all U.S. forces from Iraq in 2011, resulting in the occupation of large portions of northern Iraq by the Islamic State (ISIS).

©2006.

DID I SHAVE OFF ALL MY BODY HAIR JUST FOR THIS?

Country music fans may recall Deana Carter's song: "Did I shave my legs just for this?" It's the lament of a woman who thought her efforts to improve her appearance would help her find a worthy male companion. Apparently, the person she attracted wasn't worthy of her efforts.

That brings to mind that many of the Islamic suicide bombers shave off their body hair in an effort to be "clean" prior to their hoped-for entry into Islamic Paradise and their opportunity to ravish the promised 72 virgins.

This might strike those of a different religious persuasion as rather odd. Assuming there might be some physical manifestation of the "clean" suicide bomber that reaches Islamic Paradise, wouldn't those bits and pieces be embedded with elements of the explosives used, such as ammonium nitrate (fertilizer), and, thereby, be unclean?

But what if Allah or whoever tends the Islamic Pearly Gates, says, "Hold it, Abdul. You can't come here. Shaving off all your body hair doesn't overcome the fact you stink like fertilizer. Besides, we are running out of virgins."

Imagine, standing right behind the keeper of the Islamic Pearly Gates, is a huge crowd of Muslims -- all the innocent victims of Abdul's bombing attack on their local market. They are shouting encouragement to the Keeper of the Islamic Pearly Gates chanting, "Kill infidels, Yes! Kill us, No! Keep that hairless, stinky Abdul out of here!"

This fictional example brings us to the two fundamental questions that might be plaguing many of the adherents of Islam. The Koran (4:29-30) forbids suicide. Moreover, in a hadith, the Prophet Muhammad opines that suicide and the taking of the lives of the innocent – particularly, women and children – are prohibited.

But today's jihadists interpret these writings in such a way to make a "suicide exception" if jihad is declared and waged against the infidels. So it is that young Muslim boys (even some girls) are taught they have a duty to blow themselves up in the interest of jihad. Collateral damage is excused on the basis that if the innocent bystanders are good Muslims to begin with, then they will be in Islamic Paradise alongside the suicide bomber who killed them. Yeah, right.

Wait a minute. If all it takes to enter Islamic Paradise is just being a good Muslim, what's the point of committing suicide and running the risk that whoever controls the entrance to Islamic Paradise might not buy the so-called "jihad exception." After all, Muhammad is not around to tell us what he really meant.

That being the case, it is all a matter of interpretation -- the truth of which isn't available by resort to google.com or ask.com or Yahoo! (Of course, if you haven't been a good Muslim to begin with, the suicide gambit could overcome a lot of drinking, whoring, reading *Hustler and Playboy* and books by Al Gore, Michael Moore, Gloria Steinem and Betty Friedan.)

This raises the possibility that the earlier interpretations: i.e., don't kill yourself, don't kill the innocent, could still be in effect. So, suppose the Keepers of the Islamic Pearly Gates hold to Koran (4:29-30) where it states: *"O ye who believe! Eat not up your property among yourselves in vanities... nor kill or destroy yourselves."* And follow what Muhammad said, in a hadith: *"He who commits suicide by throttling shall keep on throttling himself in Hell-fire forever, and he who commits suicide by stabbing himself shall keep on stabbing himself in the Hell-fire."*

In other words, if young Abdul commits suicide by blowing himself up, then he shall keep on blowing himself up over and over again in the Hell-fire for all eternity. Maybe, Abdul will be asking himself: "Did I shave off all my body hair just for this?"

©2007. 1318

LET'S TALK TURKEY

Sitting around the dinner table, it is unlikely that most of us discuss what might happen in Kosovo or Serbia or Turkey this year. Yet those are countries where important news will most likely be made. The geographical proximity of Kosovo and Serbia to a Russia more than willing to light a match to the Balkan tinderbox left smoldering by the European Union bodes ill for Europe. Turkey, occupying the key terrain that connects Europe to Asia, will likely be a major player with regard to what happens in Iraq and Iran.

But, for now, "let's talk turkey" about Turkey. That phrase, by the way, is alleged to have been born of a dispute between an American Colonist and a Native American over how to divide the spoils of a turkey hunt. The Politically Correct version is that the Colonist tried to cheat the Native American; however, it could have been the other way around. It means to speak plainly about a difficult or awkward subject.

Today's Turkey faces a number of difficult challenges and awkward opportunities. Turkey has the opportunity to host the gas and oil pipelines connecting Central Asia to Europe and to do the same for the transmission of oil and gas out of northern Iraq to Europe. But to make a success of the oil and gas pipeline business, Turkey faces the challenges posed by the independence-yearning Kurds who comprise one-fifth of its population. Moreover, Turkey borders the hostile, Iraqi Kurds who also dream of an independent Kurdistan.

In order to keep its oil and gas pipelines from being blown up by the Kurds, Turkey will have to make some accommodation with its own Kurds and with the Iraqi Kurds. That's the only way for Turkey to have a stable income from the oil and gas pipeline business.

The geographical importance of Turkey is illustrated by an incident that took place in the early 1960s in West Germany. Then, Turkey was considered the weak flank of the NATO alliance against Soviet aggression. At the time, the Soviets had the world's best battle tanks. Without proper anti-tank weapons the Turks would be smashed.

Fortunately, the U.S. had the relatively inexpensive, jeep-mounted, 106-millimeter recoilless rifle. The 106 could penetrate the armor of even the heaviest Soviet tank. To get the Turks to purchase the 106 system, a demonstration for the top Turkish general officers and for NATO brass from all 14 NATO nations was set for the Hohenfels Combat Maneuver Training Area north of Munich, West Germany.

Company B, 1st Battalion, 19th Infantry, was selected to demonstrate the value of the jeep-mounted 106-millimeter recoilless rifle to those assembled in a reviewing stand overlooking the same rolling terrain that German General Erwin "the Desert Fox" Rommel had used to train his Afrika Corps. Standing on the hilltop objective of the simulated attack was a Rommel Tower, a tall masonry structure Rommel liked to mount so he could look down from high above and observe his Panzer formations in training.

It was "suggested" to the officer commanding B Company that B Company's 106-millimeter recoilless rifles "had better" score direct hits on that Rommel Tower. Unfortunately, the Rommel Tower was about 20 feet square at the bottom and weighed several tons. It would absorb a 106 shell like a catcher's mitt absorbing a fast ball.

So, the B Company Commander threw a curve on steroids. The base of the Rommel Tower was packed with enough TNT to launch it into orbit. During the demonstration-maneuver, two 106 teams stopped rolling just long enough to fire from already bore-sighted firing positions. Simultaneously, as they both scored direct hits on the base of the Rommel Tower, a hidden plunger was pressed. The Rommel Tower separated from its base and toppled over on one side.

In the grandstand, the NATO generals and admirals high-fived each other. Turkey ordered and deployed several hundred, jeep-mounted, 106-millimeter recoilless rifles, making what had been NATO's weak flank a solid bulwark against Soviet tanks.

©2008. 1356

STILL VALID: THE SOLDIER AND THE STATE

Thoughtful people will wish the new Commander-in-Chief well and hope that he will heed sound military advice during the next four years. Unfortunately, a significant number of people within the military are naturally "wary" of someone with no military or foreign policy experience. According to a recent poll conducted by *The Military Times*, 60-percent of active duty personnel polled are "wary" of Barack H. Obama. On the upside, 33-percent felt he would be "okay."

The large number of "wary" military personnel raises the issue of civilian control of the military. Fortunately, during 20 years of active duty (even though we were being sent by President Lyndon Johnson again and again into a war in southeast Asia that many of us increasingly knew that LBJ wasn't allowing us to win), I never heard that doctrine questioned. Why? In part, because the doctrine of civilian control is taught throughout the military's vast educational system.

Photographs of the members of the chain-of-command, beginning with the Commander-in-Chief, are ubiquitous in Army orderly rooms, Navy wardrooms, Air Force buildings and barracks. On January 20, 2009, clerks or yeomen in military facilities all over the world will dutifully take down the photograph of the out-going president and replace it with that of Barack H. Obama.

This is a good point to mention the work of Harvard Professor Samuel P. Huntington. While Huntington is most famous for his *The Clash of Civilizations,* a more meaningful work for military personnel is his *The Soldier and the State: The Theory and Politics of Civil-Military Relations.* In 1957, Huntington argued that the best way to strengthen civilian control of the military was to make the military more professional, to teach its members that their vocation was as hallowed as the traditional professions such as medicine, law and the clergy.

In other words, inculcate within the military the sense of a being a special and distinct segment of society, albeit subject to civilian control. Huntington's 1964 critic was Professor Morris Janowitz who, in *The Professional Soldier,* argued the opposite. Janowitz wanted the members of the military to be more civilian-like, a view that was reflected when the distinctive uniforms of the Army and Air Force were changed to look more like those of greyhound bus drivers. Note: In 2009, the Army will reclaim its distinctive (and more historically significant) Army Blue uniform.

In 1958, after several months of living for the very first time inside an army post, I began to wonder about the place of the military within the overall context of the civilian society. I found the answers in Huntington's *The Soldier and the State.* Napoleon famously said, "Every soldier carries a marshal's baton in his knapsack." Lacking a baton, I substituted a copy of *The Soldier and the State.*

In 1970, when assigned briefly to the Pentagon to help write a tiny bit of the doctrine for the All-Volunteer Army, I was pleased to find Huntington's views in vogue. Other than increasing the civilian-like creature comforts of the troops, we concluded the new force should focus on the development of a military ethos distinct from the 1960s, baby-boomer "if-it-feels-good-do-it" society. Based on the outstanding performance of the all-volunteer force in combat, not trying to mirror the ambient civilian society was the proper direction.

In 1981, while walking around the atrium balcony at Harvard's JFK School of Government, I spotted the office of Samuel P. Huntington. A knock elicited a voice that bade me enter. I rushed in, pumped Huntington's offered hand, and gushed on about how much his book meant to me. Professor Huntington was somewhat bewildered by someone still so enthusiastic about a book he had written back in 1957.

Now, I'm so glad that I took the opportunity to thank him. On December 24, 2008, Samuel P. Huntington (81) passed away.

©2008. 1404

THE MUSLIM BROTHERHOOD:
EXCHANGING DICTATORSHIPS

All across the Crescent of Islam, we are seeing secular, Islamic dictatorships under attack from the radical Islamic fundamentalists who want to turn those secular Islamic dictatorships into radical, Islamic-fundamentalist dictatorships like the one in Iran. As usual, the radicals' pro-democracy façade duped the western media.

The uproar in Egypt recalls the time when Wonder Wife (Penny) and this author were in South Korea traveling with Arnaud and Alexandra de Borchgrave, Admiral Elmo and Mouza Zumwalt; Boston University president, John Silber; and Madame Jehan Sadat, the widow of the assassinated Egyptian President Anwar Sadat. For someone who started out as a paperboy for *The*

Anadarko Daily News, that was an exciting trip. At the time, Wonder Wife was working as a stringer for the *Voice of America*.

We arranged a *Voice of America* interview with Madame Sadat. We listened in awe as the beautiful Madame Sadat recounted how her husband signed the peace treaty with Israel, traveled to Israel to close the deal, and then was assassinated by the Muslim Brotherhood. She told how, as first lady of Egypt, she founded a group to promote the rights of Muslim women.

Madame Sadat is good with names and faces. A year later, we made eye contact with her in Dulles International Airport. Naturally, we did not approach until she motioned for us to come sit with her. Madame Sadat thanked Penny for the *Voice of America* interview. She said it helped her efforts to improve the lot of women in the Muslim world. How odd that the Obama Administration has been promoting the Muslim Brotherhood which killed Madame Sadat's husband and now demands that the peace treaty between Egypt and Israel be revoked.

Given the Obama Administration's affinity for the Muslim Brotherhood, some Internet wag suggested the U.S. and Egypt swap presidents; however, that would not work because the Egyptians demand that their presidents be Egyptian citizens.

During the current Egyptian crisis, Arnaud de Borchgrave, who speaks at least five languages, has a much better grip on what is really happening than the mono-lingual American mainstream media who must rely on the relatively few Egyptians who speak English.

Writing for United Press International, de Borchgrave, who has interviewed Egyptian President Hosni Mubarack a dozen times over the last 30 years, recalls advice offered by Mubarack just a week after the 9/11 attacks on America.

President Mubarack told de Borchgrave: "I know you want to retaliate massively, but there is one thing you must not do. Do not send American troops to fight a new war against the Taliban regime in Afghanistan. Such an operation must be conducted by Muslim troops alone. If U.S. troops and other NATO contingents are dispatched, America will find itself cast as the villain in a war against Islam which is precisely what the Taliban want."

Stratfor, one of the private intelligence sources to which this columnist subscribes, suggests President Mubarack may be residing in Sharm el-Sheikh, at the mouth of the Gulf of Aquba. Per the Egyptian-Israel peace treaty, neither side is supposed to have troops there; however, about 800 Egyptian troops are reported in Sharm el-Sheikh. So far, no public protest from Israel. Should President Mubarack decide to depart Egypt, the coastline of Saudi Arabia is only 15 miles away.

Annual toll revenues from the Suez Canal are about $4.5 billion dollars. So, the Muslim Brotherhood might not want to close the canal, although all it takes is one sunken ship in one of the canal's narrow stretches. In normal times, the U.S., as the world's *de facto* guarantor of freedom of the seas, might consider closure of the Suez Canal by the Muslim Brotherhood as an act of war. But then, given the Obama Administration's support for the Muslim Brotherhood, these times are not normal.

©2011. 1514

OBAMA WORLD: THE 4TH OPTION

In 2000, Vince Flynn wrote *The Third Option*, a novel about how the U.S. might deal with radical Islam. In order of likely use by our government, he listed three options: Diplomacy, Conventional Warfare, and use of Special Operations. The latter is to use highly-trained assassins to capture, interrogate, and/or kill radical Islamist leaders such as Osama bin Laden and others.

Has diplomacy worked? Well, we are still being attacked by suicide bombers and improvised explosive devices (IED). Hugo Chavez, Mahmoud Ahmadinejad, and Vladimir Putin, and the Muslim world still hate us. The Arab Spring turned into the radical Islamist Winter. The Palestinians are still shelling Israel. The U.N. almost always votes against us. Many of our old allies are now neutrals. Mr. Obama's current "follow-rather-than-lead" foreign policy is sending our traditional allies in search of more reliable protection from Islam, from Russia, and from Red China.

The 2d Option: Conventional Warfare (Infantry, Armor, Artillery, and Airpower) quickly wiped out Saddam Hussein's conventional forces. But radical Islam replaced Saddam's conventional forces with unconventional forces which were not impressed with more voting booths, better sanitation, electricity, medical care, votes-for-women, and schools. So, we fled what Mr. Obama called the "bad war" in Iraq for what he called the "good war" in Afghanistan.

Unfortunately, the Special Operators who so quickly routed the Taliban/al-Qaeda in Afghanistan were replaced with Conventional Warfare forces which, once again, do not do well against the unconventional Islamist forces that are trying to expel the Judeo-Christian Crusaders from the Graveyard of Empires.

The 3d Option is to field a relatively small force of highly-trained assassins to find the leaders of radical Islam and...well, assassinate them. While the 3d Option has already been used with positive impact on scores of radical Islamists – the most notable being Osama bin Laden – the 3d Option causes some moral, ethical, and constitutional problems for some on the Left who think in terms of a Disney World where all the woodland animals -- instead of eating each other -- sit side-by-side on a long log singing "We Are the World." Moreover, the 3d Option doesn't seem to them as sportsmanlike as sending thousands of young Americans off to fight while trying to observe the Rules of Engagement of Conventional Warfare.

The Obama Administration just published its new defense strategy. Let's call it: the 4th Option. It reduces our Army and Marines forces by 13-percent. It cuts the defense budget in half. It abandons the concept of defending the USA on both our Atlantic and Pacific sides and focuses only on the Asia-Pacific area. Memo to Enemy: Only attack us in the Asia-Pacific area. Memo to

Pentagon: A strategy that depends on enemy cooperation is bound to fail.

Option 4 is ambivalent as to whether the Navy can operate 11 carriers or just ten. It proposes to eliminate the F-16, F-18, and Harrier fighter-jets and replace them with the F-35 fighter which the new defense strategy admits we may not be able to afford in the numbers we need.

But the most disturbing aspect of Mr. Obama's 4th option is rhetoric that envisions a force that is more reflective of the racial, ethnic, and gender mix of American society than ever before. This suggests a military force where politically-correct politics are more likely to win promotion to flag rank than demonstrated war-fighting proficiency.

At this point, it might be well to remember the words of George Orwell: "We sleep safely in our beds because rough men stand ready in the night to visit violence on those who would harm us."
©2012. 1607

BENGHAZI: AN IMAGINARY HEARING

An Article 32 Hearing is a procedure under the Uniform Code of Military Justice (UCMJ) that is similar to a "preliminary hearing" in a civilian court. No charge can be referred to a general court-martial for trial until a thorough and impartial investigation has been made. Let's listen in on an imaginary Article 32 Hearing being conducted by a senior officer appointed to do so:

Investigating Officer: "For the record, sir. Please state your last name."

"CINC. Sounds like: sink."

"Thank you, Mr. Cinc. What is your current address?"

"Sixteen Hundred Pennsylvania Avenue, Washington, D.C."

"Mr. Cinc. Where were you at 5: 00 p.m. on September 11, 2012?"

"I was at home. Actually, I have this home office. You're not with the IRS are you?"

"No, Mr. Cinc. I am not the IRS. I am conducting an Article 32 Hearing. So, what were you doing at 5:00 p.m.?"

"I was having a meeting with Mr. Piñata, the Secretary of Defense."

"Don't you mean Mr. Panetta?"

"Sorry. Oval Office joke. He takes such a beating."

"What were you discussing?"

"Important stuff. You know. Gays in the military. Girls in ground combat units. Mothballing ships. Grounding aircraft. Procuring more white flags. That sort of thing."

"For the record, the U.S. diplomatic mission in Benghazi was attacked at 3:42 Washington time. At 5:00 p.m., did you and Mr. Panetta discuss those on-going attacks?"

"Now, that you mention it. Yes, we did."

"Did you do anything about it?"

"Actually, that is sort of below my pay grade. I told Panetta to take care of it."

"Mr. Cinc. Are you aware that your ambassador to Libya, one of his assistants, and two former Navy SEALs were killed during a firefight that lasted for another six hours after you spoke to Mr. Panetta?"

"Technically, those foreign service types work for the Secretary of State. If I mess in her stuff, she can be ...well, rather difficult. The former navy guys were probably defense contractors, not very popular these days."

"Mr. Cinc. After you spoke with Mr. Panetta at 5:00 p.m., did you ever check back with him?"

"Nah. I had some other stuff I wanted to do."

"What kind of other stuff?"

"Don't recall exactly. Just stuff. Packing for a Las Vegas fund-raiser."

"Mr. Cinc. As I read Clause 1, Article II, of the U.S. Constitution and Article 92 (3) of the UCMJ, it appears that you could be charged with Dereliction of Duty."

""I had no idea. Is that something serious? You see, I never had any military service."

"In addition to imprisonment and a fine, it could mean that you can no longer hold a federal office."

"Wow! Hmmn. Okay. Let's make a deal. Maybe you could charge me with a lesser offense? You know, so I could still keep my federal job."

"Well, Mr. Cinc, you did wander off somewhere during the firefight in Benghazi. You left it to others to perform your prescribed duties. You might plead down to Article 86."

"Article 86. What's that?"

"Absent Without Leave. In the military, we call it: AWOL."

"Okay, I'll plead to AWOL. May I go now?"

"Mr. Cinc. My only job is to conduct this investigation and report my findings. It will be up to your employers to decide your future."

©2013. 1663

COMING SOON: THE OBAMADRONES

As a public service for readers who fear being hit by an ObamaDrone, here are the 22 drone-avoidance tips currently in use by al-Qaeda. Source: Associated Press. These have been edited only for brevity and clarity; however, some parenthetical comments have been added.

"**1.** If you are good with computers, buy the Russian-made 'sky-grabber' device for $2,595 and use it. (Is there a discount for two?)

2. Or, buy the Russian-made 'Racal' device that broadcasts in confusing frequencies. (No price given. Try eBay.)

3. Spread reflective pieces of glass on your car or roof. (Aren't broken mirrors bad luck?)

4. Use skilled snipers to shoot down low-flying drones. (But if your guns are grabbed by the feds, this will become much harder.)

5. Use an ordinary water-lifting dynamo with a 100-foot copper pole. (I have no idea what this one means.)

6. Run microwave ovens in various places to attract the drones. (Apparently, the Yugoslav Army did this to confuse incoming NATO missiles.)

7. Keep moving. Have no permanent headquarters. (For a mobile society, this should be relatively easy.)

8. Give early warning of drones and stop moving. (Conflicts with 7 above.)

10. Hide under thick trees because they are the best cover against the drones. (The Pine Beetles make this more difficult.)

11. Stay in places unlit by the sun. (For non-Muslims, local pubs should be a welcome choice.)

12. Don't use your radios. (Bad news for teens with boom boxes. Good news for anyone with a scintilla of musical taste.)

13. Under attack, multiple occupants should flee rapidly in different directions. (Excellent example: Office buildings toward 5:00 p.m.)

14. Use buildings with lots of entrances and exits. (Government buildings.)

15. Use underground shelters. (But not during super-storms like Hurricane Sandy.)

16. Avoid open areas. (Bad news for national parks and recreation areas.)

17. Form anti-spy groups. (Where's the John Birch Society when we need it?)

18. Set out groups of dummies to mislead the enemy. (ACLU and AARP meetings make good decoys.)

19. When under fire, scatter in all directions. (Congress is a good model.)

20. If you just absolutely have to hold a meeting, use forests or caves. (Too bad teleconferences are already out.)

21. Set forest fires to create smoke over target areas. (Some government agencies are good at this.)

22. Top leaders whose voices have been 'tagged,' should stop broadcasting." (Rush Limbaugh and Sean Hannity, watch out.)

So, there you have it, folks. Take it from al-Qaeda. The experts on drone-avoidance.

©2013 1665

DENIS THATCHER AND THE GROCER'S DAUGHTER

The late British Prime Minister Baroness Margaret Thatcher is being praised for her revitalization of Britain's economy, for curbing trade-union excesses, and for re-establishing Great Britain as a world power. She made it possible for more than a million families to buy, instead of rent their rundown government housing, which, due to pride-of-ownership, they converted from dilapidated to decent. Under Thatcher, individual incomes rose by over 80-percent. Pay for women rose to record levels and has remained so.

She rose from selling vegetables in her father's grocery store, to break the "glass ceiling" that inhibited women in British politics. The cheeky Commoner irritated the rich aristocrats in her own political party -- men whose high station in life was due to a spot of unskilled labor in the middle of the night. After winning an Oxford scholarship, she took honors in Chemistry. Her first of many female firsts.

But along with her Horatio Alger story, there's a "My Fair Lady" story. She met and married her "Professor Higgins" in the form of Denis Thatcher, a leading figure in Britain's plastics and paint industry and already a self-made millionaire. But, instead of teaching his pupil upper-class diction, Denis paid her way through law school. Along the way to becoming a barrister, Margaret, the Commoner, was also working her way up the ranks within the male-dominated, aristocratic Conservative Party.

Meanwhile Justin Dart, the CEO of America's Dart-Kraft Industries (think Tupperware™) and Denis Thatcher (think plastics) became close friends. When Dart learned Margaret was both a chemist and a lawyer, the future Prime Minister became his British Patent Law barrister. When in London, Justin Dart was always the Thatcher's house guest.

One day, Denis came home excited from hearing a speech by then former California Governor Ronald Reagan. Houseguest Justin Dart pops up and says:"I'm one of Reagan's five-closest political advisers. I'll arrange for Ronnie to meet Margaret."

At the time they met, Margaret was a Member of Parliament and the leader of the then out-of-power Conservative Party. When they met in her parliamentary office, it was conservative political love at first sight. Thus it was that the son of an alcoholic shoe salesman met the daughter of a man who owned a corner grocery store. And so it was that a Pope from Poland (of all places), Margaret Thatcher, and Ronald Reagan, would team up to end the Cold War on terms favorable to the western democracies and collapse what President Reagan called: the "evil empire."

More good news: Any male who has the honesty to do so can take part in this grand history by joining a club that has no annual dues, no annual meetings, and has only one requirement: You must admit that you married a woman who is smarter than you are: It is called: "The Denis Thatcher Society." (This columnist is a charter member.)

While Denis was shy, Margaret was outspoken. At the Williamsburg, Virginia, Big 7 Summit in 1983, President Reagan started to introduce Prime Minister Thatcher by saying, "Margaret, if your predecessors had been a bit more clever..." But the "Iron Lady" stole his punch line by saying, "Yes, Ronnie, I know. I would be hosting this Summit instead of you."

©2013. 1672

POLITICAL COVER-UP 101?

Today, two-thirds of the continental USA is covered with ice and snow. A perfect time to expose the Global-Warming Hoax. But then, why waste precious newspaper space on something which is so chillingly obvious -- even to the most mentally challenged person in the village? (Let's do clean up the planet. But for the correct reasons.)

Instead, here's a real issue. What would we do right now if America suffered a massive electrical power outage? We could burn wood. But most homes rely on natural gas, or propane, or fuel oil, or coal. To work, all fuel sources need at least a spark of electricity. A back-up generator helps; however, generators run on either gasoline or propane which could eventually run out, leaving even hospital emergency rooms without power. So, while most everyone is praying their electricity stays on, consider this little-known story:

Kudos to *The Wall Street Journal* for picking up last week on what should have been a huge story that only surfaced in print this last December in *Foreign Policy Magazine* and was now just "outed" again by, Mr. Jon Wellinghof, the former chairman of the Federal Energy Regulatory Commission.

At a power station near San Jose, CA, at 12:58. a.m., on April 16, 2013, persons still unknown removed two 75-pound manhole covers, climbed down a ladder, and cut a number of power cables.

Shortly thereafter, snipers started firing at the power station's transformers. One hundred and ten rifle shots were fired into the oil-filled radiators of 17 transformers, spilling 52,000 gallons of oil, causing the over-heating transformers to go off-line very slowly.

But timely rerouting of electric lines by Pacific Gas & Electric (PG&E) employees to other power stations prevented a massive power outage across Silicon Valley -- ground zero of America's computer industry.

At first light, investigators found over 100 finger-print free AK-47 shell casings. (Wonder who uses AK-47s?) They found piles of rock, used as firing positions that had to have been put in place in advance of the actual attack. The attackers knew better than to shoot the 17 transformers where they would explode instantly, summoning the police. The slow, but ruinous, draining of the oil-filled radiators provided time for the attackers to slip away undetected.

Last week, Mr. Wellinghof said he was going public now out of concern that national security is at risk and that critical electric-grid sites are not adequately protected. Also, a former official of PG&E said he feared the incident could have been a dress rehearsal for a much larger event.

"This wasn't an incident where Billy Bob and Joe decided, after a few brewskis to come in and shoot up a substation. This was an event that was well thought out, well planned and they targeted key components." When asked, the FBI, which works for Obama-appointee, Attorney General Eric Holder, said, "It does not think a terrorist organization caused the attack." Hello?

Somehow, the equally well-planned attack on the U.S. Mission in Benghazi, Libya, on September 11, 2012, comes to mind. Does anyone detect a pattern of playing politics with both domestic and international issues? You decide.

©2014. 1716

WARM-WATER PORT: CHECKMATE. GAME OVER.

Not since the Cuban Missile Crisis of 1962 or the collapse of the Soviet Union in 1991 has Russia been so much in the news. We witnessed 18 days of the Sochi Winter Olympics, along with rioting in Ukraine, then followed by the Russian occupation of the Crimea -- home of Russia's naval base at Sevastopol.

Vladimir Putin, the president of the Russian Federation, spent about $50 billion dollars to put Russia's best ski, skate, sled (take your pick) forward in Sochi. By almost all accounts, Putin's Olympic efforts elevated Russia from the previously held impression of Russia as a third-world country with nuclear weapons to a more modern state ready to rejoin the community of peaceful maritime-trading nations.

All the Sochi glitz, however, does not fix Russia's immutable geographic problems: 1. A lack of defensible terrain features to protect Russia from invasion from either the East or the West. 2. Russia's Baltic seaports freeze in winter just as our Great Lakes and Niagara Falls are frozen over today. 3. Russia's only year-round, warm-water port is at Sevastopol on the south end of the Crimean peninsula which, until the recent seizure of Crimea by Putin, was, by treaty, part of Ukraine. 4. In winter, Russia's only way to trade with the rest of the world by sea is from Sevastopol across the Black Sea, through the Bosporus, across the Sea of Marmara, through the Dardanelles, across the Aegean

Sea, into the Mediterranean, on through the Strait of Gibraltar and, finally, out into the Atlantic Ocean.

Ergo: Russia's warm-water port at Sevastopol is a vital national interest. Moreover, Russia is spending billions to improve its Mediterranean naval base at Tartus, Syria. The Sevastopol-Tartus connection explains, in part, Putin's continued support for Syria's brutal Assad Regime.

Russia also has demographic problems: Abortion is often used for birth control. The birthrate of ethnic Russians is so low that other ethnic groups, added together, will eventually outnumber the ethnic Russians. The life-expectancy of Russian males is only 64.3 years which is due, in large measure, to alcoholism and to the shoddy state-run, health-care system. Dare we call it: StalinCare or PutinCare? (Years ago, we visited a hospital near Zagorsk that did not even have running water.)

But despite facing a very poor geographic, demographic, and public-health Chess board, President Putin is a Grand Master at International Chess. Savoring America's current lack of military/foreign-policy leadership, Mr. Putin "rooked" Knights Gates and Hagel and Bishops Clinton and Kerry who, it appears, must have been playing "*Poddavki*," a strange Russian form of checkers in which the object is to lose all your men.

Recall, Khrushchev put missiles in Cuba after Kennedy's debacle at the Bay of Pigs; Kennedy's weak showing in Vienna vs. Khrushchev, and the U.S. failure to take down the Berlin Wall. Similarly emboldened, Mr. Putin, with no fear of Mr. Obama's now Queen-led forces, swept the Middle East so easily that Mr. Putin decided to solve Russia's warm-water port problem once and for all by military seizure of the Crimea. Moreover, Putin has now maneuvered the Russian-majority Crimean Parliament to vote for a referendum which, if approved, will make the Crimea part of the Russian Federation. Checkmate. Game over.

©2014. 1720

UKRAINE, ISTANBUL: THE LOST LESSONS OF WORLD WAR I

If you watch the 24-hour TV news cycle at all, it is a good bet you have been learning more about Donald Trump and Mrs. Bill Clinton than learning what is happening with Ukraine. While electing a president to pull America up out of its current morass is vitally important, we ignore at our peril what Russia's Vladimir Putin is doing in Ukraine.

Conventional wisdom tells us that World War I started because a Serbian terrorist assassinated the heir to Austro-Hungarian Empire in Sarajevo. Yes, that was the spark. But the rest of the story is often told from the perspective of what happened on the Western Front between Germany, Belgium, France, Great Britain, and the United States. Scant attention is paid to the war on the Eastern Front and how the vital interests of the Russian, Austro-German, and Ottoman Empires were centered on the richness of the grain and minerals of Ukraine and conflicted over the centuries-old desire of the Russian

Tsars to control Constantinople and have access to the year-round warm waters of the Mediterranean Sea.

Now, along comes a history that points us to the major underlying cause for World War I, a history that will come as a revelation to many. The book is: *The End of Tsarist Russia: World War I & the Road to Revolution* by Dominic Lieven (2015).

The collapse of the Russian Empire led to a Communist Revolution which led to Russia being excluded from the shaping of the Treaty of Versailles, the foolish treaty that caused the instability that led to Hitler and World War II that led to the Cold War that led to Vietnam and to a political and social revolution in the 1960s that confounds us to this very day. For those who understand history as a continuum of events rather than disjointed happenstance, *The End of Tsarist Russia* is a must-read.

But what if Russia had been among the victors and had been represented in Paris as the Western Allies made the decisions that divided up Germany, Austro-Hungary, and the western portions of the Ottoman Empire, that gave mandates to the victorious powers over North Africa, the Middle East and Africa? Versailles even created a geometrically-shaped Iraq whose made-up borders mixed together an indigestible stew of Sunnis, Shia, and Kurds.

If Russia had been at the peace tables in Paris and Versailles, you can bet your bottom ruble that the post-World War I map of Europe would have looked vastly different. A victorious Russia would have given the Ottoman Turks the punishment they so richly deserved.

Constantinople and the Bosporus Straits would be Russian. The Ukrainians, who are only about half Russian, would have been pulled fully into the Russian orbit as would have the almost-all Russian Crimea. The question of whether Russia or Germany would be Europe's top dog would have been settled in Russia's favor, making Germany too weak to start another world war, ever.

If Putin is to restore Russia to its former Tsarist glories, he must have Ukraine. After that, Putin must have the Bosporus and Constantinople (now Istanbul). Ergo: If there is to be a World War III, keep your eye on Ukraine and Istanbul.

©2015. 1799

BLACK SEA MATTERS

Actually, all seas matter; however, the Black Sea matters even more because the world may soon be shaken by a geo-political earthquake, running from the Russian naval base at Sevastopol on the Black Sea, to western Turkey at Istanbul, resulting in a shooting war tsunami that washes up on the shores of Syria. The conflicting interests of the major forces along this geo-political fault line are even more volatile than those mentioned in this column last week regarding the clash of the German, Austro-Hungarian, and Russian Empires that led to World War I.

If Vladimir Putin is to achieve his dream of a restored Russian Empire, Ukraine must be sucked back into the Russian orbit, the Black Sea must become a Russian lake, both sides of Turkey bordering the Bosporus and Istanbul must yield to Russian control, and the Russian naval and air bases in Syria must be secured.

Syrian dictator, Bashar al-Assad, must play both ends against the middle. Assad, an Alawite Muslim, is the puppet of the Shiite Mullahs in Iran while, at the same time, providing his seaports at Tartus and Latakia to the Russian Orthodox, Vladimir Putin. Strange religious bedfellows. Meanwhile, the Syrian religious-political, civil war rages on with Syria's many Christians bearing the brunt of the fighting between the Iranian-backed Shia and the Saudi-backed Sunnis.

President Obama's premature pullout of U.S. forces from Iraq created a power vacuum being filled by ISIS with its dreams of carving out a Caliphate from pieces of Syria, Iraq, Iran, and southern Turkey. At the same time, the Kurds are making a righteous claim to parts of Turkey, Iraq, Syria, and Iran. Turkey, sometimes called "the sick man of Europe," is led by Recep Tayyip Erdogan, who is transforming Turkey from a secular Muslim nation (acceptable to its NATO allies) into a radical Islamist state, increasingly unacceptable to NATO and, at the same time, more offensive to the Russian Orthodox Christians in Russia.

In sum, we are seeing a clash of the Russian, Ottoman, Persian, and Saudi Empires concentrated along a line running from the Black Sea to Damascus, Syria. Millions of people are fleeing this cauldron of conflict and are invading the Balkans and, especially, the socialist-welfare states of Western Europe.

This poses an existential threat to the western European states that were able to turn back armed Muslim hoards at Tours in 732, at the Battle of Lepanto in 1571, and at the gates of Vienna in 1683. Ironically, in 2015, it is entirely possible for unarmed Muslim masses to achieve what the armed Muslim masses could not -- a Europe living under the scimitar of Islam. Meanwhile, the movement of migrant millions includes thousands of displaced Christians. Trying to figure out who is who is like trying to pick out the fly specks from the pepper.

The response to all this from the Obama Administration is to make matters even more dangerous by providing the Iranian Mullahs with $150 billion dollars to spend on even more terrorism and a sure path to nuclear hegemony over its Sunni rivals and to the eventual extinction of Israel. But rather than face extinction, Israel may decide to make Iran a neo-Stone Age nation.

©2015. 1800

GRAND STRATEGY: CHINA OPTS FOR THE BLUE WATERS

International commerce runs on oil. What drives international affairs these days is that Saudi Arabia needs to sell oil and Red China needs to buy oil. But there is a lot of water between the oil of the Middle East and the factories of Red China.

Prior to the advent of Team Obama, the Red Chinese could count on the United States to help the Saudis provide them with oil and to use the U.S. Navy to guarantee freedom-of-the-seas to all nations engaging in peaceful commerce.

Now, the Red Chinese view our problems in Libya, our premature retreat from Iraq, the rise of ISIS in Iraq and Syria, Iran's proxy control of the Red Sea and the Suez Canal via Yemen, and how a nuclear-armed Iran could shut down the Persian Gulf, as a serious threat to its supply of oil from the Middle East.

So, China's recently announced military strategy calls for the creation of a robust blue-water navy designed to keep open the waters between the Middle East and Chinese ports and, more ominously, to push the U.S. Navy out of East Asian waters so the Chinese can seize the supposedly oil-rich Spratly Islands that lie in the waters between the Philippines, Malaysia, and Vietnam.

Historically, with the exception of the period between 1405 and 1433, under Admiral Zheng He, the Chinese have focused on land power rather than sea power. But with the U.S. Navy shrinking below pre-World War II levels and U.S. foreign policy in world-wide retreat, the new Chinese strategy proclaims: "The traditional mentality that land outweighs sea must be abandoned... and great importance has to be attached to managing the seas and oceans and protecting maritime rights and interests."

Of course, if the United States re-imposed the *Pax Americana* on the Middle East and reestablished our guarantee of freedom-of-the-seas, the Red Chinese would not need a blue-water navy nor would they be trying to perfect a territorial claim to one of the Spratly atolls by raising it up out of the water with sandbags stuffed with Chinese soil.

But the Chinese, taking the long view of history, probably recall America's weak response to the sinking of the *HMS Lusitania.* On May 7, 1915, without warning, the German submarine U-20, sank the British passenger liner the *HMS Lusitania*, killing 1,198 men, women, and children -- to include 128 Americans. This atrocity might have been prevented if President Woodrow Wilson had made it abundantly clear at the outset of World War I in August, 1914, that atrocities committed by Germany on the high seas would compel him to ask Congress for a Declaration of War. Instead, after the widower Wilson married the widow, Edith Galt, the two played golf almost every day of World War I. [Sound familiar?]

So, unless the United States makes it abundantly clear that the Red Chinese will not be allowed to make the Spratly Islands part of China, the CHICOMs will start construction of a military airfield on top of that sandbagged Spratly atoll. But don't worry. President Obama has a secret weapon: Global warming. The melting of the polar ice caps and the rise of the oceans may outpace the CHICOM's supply of sandbags.

©2015. 1784

MOSQUITOES: HUMANKIND'S DEADLIEST ENEMY

In Vietnam, we discovered a simple way to avoid Malaria and Dengue Fever. And the method will work for the deadly Zika Virus as well. Here's what you need to know: Mosquitoes become infected when they feed on a person already infected with a virus or parasite. Infected mosquitoes can then spread the parasites or virus to other people through bites. Fortunately, the female *Anopheles Gambiae* mosquitoes that carry the *Plasmodium Falciparum* parasite and the female *Aedes Aegypti* mosquitoes that carry Dengue Fever and the Zika and Chikunqunya Viruses -- hatch, fly around, and die within less than a mile of where they were hatched.

Ergo: If you can stay at least a mile away from people who have any of these dread diseases in their blood streams, it is unlikely that you will be bitten by a disease-carrying mosquito.

In Vietnam, close contact with the often Malaria-infected North Vietnamese soldiers could not be avoided. So, in addition to choosing night defensive positions at least a mile away from infected populations, we took the anti-malarial Primaquine-Chloraquine and Dapsone tablets. We rolled our sleeves down and buttoned our collars at sundown and, whenever possible, we slept under mosquito netting. Had we not taken all these laborious and time-consuming steps, Malaria and Dengue Fever would have killed or disabled far more of our troops than the NVA and the Viet Cong combined.

Unfortunately, the Obama Administration's program of importing so-called "refugees" from the Middle East and Africa -- with virtually no health screening and spotting them in locations all across the United States -- increases the likelihood that many Americans will come within a mile of populations who are already infected with Malaria or Dengue Fever or the Zika Virus. So, if a mosquito bites one of these infected "refugees" and that mosquito bites you, chances are you will be infected as well.

Ironically, prior to the publication of Rachel Carson's scientifically-suspect *Silent Spring* in 1962, the use of DDT had almost eliminated the scourge of mosquito-borne diseases. But Carson claimed DDT softened bird shells. Her wildly popular book led to a Hobson's choice between certain species of birds and human life. Since the banning of DDT in 1972, 60 million people -- mostly children living in third-world countries -- have died from Malaria. Go figure.

Whether by accident or design, this planting of possibly infected populations here and there across the United States could pose a greater threat to the security of America than al-Qaeda or ISIS. As the history of warfare attests, disease has killed more soldiers, sailors, marines, and airmen that all of the bombs, bullets, artillery shells, rockets, and IEDs ever exploded.

Today, scientists are on the verge of "editing" the genes of mosquitoes so the females produce generations of sterile offspring, leading to the extermination of the entire mosquito species. The June, 2016, issue of *The*

Smithsonian Magazine explains how "new technology gives us the power to wipe out mankind's deadliest enemy." Unfortunately, the same geniuses who banned DDT are opposing the elimination of the mosquito as a species of insect life. Others contend the elimination of the mosquito will result in a population explosion our agricultural production cannot sustain. We report. You decide.

©2016. 1838

BIN LADEN: COULD HE HAVE BEEN STOPPED?

Could President Bill Clinton have averted the 9/11 attacks? Sean Naylor's *Relentless Strike: The Secret History of Joint Special Operations Command* (2015) reveals President Bill Clinton called off two Delta Force operations that could have nailed Osama bin Laden long before September 11, 2001.

But *Relentless Strike* is just one of several books about "special operations" that merit reading: Tony Geraghty's *Inside the S.A.S: The Story of the Amazing Elite British Commando Force* (1980), Christopher Robbins' *Air America from World War II to Vietnam: The Explosive True Story of the CIA's Secret Airline* (2001), and Major General John K. Singlaub's *Hazardous Duty: An American Soldier in the Twentieth Century* (1991).

A common theme emerges from these histories: Be it the famed "Flying Tigers" of pre-World War II that led to the creation of the CIA's post-World War II Air America or the creation of Great Britain's Special Air Service (SAS) or U.S. Special Forces (AKA Green Berets) or the Army's Delta Force or the Army's Ranger Regiment or the Navy's SEAL Team 6, all of these "special" forces had to overcome the objections of old-fashioned generals and admirals, who fought against every dollar allocated to "special forces."

Prior to the Obama Era, it could be said that our all-volunteer "conventional" forces were "special" -- fit, strong, and combat-ready -- as evidenced by the quick victories of Gulf War I, the decimation of the Taliban in Afghanistan shortly after 9/11, and the quick toppling of Saddam Hussein in Iraq. But that is no longer the case. More training hours are now devoted to racial/gender/cultural sensitivity and menstrual-cycle/lactation-understanding training than are devoted to learning how to move, shoot, and communicate.

The Navy's official report on the January 12, 2016, capture of ten American sailors aboard two highly armed Riverine Command Boats in the Persian Gulf states: *"...This incident was the result of failed leadership at multiple levels from the tactical to the operational. The report found the crews were poorly prepared, their boats not properly maintained, communication almost entirely lacking, and their conduct after being captured by the Iranians was not up to military standards..."*

The main support, however, for "special forces" has come from American presidents or British prime ministers who want to have highly competent forces at their beck and call. But not all of our commanders-in-chief, Bill Clinton being a prime example, have been willing to use "special forces."

Shortly after Osama bin Laden bombed the U.S. embassies in Nairobi, Kenya, and Dar es Salaam, Tanzania, and attacked the *USS Cole*, Delta Force was assigned the task of killing bin Laden. In 1998, a Delta ground force and SEAL TEAM 6 snipers were ready to insert operators on a dry lake bed near bin Laden's compound outside Kandahar, Afghanistan. The SEALs and the cargo planes carrying attack helicopters were ready for take-off. At the very last moment, President Clinton decided the operation was "too risky." In 1999, after training for months at Ft. Bragg and White Sands Missile Range, Delta was all set to kill bin Laden with an AGM-114 Hellfire missile. President Clinton scrapped that mission as well. As they say, the rest is history. We report. You decide.

©2016. 1846

MARIJUANA: HOW BIG MJ THREATENS NATIONAL DEFENSE

Millennials by (about 68-percent) and the mainstream media, in general, tend to favor the recreational use of marijuana (MJ). Older conservatives (71-percent) tend to oppose MJ's recreational use. See: Pew Research Survey, March, 2015. Each side thinks it is correct; however, when it comes to national defense, conservatives take a longer and, perhaps, the more prudent view. Here's why:

"Approximately 71% of the 34 million 17-to-24-year-olds in the U.S. would not qualify for military service because of reasons related to health, physical appearance and educational background, according to the Pentagon." See: *Time Magazine*, June 29, 2014. Prior illegal drug use, to include MJ, is one of those disqualifiers.

Article 112a of the Uniform Code of Military Justice (UCMJ) lists marijuana along with opium, heroin, cocaine, and meth as a forbidden substance. Why? Because we need our soldiers, sailors, airmen, and Marines to be alert and be in possession of their full mental capacities at all times. They endure hostile fire and, even in non-combat situations, they must operate highly dangerous machinery. The military is no place for someone stoned on marijuana.

Unfortunately, and despite federal laws against the recreational use of marijuana, Colorado, Washington, Oregon, Alaska and D.C. have claimed a Tenth Amendment power to make MJ legal. Twelve more states are threatening to use the Tenth Amendment to do the same. Given the tendency of young people to experiment with and even to fall into habitual use of marijuana, this trend could continue to shrink the already very small pool of military-qualified 17-to-24-year-olds.

The Commerce, Due Process, Equal Protection and Privileges or Immunities Clauses of the 14th Amendment have been used by Big Government Democrats and Republicans alike to erode the powers of the individual states which the Founders thought would be protected by the Tenth Amendment which states: *"The powers not delegated to the United States by the Constitution, nor prohibited by it to the States, are reserved to the States respectively, or to the people."*

While constitutionalists applaud when the states stand up for their rights under the Tenth Amendment, many conservatives are appalled when the Tenth Amendment is used to legalize MJ and capture a way to collect more "sin taxes." In 2012, the Obama re-election campaign promoted Colorado's pro-MJ Amendment 64 as a way to bring out the youth vote and carry Colorado for President Obama. Moreover, Big MJ is a multi-billion-dollar industry and a vote to aid Big MJ always raises the question: *Qui bono?* Who benefits?

Elected officials who are perceived in any way to support Big MJ do so at their peril because, inevitably, some young people in their districts will be harmed by MJ and the parents of those harmed by MJ are likely to seek retribution during the next election cycle. Moreover, fairly or unfairly, a vote in favor of Big MJ raises the specter of money under the table.

While most Americans favor the use of MJ to relieve pain for end-of-life hospice situations, the nation is almost evenly split over recreational use of MJ. But factor in MJ's long-term, negative impact on our national defense and we could see a shift away from the legalization of MJ.

©2016. 1854

THE DRONE AS "DEUS EX MACHINA."

The "deus ex machina" is a literary device used by fiction writers who, usually by accident, have painted their plot into a seemingly hopeless corner. Even the great Greek playwright, Thucydides, sometimes had to use a crane (machina) to drop onto the stage an unexpected power, such as a Greek God (Deus) who would, in the process of rescuing the good and/or punishing the bad, resolve the, otherwise, hopeless situation.

Now, fast forward from ancient Greece to the 21st Century and to the advent of the Remotely Piloted Aircraft (RPA), popularly referred to as drones. Experts say, by 2020, the drone industry will be a $127 billion-dollar enterprise. By 2020, the FAA expects over 2.7 million drones to be in commercial and private use. By February of this year, over 350,000 drones were registered with the FAA. In Switzerland, commercial drones are already being used to deliver needed supplies to isolated Alpine villages.

But drones can also be used for less benign purposes. For example: Let's say, Mr. Jones does not like the party noises emanating from Mr. Smith's backyard swimming pool. In the wee hours, Jones has his drone drop some algae into Smith's pool, turning the water a slimy green. Or, a demented Mr. Jones could have his drone drop poison into Smith's unattended cocktail glass, i.e. murder-by-drone. Or, let's say you are a high-profile government official in the war against political Islam. If the radical Islamists can fly huge big airliners into the World Trade Center and the Pentagon, using a drone for targeted assassinations of U.S. officials is well within their range of skills.

Then too, let's say you are an American President who does not want to add to the prison population at Gitmo (AKA Sandals-by-the Sea where the detainees enjoy a custom-made soccer field, four Halal meals-a-day, imported dates, honey, and roasted meats (no pork) which can be worked off using treadmills and stationary bikes. Plus, detainees have local Wi-Fi, Al-Jazeera TV, art classes, and a 10,000-volume library, to include DVDs and computer games.) Even so, most detainees want to return to the squalor of the Middle East. Mr. Obama, rather than capturing terrorists for their intelligence value, has been using drones to kill the terrorists on-the-spot, skipping all that messy time and expense of housing them at Gitmo. Viola! A modern-day "deus ex machina."

By now, about 77-percent of the original Gitmo population has been released. Unfortunately, over 20-percent of the former detainees are known to have rejoined the battle against U.S. forces. But one wonders what the freed 80-percent think about their all-inclusive Sandals-by-the-Sea captivity?

Gitmo aside, the reality is that drones are here to stay. We can no longer look up into the U.S. skies and only fear death-by-meteor. If your Christmas present "deus ex machina" weighs more than .55 pounds, pay the $5.00 fee, get it registered, or risk a $27,500 fine.

Moreover, even non-commercial drone pilots would be well-advised to take the free FAA commercial drone pilot exam and use that knowledge to lower the risk of doing something stupid like downing a "real" airplane. See:www.faa.gov/uas/. Meanwhile, there is this suspicious looking hummingbird that keeps looking in our windows. Even in December...

©2016. 1866

AN OPEN LETTER TO KIM JONG-UN

Dear Mr. Supreme Leader:

Please forgive the informality of this letter; however, you have been in the news a lot lately and I feel like I am getting to know you. So, in the interest of world peace and your personal welfare, I feel compelled to give you some free advice.

First of all, I think you have made a risky career choice. Just off the top of my head, I recall the lives of some relatively recent and infamous dictators who did not end well. For example: Benito Mussolini, Adolph Hitler, Nicolae Ceausescu, Saddam Hussein, and Muammar Gadhafi. While Joseph Stalin might have died in bed from a stroke, there are rumors he was smothered by Nikita Khrushchev.

But you don't have to be an all-out despotic dictator for some people to want to kill you. Here in America's representative democracy, we lost Abraham Lincoln, James Garfield, William McKinley, and John F. Kennedy to assassins. That, however, does not count unsuccessful assassination attempts directed at: Andrew Jackson, Theodore Roosevelt, FDR, Harry Truman, Richard Nixon,

Gerald Ford, Jimmy Carter, Ronald Reagan, George H.W. Bush, Bill Clinton, George W. Bush, and Barack Hussein Obama.

Granted, you have yourself surrounded by supposedly loyal folks who guard you day and night. But I need to warn you about a possible coup d'état. You see, you are playing a very dangerous game against a very unpredictable President of the United States. Even though you hold over ten million citizens of Seoul hostage with your thousands of artillery pieces within shooting range of downtown Seoul, what if you overplay your hand? What if some of the folks around you decide you are going to get them all killed? They have loved ones: parents, wives, children, grandchildren, and other relatives.

Here's what might happen: 1. You could be deposed by a military coup that would continue your anti-western policies; however, not by playing nuclear roulette with the USA. 2. You could be deposed by a military junta that wants a better life for the poor people of North Korea, a life more like the relatively abundant life being lived by your ethnic kinsmen and women in South Korea.

Believe me; we have been shopping in downtown Seoul. It is a Disney Land for shoppers. Last time Wonder Wife and I were there, we had to buy extra suitcases to ship all our bargains back to the USA.

Okay. So, I understand you inherited this dictatorship business from your father and he inherited the business from his father. But, unless you just happen to like it, nothing is forcing you to continue with their business model.

You could become a real hero to your people by providing them with food. We can send you food. We are up to our hips in food. You could provide your people with health care. We have a half-vast, health-insurance model we are about to scrap and you are welcome to it.

Bottom line: there are better career choices to which you should give serious consideration. Our President might set you up with a casino: pretty girls. Johnny Walker Red, endless buffets, and a better barber. Think about it.

Sincerely,
William

©2017. 1897

CHAPTER FOUR

ECONOMICS: THE DISMAL SCIENCE

THE PHANTOM OF THE SOCIAL SECURITY TRUST FUND

Stop the presses! Your intrepid observer just located the Social Security (SS) Trust Fund. It is in a federal building in Parkersburg, W.Va. Slipping through the vault door, I expected to see a huge pile of dollars lying about. Wrong. Instead of dollars, I found a stack of IOUs from the U.S. Government. I was about to sneak back out when an apparition dressed in a black cape and wearing a white mask over the right side of his face challenged me with, "What are you doing inside the Trust Fund?"

"I came to visit the SS tax dollars that my employers and I deposited here. But they are gone. And, who the heck are you, anyway?"

"I am the Phantom of the SS Trust Fund. And I see you are one of those dolts who think your employers actually paid into my massive Ponzi scheme."

"Wait a minute. I paid 6.2-percent and my employers paid 6.2-percent."

"Wrong. Your employer simply reduced your pay by the amount he or she was required to pay in SS taxes. You paid all 12.4-percent of it."

"Ouch. Well, what have you done with our, I mean my, SS tax dollars?"

"Back in the early days, not many of you lived long enough to collect your Social Security. So, I took in a lot more than I paid out. But then, President Lyndon Johnson got Congress to siphon off the so-called surplus to pay for his Great Society programs."

"So, that explains why you wear a mask. You have taken my money. But I have no ownership stake in it. Only some IOUs. But why only half a mask?"

"Because, even though I have stolen your opportunity to make much wiser investments than SS, I am not all bad. By the way, I don't really have to pay you a penny. I have won two court cases: *Helvering v. Davis* (1937) and *Fleming v. Nestor* (1960) that ruled you have no contractual rights to get back any of your SS tax dollars.

"But I enjoy my power over you. So I will pay out until I start receiving fewer dollars than I take in. That will happen in the year 2018. By then, there will only be two of you suckers to support each SS retiree. So, thirteen years from now, Congress will have to either cut SS benefits and/or raise the SS taxes on those two remaining workers."

"Isn't there some other way to fix a system that is headed for the financial rocks?"

"Well, there was. Maybe, there still is. Back in the 1980s, Congress should have followed the example of 11 South American countries that let their tax payers own a portion of their SS taxes by investing them in stocks and/or bonds. Now, their SS Trust Funds are solvent, and the private investments are creating a growing, and stable, middle class."

"Is it too late for me to put a portion of my SS taxes into some investments that will help me have more retirement money than the present system?"

"If you are over 55, it is too late. But one idea floating before Congress would let those under 55 invest up to four percent of their SS taxes in some conservative investments. But don't hold your breath for that. Powerful lobbies like the AARP and the labor unions have their own mutual funds. They don't want SS to compete with them. Also, the Left-wing Democrats don't want you to own even a portion of your SS taxes."

"Why not? Isn't the American dream to own a greater stake in society, to move up the economic ladder to financial independence?"

"Naw. We want you to be more dependent on government, not less. If you become financially independent, you might vote Republican."

With that, the Phantom of the SS Trust Fund, like my SS taxes, disappeared in a puff of smoke.

©2005. 1203

PETITION ON BEHALF OF AMERICA'S CANDLE-MAKERS

In 1845, on behalf of France's candle-makers, the French economist, Frederic Bastiat, published a satire known as "The Petition of the Candle-makers." The petition was addressed to the French Chamber of Deputies. Bastiat argued that the sun was producing so much light as to drive French candle-makers out of business.

To combat the adverse effect of the sun, Bastiat wrote, "We ask you to be so good as to pass a law requiring the closing of all windows, dormers, skylights, inside and outside shutters, curtains, casements, bull's-eyes, deadlights, and blinds -- in short, all openings, holes, chinks, and fissures through which the light of the sun is wont to enter houses, to the detriment of [France's candle-makers]."

A modern-day Frederic Bastiat might appeal to the U.S. Congress on behalf of U.S. candle-makers as follows:

"We are suffering from the ruinous competition of foreign rivals who apparently work under conditions far superior to our own. Even at the current price of $140 dollars-per-barrel, we consume 21 million barrels of oil each day. That is enough oil to light the Las Vegas Strip and even the 10,000-square-foot home of Al Gore and the 28,200-square-foot home of John Edwards.

"Therefore, in addition to asking that you be so good as to pass a law requiring the closing of all windows, dormers, skylights, inside and outside shutters, curtains, casements, bull's-eyes, deadlights and blinds; in short, all openings, holes, chinks, and fissures, we ask that you take steps to increase the price of crude oil by restricting America's ability to add to its oil supply. We ask you to be aware that a return to crude oil priced at $30-per-barrel or gas at $1.20-per-gallon would encourage the use of electric-powered lighting to the detriment of those hard-working Americans who produce "green" candles from tallow, beeswax and cotton.

"We ask you to continue your prohibitions against off-shore oil exploration in over 80-percent of our coastal waters (est. 102 billion barrels), against oil exploration in 2,200-acres of the Arctic National Wildlife Refuge (ANWR) (est. 10 billion barrels), against the issuance of permits to produce oil from shale in Colorado, Utah and Wyoming (est. 800 billion barrels) and we urge you to add prohibitions against the use of horizontal drilling to produce crude oil from the Bakken Oil Formation (est. 10-500 billion barrels) that lies under North Dakota and Montana. We ask that no more gasoline refineries or nuclear power plants be permitted. Please prohibit our 200 years of coal from conversion into synthetic fuels.

"By returning to a tallow/beeswax/cotton-based economy, the production of cattle, sheep and pigs will be increased. We shall see an increase in cleared fields, meat, wool, leather, and especially manure which, prior to ethanol, was the basis of all agricultural wealth.

"If America consumes more 'green' oils, we shall see an expansion of the olive oil, corn, cotton and rapeseed industries. These rich yet soil-exhausting plants will come at just the right time to enable us to put to profitable use the increased fertility that the breeding of cattle will impart to the land.

"Our moors will be covered with resinous trees. Numerous swarms of bees will gather from our mountains the perfumed treasures that today waste their fragrance, like the flowers from which they emanate. Thus, there is not one branch of agriculture that would not undergo a great expansion.

"But what shall we say of the specialties of American manufacture? Henceforth you will behold gilding, bronze, and crystal in candlesticks, in lamps, in chandeliers, in candelabra sparkling in spacious shopping malls and on the Home Shopping Network.

"It needs but a little reflection, gentlemen, to be convinced that there is perhaps not one American from the wealthy stockholder of the Tallow-R-Us Corp. to the humblest vendor of matches, whose condition would not be improved by the success of our petition.

"Gentle Congresspersons, by granting our petition, you can return America to the way it was prior to1935 -- before President Franklin D. Roosevelt imposed the Rural Electric Administration (REA) upon us."

©2008. 1376

ECON 101: NOTHING HAPPENS UNTIL A SALE IS MADE

Recently, a great book of newspaper clippings called: "Days of Glory" brought back memories of this writer's earliest involvement in the newspaper "business." (Yes, newspapers are businesses with costs that must be met in order to remain in business.)

After school, we paperboys folded the papers we would throw on dozens of doorsteps before dark. Back then, the pressmen poured molten lead to make the galley plates. To avoid burns from splattered lead, you soon learned not to walk through the pressroom.

As the junior paperboy, I had the most economically depressed part of town. On Saturdays, trying to collect for the papers in an area of mostly poor whites and then segregated blacks, was an interesting exercise in socio-economics. The latter almost always paid right on time, but some of the former required some adult supervision.

My route included several anti-social canines who took a keen interest in boys on bikes. But a very mild solution of vinegar dispensed via water pistol caused them to lose interest in my particular bike.

The smell of newsprint and printing presses and even getting splattered with hot lead has a certain allure. After a break of about 30 years, I was back in the newspaper business, writing a weekly column syndicated up and down the Great Plains. Fondly, I recall that the first newspaper to join the syndicate was *The York News-Times*.

Eventually, Wonder Wife and I became part-owners of a community newspaper. My role as editor-in-chief led to a long string of writing assignments for the nation's largest-circulation newspaper.

But we soon learned part ownership of a community newspaper wasn't all glamour. Every column-inch of printed surface must be supported by advertising. If a news story takes up, say, 20 column-inches of space, then at least 20 column-inches of advertising must be sold to recover the cost of producing that news story.

In a free-market economy, nothing happens until a sale is made. For our economy to function, willing buyers must be put together with willing sellers. Bringing sellers and buyers together is the essential function of a community newspaper.

Unfortunately, in today's economy, few sales are being made. While government is growing, hiring more government workers only grows the economy for those particular workers and their families.

Government has no wealth other than the taxes it can extract from taxpayers. With 47-percent of the population paying zero federal income tax (the federal government's revenue source), April 15 was Tax Day for 53-percent of us and was, as the Heritage Foundation points out, Pay Day for the 47-percent who are enjoying "free" federal government services.

Professor Thomas Sowell suggests we are approaching "a point of no return" when newly-minted citizens (formerly known as illegal immigrants) are rounded up by ethnic- and union-activists to vote in a permanent radical-Left majority. A majority that pays no federal income tax would be able to elect even more politicians who promise them even more government "pork" at the expense of the tax-paying minority.

Currently, commercial lenders are uncertain what big government is going to do to them. Community banks with high debt-to-equity ratios are trying to get rid of non-performing liabilities so they can start making small business loans again.

Small business owners who can't obtain financing are reluctant to hire. Because ObamaCare negatively impacts businesses with 50 employees or more, one solution is to cut the work force down to 49 workers, or fewer. Ouch.

Newspapers are not public utilities that can raise their rates willy-nilly to recover their costs. Printing more news pages to attract more readers cannot be done unless there are advertising pages to support the news pages. So, until sellers are able to sell and buyers are able to buy, these are perilous times for America's community newspapers.
©2010. 1471

ARIZONA: MORE ECONOMICS THAN RACE

Currently, about 460,000 illegal aliens from Mexico and points South are in Arizona. Arizonans contend the illegal aliens are adversely impacting their standard of living. Is this simply an Anglo vs. Hispanic conflict? Or, is the underlying problem one of economics?

Recently, *Washington Post* columnist, George Will, observed the United States is the only "developed" country with a 2,000-mile-long border with a "developing" country. What happens, when a woefully undeveloped region, such as northern Mexico, shares a virtually unguarded border with a highly developed U.S. State, such as Arizona?

Answer: People stream from the developing country into the developed country seeking a higher standard of living. If the stream is allowed to become a flood, the standard of living in the developed country spirals downward toward the standard of living in the developing country.

This would suggest the root cause of the current chaos in Arizona has more to do with economics than race. Race, of course, is always the Obama Regime's knee-jerk response to any issue.

Based on Mexico's climate, geography, minerals, and her people, Mexico ought to be one of the world's most prosperous and powerful countries. She has great people with the ability to become skilled workers. Tourists love her balmy climate. Mexico has beautiful coastlines on two major bodies of water. She has silver, copper, gold, lead, zinc, wildlife, fish, timber, petroleum and natural gas in abundance.

Overall, Mexico has sufficient rainfall; however, northern Mexico is extremely dry. But that's a water-distribution problem. The kind of problem an effective government could solve by building dams, by piping water from wet regions to dry regions. But Mexico does not have an effective government.

Instead, Mexico has a long history of bad and corrupt government which, according to the *CIA World Fact Book*, has led to: *"a scarcity of hazardous waste disposal facilities; rural to urban migration; raw sewage and industrial effluents polluting rivers in urban areas; deforestation; widespread erosion; desertification; deteriorating agricultural lands; serious air and water pollution in the national capital and urban centers along the U.S.-Mexico border."* No wonder her people want to leave.

But the chances of getting Mexico to fix its governance problem are somewhere between slim and none. So, what are the people of neighboring Arizona to do? Wait for the U.S. Government to do its sovereign duty and secure the border? Fat chance the Obama Regime will do anything other than complain that Arizona's new immigration law is misguided and try to use Arizona's dilemma for partisan political advantage.

CNN's Jack Cafferty says: *"What's misguided, Mr. President, is the federal government's ongoing refusal to enforce the laws that are already on the books. Read the Arizona law. Parts of it are word-for-word the same as the federal statutes which continue to be all but ignored."*

Columnist Peggy Noonan writes: *"Arizona is moving forward because the government in Washington has completely abdicated its responsibility. For 10 years – at least – through two administrations, Washington deliberately did nothing to ease the crisis on the borders because politicians calculated an air of mounting crisis would spur mounting support for what Washington thought was appropriate reform – i.e., reform that would help the Democratic and Republican parties."*

Cable news pundit, Rich Galen, suggests Mexico, by warning its citizens that it is now dangerous to travel in

Arizona, is taking hypocrisy to a new high. Excuse me, if you want to experience dangerous travel, try Mexico where drug cartels slaughter not just each other, they kill and/or kidnap thousands each year.

Unfortunately, the flood of illegal immigrants is making Arizona more like northern Mexico when what is needed is to make northern Mexico more like Arizona. Meanwhile, the citizens of Arizona are doing what they can to defend their standard of living. The fault lies with the Mexican and U.S. governments, not with Arizona.

©2010. 1473

THE ECONOMY: STOCK UP ON WHEELBARROWS?

The dismal "science" of economics is difficult. But the Misery Index – a term once favored by former President Carter -- is fairly easy to understand.

The Misery Index is the rate-of-unemployment plus the rate-of-inflation expressed as a point value. When President Ford's Misery Index was 12.66, candidate Carter used that against Ford. Ironically, Carter ended his own presidency with a Misery Index of 19.72 -- the highest since World War II. President Ronald Reagan, employing free-market principles, took the Misery Index down to 9.72, setting off 25 years of generally high employment and relatively low inflation.

In 2008, the sub-prime mortgage crisis revealed President Clinton and the Democrats in Congress, in the years subsequent to Clinton, had been pushing for home mortgages for poor people who could not even pay their phone bills, much less make their mortgage payments. Moreover, the main malefactors: Congressman Barney Frank and Senators Christopher Dodd and Charles Schumer pushed for regulations that punished banks if they failed to make mortgage loans no sane banker would ever make. Like the debates leading up to the Smoot-Hawley Tariff Act of 1930, which triggered the Great Depression, the sub-prime mortgage crisis in the U.S. produced a world-wide economic morass.

Looking back over the history of the 20th Century we see how foolish decisions on the part of European governments and Japan made America rich. The belligerents on both sides of World Wars I and II needed enormous amounts of capital to pay for munitions. The United States, that great maritime nation protected from invasion by two great oceans and possessed of an un-bombed means of production, provided capital and munitions for the Allied Powers. So, even before the end of World War II, the British Pound Sterling was replaced by the U.S. Dollar as the world's benchmark currency, the paper money by which the value of all other paper financial instruments is determined.

In 1945, President Truman inherited an economy that was inflated because we had a lot of wealth chasing too few consumer goods. So, Truman's starting Misery Index was 13.63; however, by the time Truman left office, the switch from war production to the production of consumer goods and America's strong financial position as the world's creditor reduced that number down to 3.45.

But, as we can see from the time of the sub-prime mortgage crisis and right on through the recent G-20 Economic Summit in South Korea, the relative financial position of the U.S. to the rest of the world is weakening. Indeed, almost all of the western developed nations are showing financial weakness. Conversely, Red China, India, and Indonesia are gaining financial power.

The reasons for the decline of the western developed nations are abundantly clear: over consumption of consumer goods and over-borrowing to pay for that over-consumption. Unfortunately, the Federal Reservists, the Obamessiahs in the White House, and the EarMarxists in Congress seem clueless. Government overspending and printing more paper money to borrow from ourselves to pay debts for which we do not have the capital to repay in the first place is the path to the kind of inflation that robs the elderly, in particular, of their savings.

Moreover, using "stimulus" money to create a job for a government bureaucrat means the salary and benefits to pay for that new bureaucrat must be taken from the pockets of taxpayers. That is not economic growth. Historically, reducing taxes on individuals and businesses and lifting government restrictions on free-market capitalism result in the creation of real.

Unless we reverse course, we could be like Germany in 1923 when the wheelbarrow used to carry the millions of German *Papiermarken* it took to buy a loaf of bread had more intrinsic value than the essentially worthless paper money inside the wheelbarrow.

©2010. 1502

ECONOMICS 101: THE CONSUMER ALWAYS PAYS

All too often, someone says: "The government is going to pay for it." While it would be nice to have some kind of government fairy godmother to pay the expenses of government, the truth of the matter is that for governments to have money governments must take the money away from people in the form of taxes.

Another fact that seems all-too-often misunderstood is that successful business enterprises pay taxes. But the fact of the matter is that successful businesses only "appear" to pay taxes. That is because to stay in business all the operating costs of the business are borne ultimately by the consumer. In other words, if more taxes are imposed on a business, the business simply adds the cost of those taxes onto the price of the goods and/or services it provides to its customers.

So, whether we buy a loaf of bread or a gallon of gas or a kitchen appliance or a kilowatt of electricity, all of the costs of producing those items and providing them are passed on to us – the ultimate consumers or users.

Recently, the Obama Administration dictated that religious institutions must provide insurance to their employees that must include insurance coverage for contraception devices, birth-control pills, tubal ligation, and "morning-after" abortion-pills. The leaders of the Roman Catholic Church and some of the major Protestant Evangelical groups rose up in protest. They were not about to pay for insurance coverage that ran counter to their basic religious beliefs. Nor did they want to pay for what they saw as a disregard for the religious freedoms guaranteed by the First Amendment.

Responding to the uproar, the Obama Administration used an accounting trick. Mr. Obama said he would "force" the insurance companies to provide the offending services for "free" and the religious institutions would not have to pay for them. Hello? The insurance companies offer no goods, services, or protections for free. Someone has to pay for them. Guess who?

Like all corporations or businesses, the insurance companies must "socialize" all their costs across their customer base which has to include everyone and every institution that is insured, to include (drum roll) those Catholic-run hospitals, like Holy Cross Hospital, and other Catholic charities.

So, saying that the insurance companies must provide the contraceptive services and abortion drugs for "free" changes nothing. The only realistic step the Obama Administration could take to solve this dilemma would be to exempt religious institutions from ObamaCare. According to a recent article in *Commentary Magazine*, the Obama Administration has already issued 1,168 ObamaCare waivers, many of them going to labor unions and other major Obama campaign contributors.

One wonders why Mr. Obama is so deaf to the concerns of Roman Catholics and some Protestant Evangelicals? Wesley Pruden, writing in *The Washington Times*, says, "Mr. Obama, like the rest of us, is a man formed by the earliest influences in his life. He spent his most formative years in Indonesia, about as far from America as a man can go before he meets himself coming back. He grew to manhood in Hawaii, and finally ended up at Harvard for a little book learning and a lot of attitude adjustment. All worthy places in their own way, to be sure, but hardly places to absorb the faith, practice, culture and lore of America."

Professor Cal Jillson, at Southern Methodist University, says of Mr. Obama: "He doesn't have a natural feeling for the depth of emotion of how some Americans hold their religious views." According to CatholicNews.com, 54-percent of Roman Catholics voted Mr. Obama into the White House. It will be interesting to see what happens this November.
©2012. 1610

ECONOMICS: WHAT'S IN A LANGUAGE?

This is not to say today's Germans are better than today's Italians, Spanish, French, or Portuguese. But it is a fair question to ask: After disastrously losing two wars in the 20th Century (largely, of their own making) and suffering through the Cold War as a nation split in half, how is it that Germany today is the ruler of Europe's economy?

Why does the entire world hang on almost every word coming from the mouth of German Chancellor Angela Merkel and is largely dismissive of the leaders of France, Spain, Italy, Portugal, and even the United States?

Why do many Europeans think they should work only 35 hours-per-week and then retire at age 50 with virtually the entire benefits of full-time employment? Perhaps, "language" can provide part of the answer.

The German noun for "work" is *werk*. The German verb for "work" is *wirken*. But, most often, the Germans refer to "work" as *Arbeit* -- pronounced in English as: r-bite.

In German, the *Arbeitgeber* is one who "gives" work to another. In Germany, providing someone with *Arbeit* is highly honorable. Contrast that with the French-English word: "employer" which has its roots in: to exploit, to use someone, to rule, to master, and to oversee.

The French noun for work is: *le travail*. The French verb for work is: *travailler*. Both noun and verb are rooted in the Latin word: *tripaliare,* to torture, which is derived from *tripalium* – an ancient torture device composed of three poles. Thus, in French, work and torture are the same. In Italian, work is *travagliare;* in Spanish, *trahahbor;* and in Portuguese, *trabalhar.* All these words plus "travail," often used in English for toil and trouble, derive from *tripalium* -- the torture device.

So, if your cradle languages are telling you that employers are exploiters of the workers and that "work" is just another word for torture, you might dread going to work and also want to stop doing work as soon as possible.

As related in a previous column, the renowned German sociologist, Max Weber, (pronounced: machs vay-burr), marveled, in 1904, at the work ethic he observed in America. Back then, many Americans believed working hard would find favor with God and that working hard was something noble to do, a path toward Salvation.

In certain quarters, however, the American work ethic may be dead and buried. An example is Government Motors (GM) where auto workers are paid $56 dollars-per-hour, use up an enormous number of paid "sick" days, and enjoy long paid vacations. In addition, the Obama bailout pumped $50 billion tax dollars into the United Auto Workers pension fund. Now, some auto industry experts say GM's wages and benefits are so non-competitive that there is no way that GM will ever again show an actual profit.

Downtown Detroit, which was booming in 1945, looks today more like the bombed out Berlin of 1945. Today's Berlin looks like Detroit in 1945, only better.

The famous historian, Victor Davis Hanson, concludes: "If the people of the European Union want to live like the Germans, they must learn to work and save like the Germans." Germans are fond of boasting: "*Immer besser bei uns*." Meaning: Our way is always better! Irritating as that was when this soldier lived with the Germans for almost a decade, today's Germans are making good on their boast.

©2012. 1629

THE AFFORDABLE BOAT ACT

Columnist Ann Coulter points out that ObamaCare will force gays to buy maternity coverage, Mormons must pay for gambling addiction therapy, elderly couples must pay for pediatric dental care, and Catholic hospitals must pay for birth control and abortions. What follows is an anonymous satire going around the Internet that points out the absurdity of ObamaCare: The Affordable Boat Act:

The U.S. government has just passed a new law called: 'The Affordable Boat Act' declaring that every citizen MUST purchase a new boat, by April 2014. These 'affordable' boats will cost an average of $54,000-$155,000 each. This does not include taxes, trailers, towing fees, licensing, and registration fees, fuel, docking and storage fees, maintenance or repair costs.

This law has been passed, because until now, typically only wealthy and financially responsible people have been able to purchase boats. This new law ensures that every American can now have an 'affordable' boat of their own, because everyone is entitled to a new boat. If you purchase your boat before the end of the year, you will receive four 'free' life jackets; not including monthly usage fees.

In order to make sure everyone purchases an affordable boat, the costs of owning a boat will increase on average of 250-400% per year. This way, wealthy people will pay more for something that other people don't want or can't afford to maintain. But to be fair, people who can't afford to maintain their boat will be regularly fined, and children (under the age of 26) can use their parent's boats to party on until they turn 27; then they must purchase their own boat.

If you already have a boat, you can keep yours (just kidding; no you can't). If you don't want or don't need a boat, you are required to buy one anyhow. If you refuse to buy one or can't afford one, you will be regularly fined $800 until you purchase one, or face imprisonment.

Failure to use the boat will also result in fines. People living in the desert, ghettos, inner cities or areas with no access to lakes are not exempt. Neither age, motion sickness, experience, knowledge, nor lack of desire are acceptable excuses for not using your boat.

A government review board (that doesn't know the difference between the port, starboard or stern sides of a boat) will decide everything, including: when, where, how often and for what purposes you can use your boat along with how many people can ride on your boat, and determine if one is too old or healthy enough to be able to use their boat. They will also decide if your boat has outlived its usefulness, or if you must purchase specific accessories (like a $500 compass), or a newer and more expensive boat. Those who can afford yachts will be required to do so…it's only fair. The government will also decide the name for each boat. Failure to comply with these rules will result in fines and possible imprisonment.

Government officials are exempt from this new law. If they want a boat, they and their families can obtain boats free, at the expense of taxpayers. Unions, bankers and mega companies with large political affiliations are also exempt.

Again, this is only satire. Please do not try to sign up for an affordable boat. Besides, the web page portals are already jammed and the server crashed -- again.

©2013. 1703

HEALTH INSURANCE AND THE FAUSTIAN BARGAIN

Last week, I fell asleep re-reading Christopher Marlowe's circa 1604 A.D. play: "The Tragic Life and Death of Doctor Faustus." Soon, I was dreaming that I was Dr. Faustus, the CEO of Dewey, Cheatem & Howe -- a major health insurance company. Some fellow named, Mephistopheles, told me that his boss, Lew C. Furr, wanted to offer me a bargain that would make me and my shareholders fabulously wealthy.

When I met Lew C. Furr, he said, "Look, if you will let me operate your business for 24 years, I will provide you with 33 million new customers who will be mandated to buy your health insurance and if they don't purchase your health insurance, the government of the U.S. of A. will punish them for not buying your health insurance. Even better, most of the 33 million new customers will be too young to have health problems. That means your company won't be paying out much money to health-care providers. Such a deal!"

This Lew C. Furr character was tall, thin, and kinda toasty-looking, as if he had been standing too close to a hellacious fire for too long. He smoked cigarettes like a chimney, so I figured he would not last four years, much less eight. Certainly, not the 24 years he was asking for. So, I entered into the bargain with Lew C. Furr.

Unfortunately, the on-line enrollment system set up by Lew C. Furr was devilishly difficult for people to navigate. Rarely, would their computers connect with Lew C. Furr's enrollment system. And, when they did connect, people had to provide their most private health information to a system which was being hacked by scammers pretending to be Lew C. Furr's system.

I hurried to an Internet Cafe where I found a Miss Sissy Fuss who was trying over and over again to get enrolled; however her only partially completed form kept dropping off-line. Sissy Fuss showed me a letter from her old health insurance company saying she was no longer insured. Because she had just discovered a large lump in one breast, she was desperate. Her answering machine at home was receiving robo-calls saying, "Unless she submitted additional personal information, her application had uncorrectable errors." She feared the lump removal, radiation, and chemo therapy would wipe her out financially.

I contacted Lew C. Furr, who responded, "Sorry, Dr. Faustus, you see the 'public opinion clause' in our bargain's fine print says you will be forced to pay her medicals costs whether she is fully enrolled or not. In fact, whether or not your company ever gets paid any insurance premiums is not my concern.

"But that's where the fines come in. The fines from those who refuse to buy health insurance go into your company coffers."

"Wait," I protested. "The fines won't cover our payments to health-care providers. Under this cockamamie bargain, we can't afford to stay in business!"

"I know," said Lew C. Furr. "Again, check the fine print. It says, 'If the private insurance companies fail, then Plan B is Socialized Medicine, AKA single-payer.' You know, for a highly paid CEO, you are rather naïve."

Jolted awake, I realized this wasn't a dream. It was an actual nightmare.

©2013. 1708

EMP ATTACK: WHAT ARE THE AFTER-EFFECTS?

Two seemingly unrelated recent events should command the attention of every American. First, the North American Aerospace Command (NORAD), at a cost of $700 million, is going to move its communications gear back inside the depths of Colorado's Cheyenne Mountain. Why? Because of the growing threat of an electromagnetic pulse (EMP) attack.

Secondly, Russian President Vladimir Putin just announced that Russia will provide Iran with Russia's first-class S-300 Air Defense System. Ergo: About a year from now Iran's nuclear-weapons production facilities will be virtually immune from attack by Israel and/or the United States. Moreover, nothing in the pending nuclear-arms agreement restrains Iran's ability to produce intercontinental ballistic missiles (ICBMs). Not one word bans the production of EMP weapons. (Nuclear-armed North Korea already has a growing ICBM capability.)

So, if NORAD is sufficiently worried about an EMP attack to leave the comfort of Peterson Air Force Base and move back into the dank tunnels of Cheyenne Mountain, what's the big deal? What would be the impacts of an EMP attack on the U.S. homeland?

"According to Lowell Wood, acting chairman of the Commission to Assess the Threat to the United States from an EMP Attack, such an attack 'could cripple the U.S. by knocking out electrical power, computers, circuit boards controlling most automobiles and trucks, banking systems, communications and food and water supplies.'

"...electromagnetic pulses propagate from the burst point of the nuclear weapon to the line of sight on the Earth's horizon, potentially covering a vast geographic region at the speed of light," Wood said. "For example, a nuclear weapon detonated at an altitude of 400 kilometers (about 250 miles) over the central United States would cover, with its primary electromagnetic pulse, the entire United States and parts of Canada and Mexico."

Writing in *Florida Today*, Don Gilleland, a former executive with General Dynamics Corp. says: *"Within nanoseconds... all computer chips within line of sight of the explosion, i.e., the entire continental United States will be immediately and irreparably fried. All aircraft aloft will lose power... All ground vehicles dependent upon computers will lose power and drift to a halt.*

"There will be no electric power anywhere. Cell phones will not operate. All life-support equipment will cease to function. Delivery of all goods and services will quickly cease. Public safety, sanitation, police and fire and rescue services will immediately be overwhelmed and quickly disappear.

"Existing supplies of food and water will not be replaced. Prisons will be opened and felons will arm themselves. Money and credit cards will be worthless. Looting will be endemic. The sick and the elderly will be the first to die. Starvation and disease will attack the survivors. There is no reason to hope that government agencies, at whatever level, are remotely equipped to deal with the situation. Retaliation is possible, and the military ability exists to reduce the perpetrator to a smoldering slag heap, but by that time nine of 10 Americans will likely be dead or dying..."

Amazingly, EMP does not destroy bricks and mortar. The USA would become a land of standing-empty, uninhabited homes and factories just waiting for the Islamic Imperialists or the North Koreans to occupy. Should Congress be involved in negotiations involving nuclear and EMP weapons and ICBMs? Or, just President Obama? We report. You decide.

©2015. 1778

SOCIALISM: THE PARABLE OF THE LEMONADE STAND

Our teenage daughter decided to raise money for that cute kid you see on TV, trying to raise money for his children's hospital. Because we made sure her bedtime stories were inspired by Ludwig von Mises, Russell Kirk, and William F. Buckley, Jr., her decision to open a lemonade stand came as no surprise. The organic lemons came from a tree we planted years ago, the potable water came from our own well. She placed her cardboard lemonade stand in our front yard, adjacent to the sidewalk.

Then, arm-in-arm, along came Bernie, Hillary, Barack, Elizabeth, and Michael, followed by Michael's pistol-packing body guards. Michael said, "Kid, as a former mayor, I know you gotta have a city permit to sell those sugar-laced 16-oz. beverages."

"I don't, your Honor. But I am helping a licensed, tax-exempt charity. My sweetener is: *Stevia rebaudiana*."

"Well, we'll see about that," mumbled Michael.

"Miss," said Barack, "I don't see any minorities working here. Of folks like me, you need 13-percent."

"But sir," there's just 100-percent of me and I must keep my overhead low."

"By the way, you got ObamaCare?"

"No, sir, ObamaCare is too expensive and I don't get to keep the doctor who delivered me. So, Dad started my own health-savings plan IRA. By the time I'm old enough to need extensive medical care, I will be able to pay my own way."

"Proud of you," said, Hillary. "Back when my mother named me after Sir Edmund Hillary and when I was dodging bullets in Bosnia, I was a feminist like you."

"Ma'am, I am not a feminist. While I am for equal pay for equal work, I cannot do everything that men can do and men cannot do everything that I can do. God made us different for a reason."

"Well, I'm not sure I believe in that God stuff," said Bernie. "Also, I notice you only charge $1.00 for 16-oz. of lemonade. Under my plan, 90 cents will go for taxes. You would be wasting your time here."

"Sir, you are correct. I would have no incentive to do this work."

"Look, kid," said Elizabeth," you must pay taxes because you did not build this road here or build the sidewalk that brings your customers to you." Barack nodded his agreement.

"Beg to differ, ma'am. The taxes paid by my family helped pay for the roads. My Dad and I laid the forms and poured this sidewalk ourselves. And it is on our property."

"Speaking of property," said Bernie, "this would be a good place for low-income housing and, if your folks don't want to sell your land, we can have the state use the Power of Eminent Domain to take it. And besides, I don't believe in private property to begin with. Anyway, the state should be running this lemonade business."

"But sir, my volunteer labor keeps overhead low and every dime I make goes to that little kid in a wheelchair. Likely, the state would be selling only 8-oz. cups for $5.00. No one would buy lemonade at that price."

"Listen, kid," said Michael, "that's enough of your Capitalist crap. Okay men, she's got no permit. Shut her down!"

©2016. 1822

BREAKING NEWS: CANADA MAY BUILD WALL

Whenever possible, it is the practice of "Central View" to provide attribution to other writers. Unfortunately, the author of what follows is unknown. Edited only for space and clarity, here is his or her satirical approach to the presidential election of 2016:

"The flood of Trump-fearing American liberals sneaking across the border into Canada has intensified in the past week. The Republican presidential [victory] is prompting an exodus among left-leaning Americans who fear they'll soon be required to hunt, pray, pay taxes, and live according to the Constitution.

"Canadian border residents say it's not uncommon to see dozens of sociology professors, liberal arts majors, global-warming activists, and 'green' energy proponents crossing their fields at night.

"I went out to milk the cows the other day, and there was a Hollywood producer huddled in the barn," said southern Manitoba farmer Red Greenfield, whose acreage borders North Dakota. He was cold, exhausted and hungry, and begged me for a latte and some free-range chicken.

When I said I didn't have any, he left before I even got a chance to show him my screenplay, eh?'

"In an effort to stop the illegal aliens, Greenfield erected higher fences, but the liberals scaled them. He then installed loudspeakers that blared Rush Limbaugh across the fields, but they just stuck their fingers in their ears and kept coming. Officials are particularly concerned about smugglers who meet liberals just south of the border, pack them into electric cars, and drive them across the border, where they are simply left to fend for themselves after the battery dies.

"'These people are not prepared for our rugged conditions,' an Alberta border patrolman said. 'I found one carload without a single bottle of Perrier water, or any Gemelli [a type of pasta] with shrimp and arugula. All they had was a nice little Napa Valley cabernet and some kale chips.'

"When liberals are caught, they're sent back across the border, often wailing that they fear persecution from Trump high-hairers. Rumors are circulating about plans being made to build re-education camps where liberals will be forced to drink domestic beer, study the Constitution, and find jobs that actually contribute to the economy.

"In recent days, liberals have turned to ingenious ways of crossing the border. Some have been disguised as senior citizens taking a bus trip to buy cheap Canadian prescription drugs. After catching a half-dozen young vegans in blue-hair wig disguises, Canadian immigration authorities began stopping buses and quizzing the supposed senior citizens about Perry Como and Rosemary

Clooney to prove that they were alive in the '50s. 'If they can't identify the accordion player on The Lawrence Welk Show, we become very suspicious about their age,' an official said.

"Canadian citizens have complained that the illegal immigrants are creating an organic-broccoli shortage, are buying up all the Barbara Streisand CD's, and are overloading the Internet while downloading jazzercise apps to their cell phones. 'I really feel sorry for American liberals, but the Canadian economy just can't support them,' an Ottawa resident said. 'After all, how many art-history majors does one country need?"'

©2016. 1863

GLASS-STEAGALL: CAN IT RISE FROM THE DEAD?

What could be more boring than a newspaper column about banking regulations? But wait! What if your family were crushed by the Great Depression of the 1930s? Or, more recently, devastated by the economic collapse of 2008-09? Then, you might be interested in the history of the Glass-Steagall Act of 1933.

Prior to Glass-Steagall, commercial savings banks and insurance companies could take savings from depositors and invest those savings in the over-inflated stock market of the late 1920s. When the stock market crashed in October, 1929, the hard-earned savings of millions were wiped out as were the many commercial savings banks and the insurance companies who put the savings of millions of Americans at greedy risk.

President Roosevelt, to his credit, signed Glass-Steagall which divided banking into two categories: commercial banks that made loans to individuals and businesses and investment banks that were allowed to underwrite and trade complex financial instruments (read: higher risk stocks and bonds). From 1933 to 1999, Glass-Steagall was instrumental in averting further stock market crashes and economic busts.

But all that changed in 1999 when Democrat President Bill Clinton, with the help of a GOP-controlled Congress, repealed Glass-Steagall. That coupled with the Clinton Administration's demand that banks confer home mortgages on unfortunates who could not even pay their telephone bills, led to the sub-prime mortgage crisis of 2008-09

In 1999, the effort to repeal Glass-Steagall was led by Republican U.S. Senator Phil Gramm who, after retiring in 2002, got a job with UBS-AG, a Swiss bank that converted from commercial banking into investment banking and then lost tons of money in the 2008 debacle. Citigroup lost $27.7 billion in 2008. AIG Insurance lost billions. Both Citigroup and AIG and other investment groups were bailed out by you and me.

Now, President Trump wants to restore Glass-Steagall and erect a "wall" between commercial savings banks and the risk-taking investment banks. Surprisingly, President Trump has the support of Treasury Secretary, Steven Mnuchin, and National Economic Council

Director, Gary Cohn, both of whom are former bankers from Goldman Sachs Group, Inc., one of the leading investment-banking houses.

Even so, what are the chances that President Trump, Mnuchin, and Cohn can get the GOP-controlled Congress to reinstate a "21st Century" form of Glass-Steagall? Just like the opposition to the repeal of ObamaCare by the American Medical Association, AARP, and the major hospital chains (follow the money trail), it is likely that Wall Street, which actually prefers Democratic Administrations to Republican, will find a way to route millions of campaign contributions to members of the House of Representatives in return for the continued entombment of Glass-Steagall.

Meanwhile, the convoluted post-2009 crash regulations of Dodd-Frank make it very difficult for commercial banks to underwrite mortgages and small business loans. After all, why would Wall Street mess around with small loans to individuals and small businesses when it is so much easier to make big money in today's stock market?

If readers find it difficult to obtain a home mortgage or a small business loan in a timely fashion, this look back at the demise of Glass-Steagall may offer the small comfort of better understanding: however, comfort is a poor substitute for actual reform of America's banking regulations and the resurrection of Glass-Steagall.

©2017. 1888

CHAPTER FIVE

GOVERNMENT

BIG BROTHER REALLY IS WATCHING YOU

Recently, we went to the expense of hiring a webmeister to create a website so this weekly column can be posted on the Internet. Now that the web page is up and running on the internet, I'm beginning to learn there is an Orwellian Big Brother aspect to web pages.

For example, many websites are backed up with a statistical package designed to tell the owner of the website some pretty amazing things. You are probably already aware most websites have "hit" counters that record how many people have looked in on the website each day, even each hour. That's a good idea because someone offering products for sale or just doing advertising on a website needs to know if he or she is wasting their money or not. Unfortunately, the technology doesn't stop there.

For example, the statistical program attached to **www.central-view.com** reveals who is looking at the columns and for how long. That's the part that bothers me because I feel like I am, somehow, invading the privacy of my readers.

But other features I like. For example, by telling me how long each column is viewed, the program reflects which columns drew the most interest and which the least. This is not the reason we put up the website; however, I am delighted with this feature because it becomes a guide as to which subjects are of interest to readers and which are not. So, in that context, the program is both helpful and innocuous.

But put this kind of information into the hands of a dirt-digging political consultant and such programs can be abused. By hacking into certain websites (and it can be done) the political hatchet person can find out who is watching pornography on the internet or spending internet time with radical hate-groups or is spending time in sex chat rooms or using the internet for all kinds of nefarious purposes.

This Big Brotherism can even extend into your satellite TV viewing choices. The companies that sell programming for your satellite dish can tell what you are watching and how long you watch it. If you've ever been on the phone with your satellite program provider adjusting your satellite receiver, you know what I mean.

One might think those who do political "opposition research" wouldn't stoop so low as to hack into internet viewing statistics or TV satellite records. But if the past is any indication, they will. For example, when Judge Robert Bork was up for Senate confirmation to the U.S. Supreme Court, the liberals went after his video store rental records to see if he had checked out any porno films. He had not. That was low-tech. But it makes the point.

Ever wonder why the sitcoms offered by ABC, CBS, NBC and FOX are so inane? It's because they are written for a 14-year-old audience. Why 14-year-olds? Because the geniuses in Hollywood and New York have this cockamamie idea that brand-choice loyalty is determined around age 14. Ergo: They must capture the hearts and minds of 14-year-olds so those skulls-full-of-mush will buy Happy Loops cereal for the rest of their lives. Hogwash. But that's what the TV moguls believe.

And how do the TV moguls know what 14-year-olds are thinking? Evidently, that age group spends a lot of time on the internet visiting websites. From those visits, the TV moguls pick up tons of information about teen preferences. Those preferences are then factored into prime-time TV programming. Duh.

Although 14-year-olds are welcome, Central View is written for a much more sophisticated audience and so I invite you, gentle reader, to look in on: **www.central-view.com** each week. Stay as long as you wish, I won't assume you are a slow reader. There will, however, be a test on domestic politics and foreign policy. Just kidding. *NB: the tracking software has been removed.*
©**1999. 904**

IMMIGRATION: THE KENNEDY-MCCAIN FANTASY

One wonders what they are imbibing in that U.S. Senate cloakroom where Senators Kennedy, McCain, Kyl, Graham, Martinez, Salazar, Specter and Feinstein meet twice daily to strategize their immigration legislation. Apparently, they think some 12 to 20 million illegal immigrants will line up, sombreros-in-hand, to each pay a $5,000 fine, process for some kind of yet-to-be-invented super-ID card, then line up again on the Mexican side so they can step back over our border and be admitted into the U.S as part of a guest-worker program. Wrong.

Then, there are those who think federal agents can deport some 12 to 20 million illegal immigrants and tell them to get in line behind millions of applicants for legal immigration who have been waiting to come here and work. Wrong.

The problem is that previous federal governments, both Democrat and Republican, failed to control our borders and failed to enforce the immigration laws already on the books -- except with regard to those who dutifully applied for legal immigration. As a result, we really don't know who is here. But, just to be conservative, let's assume the low estimate of 12 million illegal immigrants is correct.

That being the case, by the time the Kennedy-McCain legislation could be implemented; a profound demographic shift will have already taken place. The shift will stem from the operation of the 14th Amendment to the U.S.

Constitution, the first sentence of which reads, "1. All persons born or naturalized in the United States, and subject to the jurisdiction thereof, are citizens of the United States and of the State wherein they are born."

Let's further assume that 12 million number includes just three million females who give birth within the next year. That's an additional three million 14th Amendment U.S. citizens, all the progeny of someone who violated U.S. law to get here.

The illegal-immigrant mothers, of course, must remain here to care for their U.S. citizen-babies. We are good people so we allow the father and any siblings to remain or, if not here already, to enter the U.S. to be with the U.S. citizen-baby and its mother. Add the mothers and the fathers to the 14th Amendment babies and the "legacy" number rises to five million. If the actual number of current illegal immigrants is closer to 20 million, the demographic impact is far more dramatic.

Lawyers could argue that an illegal immigrant mother and her unborn child are not "subject to the jurisdiction" of the U.S. at the time of birth. The case, however, would take years to reach the U.S. Supreme Court. The 14th Amendment can be amended; however, ratification would take about a decade. In other words, it's too late.

Those who want to maintain a white majority in America should understand that human reproduction is just a matter of "unskilled labor in the middle of the night," and get busy. The fashion among liberal whites is to have fewer children via contraception, abortion, gay-marriage and even anti-menstrual-period pills. Demographers say conservative families tend to be larger. So, there is motivation on the part of liberal political strategists to import (or let stay) more people who will vote Democrat.

So, if the Kennedy-McCain fantasy won't work and federal agents can't deport 12 to 20 million kicking and screaming illegal immigrants, what could happen?

First, the only thing left for a sovereign nation to do is reestablish its sovereignty by getting iron-clad control over its borders. Second, sovereign nations find out who is inside their borders.

With those two actions completed, it would then be time to figure out who is supposed to be here and who isn't. The next step would be to determine the conditions under which those who entered the United States illegally could correct for their illegal actions and get on the path toward legal status. The Kennedy-McCain legislation has the cart before the burro.

©2007. 1319

AIRLINE SECURITY: THE SYSTEM WORKED: FOR AL-QAEDA

When the wealthy Nigerian businessman, Alhaji Umaru Mutallab, learned that his son, Umar Farouk Abdulmutallab, had left his $2,000,000 apartment in England for Yemen to join al-Qaeda, the father informed Nigerian security officials and the U.S. Embassy.

Undeterred, young Umar, with no luggage, paid $3,000.00 cash for a one-way ticket to cross three-continents: from Africa, to Europe to North America. The radical Islamist walked right through Nigerian and Dutch security carrying a concealed detonator syringe and wearing underwear stuffed with PETN explosive.

Later, Umar told authorities in Detroit that he had intended to kill himself and his 278 fellow passengers. But he messed in his pants -- so to speak – inadvertently, setting fire to his underwear. (So now, if and when he gains access to those 72 virgins, he may have some, well… performance issues.)

Granted, airline security is less than perfect; however, the Transportation Security Administration (TSA) really has been trying to improve safety and is also trying to speed up the flow of passengers to catch their flights. For example, a few years ago, the TSA conducted a two-year test of what it called: the Registered Traveler Program.

The results were promising enough that the TSA allowed three private companies to establish Verified Identity Pass Programs at selected airports for individuals who were willing to submit to retina scans, fingerprinting, and to provide personal background information akin to getting a top-secret security clearance. Wonder Wife and I were among some 250,000 who jumped through all the hoops. We even paid the hefty annual fee.

Armed with our Clear Pass ID and tickets, we never once found anyone ahead of us in the special Clear Pass lane. After having our retinas scanned to prove our retinas were the same retinas scanned during the enrollment process, a Clear Pass staffer put our luggage on the conveyor belt for the regular TSA luggage/shoe X-ray.

Shoes back on, we were good to go. Unfortunately, all three vendors went out of business.

But given the success that young Umar had in evading every security screening tool known to man -- to include the fact that his father had alerted the U.S. Embassy to his son's al-Qaeda involvement -- maybe it is time for the TSA to take another look at a Registered Traveler Program.

What if we could identify, in advance, the folks who pose absolutely no airline security risks? That way, the poor TSA screeners who are, after all, just following orders, would not have to take knitting needles away from aging grandmothers and, maybe, even give back my Gerber Tool.

What would the keen intellect of Sherlock Holmes deduce from the history of these airline atrocities? Media pundit, Ann Coulter, must read Sherlock Holmes because in a recent column Miss Coulter observed: "Since Muslims took down Pam Am Flight 103 over Lockerbie, Scotland, in 1988, every attack on a commercial airliner has been committed by foreign-born Muslim men with the same hair color, eye color and skin color. Half of them have been named Mohammed." (My word, Dr. Watson, she may have found a clue!)

Almost for certain, the Keystone Kop failures that allowed a known radical-Islamist to almost commit a "man-caused disaster" (the Obamatons contend terrorist acts no longer exist) and snuff out the lives of 278 airline passengers will not cause anyone to be fired or even demoted. What is absolutely for certain is that those who could so easily be excluded from any kind of airline security concern will now be subjected to even more invasive procedures and needless delays.

Airline travel tip: Buy one of those Keffiyahs like the late Yasser Arafat used to wear on his head. That might work better than the now-defunct Clear Pass Verified Identity Pass Program.

©2009. 1456

IMMIGRATION: PRESIDENT REAGAN'S GREAT MISTAKE

Back in 1986, late-night comedians said of the Simpson-Mazzoli immigration legislation: "Simpson gets to stay, but Mazzoli has to go." But Simpson-Mazzoli turned out to be no joke. In fact, by any objective standard, the immigration bill signed into law by President Ronald Reagan in 1986 was an absolute disaster. It failed to achieve all three of its stated objectives:

1. Force U.S. employers to attest to their employees' immigration status. The fine for scofflaw employers was inconsequential. There was no punishment provision for being here illegally.

2. Make it illegal to "knowingly" hire or recruit illegal immigrant workers. The fines were a joke, document fraud was rampant, and there was little or no enforcement.

3. Bring an end to the flood of illegal immigrants being attracted to the U.S. by the 92 months of the Reagan

supply-side economics boom. Simpson-Mazzoli granted various forms of amnesty to 3,000,000 illegal immigrants and, because our borders have remained virtually unsecured and because there has been no political will by either Republicans or Democrats to enforce the puny provisions of Simpson-Mazzoli, the last 24 years have seen the number of illegal immigrants swell to somewhere between 12,000,000 and 20,000,000.

Some of President Reagan's most devoted fans consider the signing of Simpson-Mazzoli one of his greatest mistakes. Former U.S. Attorney General Ed Meese recalls President Reagan did not like the amnesty provisions of Simpson-Mazzoli, but signed it anyway. That is the kind of mistake no rational President should ever make.

But rationality, like beauty, may be in the eye of the beholder. What if a President is not in favor of border control? What if a President sees political advantage in becoming the amnesty champion for some 12,000,000 to 20,000,000 illegal immigrants who, out of gratitude, would then vote for him and for his political party?

If partisan political advantage is the goal, then total amnesty is totally rational. Moreover, if a sitting President doesn't even want to enforce the weak provisions of federal law as codified by Simpson-Mazzoli, then that President would not want a State like Arizona or any State to be enforcing federal immigration law.

Now, the Obama Administration is suing Arizona to stop Arizona from enforcing federal immigration law, citing the idea that immigration law is a field already occupied or "preempted" by the federal government.

But wait. What about the cities that have preempted federal law by legislating themselves as "sanctuary cities?" Clearly, those cities were acting in an area of the law "preempted" by federal law. Why have they not been sued? Well, if your objective is to make America one big, open-bordered sanctuary, then you don't exert the federal preemption when you don't want to do so. You only enforce the federal preemption against state laws you don't like.

Ironically, Rhode Island state troopers have been enforcing an ID-check immigration law like that of Arizona for several years; however, Rhode Island is not being sued by the Obama Administration.

If the Arizona ID-check immigration is offensive to the Obama Administration, then the Rhode Island law should be offensive as well. But then, if you are into selective-law enforcement of the law to begin with, why bother with concepts such as: equal justice and equality before the law?

This February, in *Estrada v. Rhode Island,* the U.S. Court of Appeals (1st Circuit) ruled in favor of Rhode Island's ID-check immigration procedures, citing the U.S. Supreme Court's unanimous ruling in *Muehler v. Mena* (2005) that police who have detained a suspect may also check the person's immigration status. Those rulings should bode well for Arizona.

But if Mr. Obama gets Ms. Elena Kagan confirmed to the Supreme Court, then *Muehler v. Mena* and *Estrada v.*

Rhode Island might be overturned; proving, once again, that presidential elections are as much about the Court House as they are about the White House.

©2010 1483

UNCLE NANNY: LAW OF UNINTENDED CONSEQUENCES

Uncle Nanny is a composite of thousands of know-it-all, post-flower-children government bureaucrats who issue water- and energy-wasting mandates irrespective of the Law of Unintended Consequences (LOUC), and then ride off on their Unicorns into a pixie-dusted Utopia.

Before Uncle Nanny, toilets used 3.0 gallons of water-per-flush. Now toilets are limited to 1.6 gallons-per-flush. Often, one flush isn't enough. Two flushes total 3.2 gallons for a net water loss of .2 gallons. *The San Francisco Chronicle* reports: "Skimping on toilet water has resulted in more sludge backing up inside the sewer pipes," said Tyrone Jue, spokesman for the city Public Utilities Commission. That has created a rotten-egg stench near AT&T Park and elsewhere, especially during the dry summer months. The city has already spent $100 million over the past five years to upgrade its sewer system and sewage plants, in part to combat the odor problem. Now officials are stocking up on a $14 million, three-year supply of highly concentrated sodium hypochlorite—better known as bleach—to act as an odor eater and to disinfect the city's treated water before it's dumped into the bay..." LOUC!

Uncle Nanny ordered dishwasher detergent makers to eliminate the phosphates that keep minerals from clinging to dishes. Trying to get dishes clean, some people bought new dishwashers, only to realize they still had a problem.

For years, we never had to pre-rinse our dishes. But post Uncle Nanny, even pre-rinsing in warm water didn't help. Doubling the detergent didn't help. Solution: Now, we heat water to pre-rinse the dishes. We use twice the detergent. We add a cup of vinegar to each load plus some kind of special acid capsule. We can only run a half-load of dishes at a time. Ergo: To get clean dishes, we use twice the energy and even more chemicals. LOUC!

Uncle Nanny dictated energy-efficient laundry machines and refrigerators: *"Consumer Reports"* found that not only did consumers have to pay a higher sticker price for the machines, but they also had to wash their clothes twice because of the reduced performance—using more energy in the process. Furthermore, *"Consumer Reports"* called the Department of Energy (DOE) out for overstating the energy savings from energy-efficient refrigerators. When *"Consumer Reports"* conducted its own energy use test, which they claim is much more realistic than the DOE; they found much higher energy use. LOUC!

Uncle Nanny mandated higher crock pot temperatures: We had a 75 watt-per-hour crock pot you set in the morning, returned at day's end, and enjoyed "fall-off-the-bone-tender" roasts. Unfortunately, for easier clean-up, we bought an "improved" crock pot with removable insert. But the "improved" model, instead of braising, boiled the roasts into brown shoe leather. We are back to the much higher energy-consuming conventional electric oven. LOUC!

Note: Cheaper cuts of meat did very well in the old crock pots. Now, lower income groups are, yet again, the victims of Uncle Nanny.

The New York Times says owners of the $39,828 Chevy Volt only have to drive their Volts for 26.6 years before they break even on their fuel costs. We taxpayers subsidize each Volt to the tune $256,824. LOUC!

Uncle Nanny's zany efforts cause some people to flout the law which, of course, is corrosive to the Rule-of-Law in a free society. Except for phosphates, there are illegal ways (like removing water-flow restrictors), to "fix" almost all the Uncle Nanny-created problems. But, as one revered neighbor suggests: "The day may come when we will see homemakers arrested on our southern border for dealing with illegal phosphate cartels." LOUC!
©2012. 1618.

TSA TRAVEL RULES: COMPLY LIKE A TERRORIST

For air travelers over age 75 and under age 12, the Transportation Security Administration (TSA) is working toward making your screening experience less troublesome. Already children under 12 no longer have to remove their shoes. At Chicago, Denver, and Portland seniors over 75 no longer have to remove their shoes, belts, and jackets. Soon JFK International, La Guardia, and Newark Liberty airports will be added to that list.

One of the nice things about the TSA is that you can go on their website at: **www.tsa.gov** and find detailed lists of what you need to know to be allowed on board an airliner in this country. Savvy travelers read all that information and do their very best to comply with whatever the TSA wants them to do. With practice, the experienced traveler can get very good at pleasing the TSA and sail right on through TSA screening with minimum hassle.

Unfortunately, the Islamic jihadists and other terrorists read these same instructions from TSA and learn them by heart and possibly know them even better than the frazzled TSA screeners at the nation's 499 commercial-service airports. No self-respecting terrorist is going to try to board an airliner in this country without having made sure that he or she is in strict compliance with the instructions available at: **www.tsa.gov**.

So, the next time you board an airliner, you can take comfort knowing that every last person going on board along with you has had to comply with the TSA's pre-boarding instructions. On the other hand, there are untold numbers of innocent, non-terrorists who are ignorant of the rules or, even if informed, do not follow them. For example, just last week, the TSA intercepted 30 loaded pistols that were inside carry-on baggage. Famous sports and entertainment celebrities have been caught with weapons in their carry-on briefcases or bags. Since TSA screening went into effect, hundreds of thousands of prohibited items have been confiscated by the TSA. In fact, the TSA has had to hold auctions to get rid of hundreds of swords, meat cleavers, spear guns, cattle prods, brass knuckles, and box cutters, to mention only a few prohibited items.

Needless to say, the TSA needs to do as good a job educating America's non-terrorists on how to go through TSA screening as the TSA has done with the terrorists. If the rest of us would comply the way the terrorists are complying, the work of the TSA would be easier.

Getting ready to depart the Nashville Airport last September, this writer encountered a female TSA screener with a keen sense of humor. Running late, Wonder Wife and I hurried to catch a flight back to Denver. We take pride in having our little 3-1-1 bags in perfect order. Our shoes, jackets, keys, cell phones, watches, and other metal items placed just right in those little plastic tubs. We can pass through the magnetometer without setting it off.

Having strictly compiled with TSA rules and sailing on through, I was collecting my belongings off of the conveyor belt when the TSA lady posted there said, "You obviously take pride in being ready for inspection and in following our rules; however, I want you to know that we really do not go *that* far."

"What you mean you don't go *that* far?" I asked.

With a benevolent smile, the nice TSA lady said, "Your fly is unzipped."

©2012. 1625

INTERNET IRONIES: TRUTH STRANGER THAN FICTION

A lot of the stuff going around the Internet is rubbish; however, some information is very valuable and even funny. Here are a few amusing and factual items:

U.S. Attorney General Eric Holder is opposing attempts by Texas, Florida, and 28 other States to clean up their voter registration rolls. Mr. Holder is especially opposed to the idea that voters be required to present a photo identification card prior to voting.

Last week, Mr. Holder spoke in Houston, Texas, at the annual meeting of the National Association for the Advancement of Colored People (NAACP). People who wanted to gain entrance to the hall where Mr. Holder was speaking were required to (drum roll) present a color, photo identification card.

Here's another ironic Internet item: The U.S. Department of Agriculture, which administers the Food Stamp Program, proudly publicizes (even in Spanish) that it is distributing the greatest number of free meals and food stamps in its history. Meanwhile, the U.S. National Park Service asks us to: "Please Do Not Feed the Animals." The stated reason for the policy is because animals will grow dependent on handouts and will not learn to take care of themselves.

Because the 2012 U.S. Olympic team uniforms were "outsourced" to China, Democrat Senate Leader Senator Harry Reid wants them burned. Ironically, the "outsourcer" was multi-billionaire designer, Ralph Lauren, who donated $7,300 to Mr. Obama, $35,000 to the Democratic National Committee, and nothing to the GOP.

A seven-year-old boy can be thrown out of class for calling his teacher "cute," but hosting a sexual exploration or diversity class in grade school is perfectly acceptable. The Pentagon now celebrates Gay, Lesbian, and Transgender Pride Week; however, the left-stream media never mentioned that the Army's most famous gay soldier, Bradley Manning, is currently on trial for treason.

Children are forcibly removed from parents who try to discipline them while children of "underprivileged" drug addicts are often left in squalor with their drug-addicted parents. Working Americans pay for or contribute to their own health care yet unmarried women can have child after child on government welfare and are never held responsible for their own choices; nor are the males who impregnate them.

The government's plan for getting people back to work is to provide 99 weeks of unemployment checks to not work. If you shop on-line for materials to pack an emergency survival kit, you may be monitored as a threat to the government. Your government can add anything it wants to your child's water in the name of health; however, you may not give your child raw milk from your own cow which you have raised from birth. A child needs parental approval to go on a school field trip, but not to get an abortion.

An 80-year-old woman can be strip searched by the TSA at an airport; however, a Muslim woman wearing a burqa is only subject to having her neck and head searched. Yelling Allahu Akbar!, a Muslim physician kills 13 Americans and wounds 20 at Ft. Hood; however, your government says the attack was merely "work-place violence," and Purple Hearts are not authorized.

Is something out of whack here or is it just this writer? But then, I'm one of those picky people who think that Buffalo Wings taste like chicken.

©2012. 1632

BIG GOVERNMENT: WHO GETS THE COOKIES?

Lucy and Ethyl were excited. The scheme between the White House, Ethyl's Treasury Department, and Lucy's Federal Reserve Bank to pump up the stock market by printing billions of dollars of Treasury Bonds and selling them at auction to wealthy investors and even to the Red Chinese was working. The Dow Jones industrial average was up 13 points. It closed above 13,600 for the first time since December 10, 2007.

But major investment advisers were saying more government borrowing only created an illusion. They said the economy was like a battered battlefield filled with the mournful mutter of high unemployment and snail-like growth. According to the Labor Department, 26 states just reported higher unemployment. The World Trade Organization cut back its estimates for any growth in the global economy. But as long as the illusion lasted to the November elections, Lucy and Ethyl had done their jobs.

So, Lucy and Ethyl left Washington for New York and went back to making chocolate-chip cookies. If they could reduce their cost-of-production, they hoped to stop losing money on each cookie they sold. But, finally realizing that increasing their sales volume only increased their losses, they appealed to the White House to bail-out their failing cookie business.

The White House, grateful for their illusory pump up of the stock market, responded with a new economic plan it called: Redistribution. In truth, the basic idea was old. It dated back to 1875 when Karl Marx wrote: "From each according to his abilities, to each according to his needs." Accordingly, the White House ordered Lucy and Ethyl, who had the ability to make cookies, to give their cookies to everyone who needed a cookie.

Moreover, the producers of butter, sugar, eggs, vanilla, flour, baking soda, salt, chocolate chips, and walnuts were ordered to provide their wares to Lucy and Ethyl for free. Joyfully, Lucy and Ethyl turned out tons of cookies with no worries about losing money. But their joy was short-lived. The producers, unable to make any money, stopped producing.

Soon, there were no ingredients such as: butter, sugar, eggs, vanilla, flour, baking soda, salt, chocolate chips, and walnuts. The result was that no one got any cookies at all. When Lucy and Ethyl complained to the White House, they were told most of their ingredients contributed to obesity, heart disease, and high blood pressure. Moreover, some people are allergic to nuts. Also, corn sugar was in short supply because corn is used to make ethanol for cars.

The shortage of animal fodder depressed the swine and cattle markets. Animals were being starved or slaughtered for lack of food.

So, Lucy and Ethyl switched to artificial ingredients which had two unfortunate results: The chemicals gave some people headaches and the cookies tasted awful. Not even free cookies were in demand.

No one had any money for entertainment, so Ricky lost his job at the nightclub. Because of cuts to Medicare, Ethyl and Fred had to buy additional supplemental insurance from AARP which, due to ObamaCare, got a $2.8 billion boost in sales. Lucy and Ricky could not pay their rent to Fred and Ethyl, their landlords. That left Lucy and Ethyl with only one solution: Join a union for government employees and go back to work for the government.

©2012. 1642

MIND YOUR GRAMMAR: BIG BRO IS LISTENING

On December 6, 1942, a telephone message astonished the physicists working on the Manhattan Project with these words: "...the Italian navigator has just landed in the New World," meaning that University of Chicago Professor Enrico Fermi had just proven the technology needed to make the world's first atomic bomb. At that moment, although no one knew it yet, the balance of power between Legislative Branch and the Executive Branch began to shift toward the Oval Office. Why? Because, with the eventual advent of thermo-nuclear weapons and intercontinental ballistic missiles, the decision time between devastating nuclear war or abject surrender was reduced to about 30 minutes.

Consequently, possessing accurate intelligence about potential enemy capabilities and intentions became essential to our survival and that led to massive investments in intelligence-gathering technologies. For example, now there is PRISM, which the Obama Administration is using to eavesdrop on U.S. cell phones. The recent disclosure of PRISM caused late-night comic Jimmy Fallon to comment: *"Another scandal hit the White House today. A report found that the government has been secretly collecting the phone records of Verizon customers. I knew something was up when I said, 'You hang up first.' Then my wife said, 'No, YOU hang up first!' Then Obama said, 'Uh, how about you just hang up at the same time?'"*

But U.S. Government (USG) spying on its own citizens is nothing new. The Clinton Administration initiated ECHELON -- a Top Secret electronic eavesdropping program designed to listen in on foreign countries, terrorist groups, drug cartels, and even U.S. citizens. After ECHELON was exposed by "CBS 60 Minutes," the pro-Clinton *New York Times* opined that ECHELON was "a necessity." After 9/11, when the Bush Administration obtained overwhelming bi-partisan support to enact the Patriot Act which, in effect, legalized ECHELON, the *New York Times* said the eavesdropping program it endorsed under Clinton was unconstitutional under Bush. Go figure.

People of a certain age were raised to think that our private correspondence and our phone calls were private. Of course, in the old days, the telephone operators might listen in after making a connection. Some may recall asking to be connected to the Smith household only to be told by the operator that the Smith family was away on vacation. That kind of eavesdropping was more on the order of a public service than it was spying on your private life.

To be fair, it should be noted that the Eisenhower Administration conducted a "flaps and seals" operation that could open, read, and reseal mail sent to certain U.S. citizens who were thought to have interests "inimical to the United States of America." But it was only mail coming from communist countries that got the "flaps and seals" treatment.

Now, Russia, Red China, and the U.S. Government have the ability to listen to our cell phones, to read what we place on the Internet, and even to monitor each computer keystroke -- as I am sure that at least one of them is doing right now.

While this is worrisome, and it should be, we can only hope for the rediscovery of the U.S. Constitution and the Bill of Rights. That, however, is a political question that can only be resolved at the ballot box and/or by the Judicial Branch.

©2013.1680

AMERICA: DRIFTING APART

In 1964, when President Johnson declared the War on Poverty, 14-percent of Americans were considered impoverished. Since 1964, we taxpayers spent $20.7 trillion to fight poverty. Today, the percentage of Americans living in poverty remains at (drum roll) 14-percent. Looks like we have an under-class that needed more hand-ups (Capitalism) and fewer hand-outs (Socialism).

But we have also -- at the expense of the middle-class -- developed a super-elite, upper-class, as well. Dr. Charles Murray, in his new book: *America Coming Apart: The New Cultural Divide*, tells us that 11 of the 13 zip codes in the Washington, D.C. area are populated with America's richest and highest-educated. Our nation's Capital is full of over-caffeinated, hair-on-fire, former student-council presidents passing laws or writing regulations to tell you and me how to live our lives.

Go to Georgetown, Chevy Chase, Bethesda or McLean and you will see streets filled with Rolls, Bentley, Jaguar, Mercedes, and Lexus cars. Clearly, your stimulus tax dollars, expended in the wake of the sub-prime mortgage collapse of 2008-2009, were not spent on "shovel ready" projects. The money went to hire more government bureaucrats, more consultants, to bail out union pension funds, to bail out GM, which stills owes us $7.8 billion and is now building Cadillacs in Red China; to bail out Chrysler, which is now building Jeeps in Red China, and was just bought by Italy's Fiat. In other words:

"If you want to keep your automobile industry, you can keep your automobile industry. Period."

But this new, super-elite, upper-class is split. You have the student-council types telling us how to live. Then, you have what author David Brooks calls: "Bobos." An Amazon.com review of Brooks' *Bobos in Paradise*, describes Bobos:

"...They sip double-tall, non-fat lattes, chat on cell phones, and listen to NPR while driving their immaculate SUVs to Pottery Barn to shop for $48 titanium spatulas. They tread down specialty cheese aisles in top-of-the-line hiking boots and think nothing of laying down $5 for an olive-wheatgrass muffin. They're the bourgeois bohemians--'Bobos'--an unlikely blend of mainstream culture and 1960s-era counterculture..."

But the chilling connection between Dr. Murray's findings and David Brooks' observations is that the student-council types and the Bobos are themselves the off-spring of a previous generation of super-elites. Dr. Murray says, "They reached adulthood never having known anything else, and then rose to positions of enormous influence over the rest of the country without having had an opportunity to experience first-hand how most Americans live and think..."

One is reminded of the Frederick Machetanz painting in which a lone Eskimo sits on a small chunk of ice that has broken off from the mainland. The Eskimo knows he is doomed to drift out into the Bering Sea and drown.

Last week, it was revealed that over half of the members of Congress are millionaires. Is that why

Congress -- members of both parties -- seem so indifferent to the problems of the shrinking middle-class? Maybe that lone Eskimo represents America's over-taxed and over-regulated middle-class, drifting out to sea on a shrinking patch of ice. Unless something changes in 2014 and 2016, middle-America may be lost at sea and never come back.
©2014. 1713

FAA HIRING: FLY THE DIVERSITY-FRIENDLY SKIES

Just as your aircraft reaches, say, 30,000 feet on your airline flight, say, from Denver to Chicago, the Captain says, "Hello. This is your Captain speaking. Welcome aboard Olympic Mountain General Airlines. Okay, I know some of you call us: OMG! But, seriously, passengers who studied urban sociology in college may be pleased to know the air traffic controllers who will be controlling our flight today from the En Route Air Traffic Control Centers had absolutely no previous training in air traffic control before they joined the FAA's training program.

"None. They walked in off the street, took a combination personality-biography test --designed to make sure they had an understanding of life in urban environments -- and then went on to experience for the first time the wondrous world of aviation, in general, and air-traffic control, in particular. Is this a great country, or what?

"Now, some of you with aviation knowledge may wonder what happened to the air traffic control applicants from the College Initiative Training (C.I.T.) Program, those 36 universities and colleges around the nation which for 24 years have provided the FAA with a pool of highly qualified applicants to become air traffic controllers?

"Well, the new FAA air traffic controller hiring policy has removed the hiring preference that those students and even military veterans used to enjoy and, in some cases, the FAA has disqualified them from even making application.

"Even though many of those students spent four college years in the air traffic control career track, or were military air traffic controllers, the FAA, in the name of social justice, decided those college graduates and veterans had an unfair advantage over applicants with no previous air traffic control knowledge.

"So folks, sit back and relax and know that your flight is being controlled from the ground by people who are learning about aviation and air traffic control with the fresh enthusiasm of beginners who have just learned something new and do not suffer from the, say, complacency of having studied air traffic control for four years in college or operated military control towers."

End of Satire: Gentle readers, I just worked alongside a bright young woman who just completed a four-year course in air traffic control and was told she was not eligible to be tested for the FAA career she planned. Now, she is switching to Airport Management and will have the added expense of a fifth year in college.

To make matters worse, the biographical assessment test, which is more concerned with how many sports applicants played in high school than aviation-related subjects, has been leaked to certain applicants. Over 25 members of Congress have recognized that the FAA is now more concerned with diversity than aviation safety and are protesting these changes to the FAA's hiring policies.

When interviewed by investigative reporter for Denver Channel 7, John Ferrugia, Professor Keith Kuhlmann, who teaches air traffic control at Denver's Metro State University stated, "... the FAA is taking less qualified applicants that have no clear aptitude for the job. In the end ... the policy will cost taxpayers millions."

So, the next time you fly on OMG!, you can feel all warm and fuzzy about what is happening on the ground but not necessarily about what could happen to you in the air.

©2015. 1786

MARBURY V. MADISON: A RULING TOO FAR?

No matter how you feel about the recent decisions by the U.S. Supreme Court (SCOTUS), something seems out of balance. In 1787, our nation's Founders felt a Congress elected by the people should be the foremost branch of our national government. That is why the very first article of the U.S. Constitution, Article I, created the Legislative Branch.

The Founders knew we would need a chief executive to manage the national government and so Article II created the Executive Branch. The Founders thought the Judicial Branch would be the least of the three branches of government, so the Judicial Branch was created as Article III. But then, in 1803, along came *Marbury vs. Madison*, 5 U.S. 137.

William Marbury was a wannabe Justice of the Peace (JP) who had not received his commission from the previous administration. Under the provisions of the Judicial Act of 1789, Chief Justice John Marshall could have ordered Secretary of State James Madison to give Marbury his commission. But, rather than get into a shoving contest with the Executive Branch, Marshall held that the provision of the **Judiciary Act of 1789** that enabled Marbury to bring his claim to the Supreme Court was itself unconstitutional because it purported to extend the Court's **"original jurisdiction"** beyond that which Article III established. So, Marbury did not get his commission.

On the surface, Marshall's ruling appeared to be reining in the powers of the Federal Judiciary; however, the practical effect of his ruling was both otherwise and twofold:

1. The ruling avoided a clash with the Executive Branch and

2. The ruling told Congress that the SCOTUS would decide which laws or parts of laws passed by Congress were constitutional or not. In other words, nine, political-appointee, non-elected judges would be the ultimate arbiters of what is law and what is not.

Based on your point-of-view, the SCOTUS has made good decisions and bad decisions. Arguably, the worst was *Dred Scott v. Sandford*, 60 U.S. 393 (1857). The SCOTUS held that African Americans, either free or enslaved, could not be American citizens. Fortunately, in 1868, the Fourteenth Amendment overturned the Dred Scott decision by granting citizenship to all those born in the United States, regardless of color. That it took a Constitutional Amendment to correct the Dred Scott decision suggests that *Marbury v. Madison* elevated the SCOTUS to a position where nine, non-elected judges have more power than the Legislative Branch and the Executive Branch combined.

For example, we have seen numerous cases where the elected representatives of the people in the States have passed laws that have been overturned by non-elected, Federal Judges and their rulings upheld by the non-elected judges on the SCOTUS. We have seen times when the people of the States have amended their state constitutions by overwhelming majorities, only to have Federal Judges set aside their amendments and then be upheld by the non-elected justices on the SCOTUS.

But can the power of the Federal Judiciary be curtailed? Yes, Article V provides for a Convention of the States. If 34 or more States call for a Convention of the States, the delegates (commissioners) could fix (or make worse) all sorts of things. You decide. ©**2015. 1791**

CITY VOTES VERSUS RURAL VOTES

As a pencil mark on a ballot tally sheet, a rural vote looks just like a city vote. But the reasoning process that goes into a rural vote may be entirely different from the reasoning process that goes into a city vote.

Some background: Our Founding Fathers took care to see that values and mores of those living in rural America would not be overwhelmed by the expected waves of immigration crowding into what actually did become our "teeming" cities. They did this by allocating two U.S. Senators to each state, irrespective of a state's population. For balance, they based the allocation of seats in the U.S. House of Representatives on population.

This balance between the interests of rural "geography" versus urban "population" protected the interests of rural America until 1962 when the Warren Court decided the case of *Baker v. Carr* in favor of the plaintiff, Carr, who claimed the State of Tennessee, was failing to faithfully execute its own statutes governing reapportionment. Prior to *Baker v. Carr*, the Supreme Court of the United States held that political district reapportionment within a state was a political matter for the states to decide and, therefore, out-of-bounds for intervention by federal courts. By six to two, the Warren Court ruled the federal courts can overrule the individual states with regard to how their internal political boundaries are drawn.

Baker v. Carr is known as the "one-man, one-vote" ruling. While the sentiment has a warm and fuzzy ring to it, the impact of *Baker v. Carr* was to put America's urban population at the steering wheel of government and America's rural/small-town population in the back seat. Today, about 60-percent of Americans live in cities while only 40-percent live in rural/small-town America.

Recently, the novelist, Peter Grant (AKA the Bayou Renaissance Man), invited our attention to the differences between urban thought patterns and rural thought patterns. Grant recalls meeting a city-dwelling woman with a college degree who was reduced to tears when she was told the steak on her dinner plate came about due to the slaughter of an animal. But that woman was not alone. Many urban dwellers think their food just comes from the super market. Period. Conversely, the people in rural and small-town America are financially dependent on their ability to produce food and they understand our farm-to-market economy full well.

Unless hit directly by a tornado or flood, weather is not much on the minds of urbanites. But weather can fill or empty the pocketbooks of farmers and ranchers. City dwellers are surrounded by hospitals, first-responders, law enforcement, and welfare services. They live within an artificial cocoon, depending on others to provide for their needs. For the most part, rural and small-town Americans must rely on themselves. Consequently, urbanites tend to vote for big government while many rural/small-town folks just wish big government would leave them alone.

When it comes time to cast their ballots, the urbanites tend to vote for the Democrats while rural and small-town Americans tend to vote for the Republicans. So, while the

pencil marks on ballot tally sheets may look the same. The thinking behind those marks can be vastly different.
©2016. 1860

VOTER FRAUD: INVESTIGATE OR NOT?

When it comes to voter fraud, there are generally three kinds of people: 1. Those who are practicing voter fraud and do not want the subject investigated. 2. Those who lost an election due to voter fraud and want it stopped. 3. Those who won elections, despite being subjected to voter fraud, and just want to move on with their lives and their newly-won or re-won offices.

Long before President Trump created the presidential election integrity commission, two reputable organizations: The Heritage Foundation and Judicial Watch were finding some alarming instances of voter fraud in local, state, and congressional elections. One of their key findings is that "Dirty voter rolls lead to dirty elections."

So, how can it be that the secretaries of state in so many states are maintaining dirty voter rolls when this is what is supposed to happen: In advance of Primary and General Elections, citizens are supposed to provide local election officials with their correct name, date of birth, party affiliation, address, and proof of U.S. citizenship. Then, when it comes time to vote in the Primary and/or General Elections, the citizen displays a form of government-approved identification, signs the voter rolls, and casts his or her ballot into the ballot box. Stone simple; however, recent modifications such as mail-in ballots, same-day registration, and drive-by voting are making voter fraud more difficult to detect.

The voter fraud industry -- yes, there is one led by the Association of Community Organizations for Reform (ACORN) -- figures out ways to cast the votes of people who are not eligible to vote by reason of being dead, not U.S. citizens, illegally inside the USA, voting in more than one state, or even stuffing ballot boxes. Hopefully, in the fullness of time, the on-going presidential commission will produce its findings and we can decide to believe those findings or not.

But what if a particular case of voter fraud caused an American war to be conducted with its priority being the reelection of a sitting president rather than doing what was necessary to win the war? In Robert A. Caro's *Means of Ascent: The Years of Lyndon Johnson* (1991), biographer Caro details how, in 1946, Lyndon Johnson stole/bought enough votes in the Pedernales Valley of Texas to win election to the U.S. Senate by a "landslide" 87 votes.

"Landslide Lyndon" pulled off a case of voter fraud with tragic consequences. H.R. McMaster's *Dereliction of Duty: Lyndon Johnson, Robert McNamara, the Joint Chiefs of Staff and the Lies that Led to Vietnam* (1997), reveals how Johnson and McNamara micro-managed the Vietnam War with Johnson's reelection as their top objective, rather than success on the battle fields of Southeast Asia.

If history is, indeed, a continuum of events then, when read side-by-side, Caro's *Means of Ascent and* McMaster's *Dereliction of Duty* make a compelling case that just this one 1946 instance of voter fraud in Texas led to the political failures of command by President Johnson, to the riots and societal disruptions of the 1960s, and, in 1975, to the ignominious end of the Vietnam War. Can voter fraud destroy lives, families, and have a negative impact on American history? We report. You decide.

©2017. 1899

CHAPTER SIX

HISTORY A LA CARTE

KEEP THE ANASAZI POLITICALLY CORRECT, OR ELSE!

Some people dismiss the Politically Correct or PC Movement as a bad joke. But when being Politically Correct means objective reality must be twisted to conform to the PC vision of how the world ought to be, then the PC Movement begins to take on ominous Orwellian-Hitlerian overtones.

For example, the Anasazi were an ancient people of the American southwest who disappeared mysteriously from the face of the earth. Many theories, none conclusive, have been advanced as to why this relatively advanced agricultural civilization vanished, leaving behind only the ruins of their high-rise, cave-dwellings.

One of the local jokes in Colorado, where one of the largest Anasazi ruins is found, is that the Anasazi were doomed because they built their ruins too close to the highway.

Until just recently, the hitherto supposedly, peace-loving, corn-eating, oh-so-politically-correct Anasazis were probably on their way to being lionized in a Disney movie. You know the genre: all the wild animals sit around the camp fire in peace and harmony and sing to the natives who, of course, are the only humans fit to inhabit the earth because they are "at one" with nature.

But new research found in Christy Turner's book: "Man Corn: Cannibalism and Violence in the Prehistoric American Southwest," reveals the Anasazi tortured, mutilated and then ate their enemies. So far, no one has unearthed an Anasazi cookbook giving directions for the proper preparation of Homo Sapiens a la Anasazi. But if the Anasazi partook of victims carrying a prehistoric version of Ecoli bacteria, that might explain why they disappeared so suddenly. As they say: "You are who you eat."

The evidence suggests Anasazi cannibalism was not, like the Donner Party, something done only in an extreme situation where those who died of starvation and exposure were then eaten by those still surviving. Apparently, Anasazi cannibalism was an established practice based on a communal decision that killing and eating other humans was acceptable. Presumably, the Anasazi did not eat their friends and relatives. In all probability, they did as the Aztecs and the Mayans, who generally used their slaves or enemy POWs as objects of ritual murder.

When members of the PC Movement heard Professor Turner found evidence of Anasazi cannibalism, they criticized him for being insensitive to the negative political ramifications of his findings. The PC Movement's outrage with Professor Turner is a prime example of trying to intimidate those who come across the truth from sharing it with the rest of the world because the truth does not support their political objectives.

©1999. 902

A VOYAGE TO REMEMBER

For those faithful readers who have been following our light-hearted, year-end cruise to the western Mediterranean, along coastal Spain, to Gibraltar, to the North African cities of Casablanca and Tangiers, to Seville and on to Portugal, I must report that we did not find all the answers we sought.

Wonder Wife and I did confirm that mayonnaise was invented in Mahon, Minorca, and not in Metropolitan France. But our goal of purchasing a jar of mayonnaise made in Mahon was thwarted. The nearest mayonnaise plants are in Barcelona and Seville. The only spread we found had to do with my waistline.

Our quest to determine the true nationality of Christopher Columbus became even more confused when we dined with a fellow cruiser who has just written a book on this very subject. The author says Columbus was born in Genoa – before Italy became a nation-state – but spent most of his life in Portugal. Thus, the Portuguese can make a claim that Columbus was Portuguese. The marginal notes made by Columbus on the logs of his ships were mostly written in Portuguese although some were in Catalan as well. Evidently, Columbus never wrote in Italian. [Later, we learned most of the marginal notes were written in Hebrew.]

In Barcelona, people claim the discoverer of the New World was actually a Catalonian Jew whose first voyage was financed by a wealthy Jewish merchant of Barcelona. If true, this may explain why Columbus or Colon sailed all the way around to Barcelona instead of stopping in Cadiz or Seville to report the discovery of the New World.

But his wealthy Jewish patron was not there to receive him in Barcelona. Instead, he was received by King Ferdinand and Queen Isabella. It seems while Chris was off discovering the New World, the Spanish government expelled all the Jews from Spain. How handy for Ferdinand and Isabella to step into the shoes of the Jewish financial backer of that historic voyage of discovery and reap the financial rewards.

So, when Columbus Day rolls around, it looks like our traditional Italian menu will have to be modified somewhat. In addition to Italian meatballs and pasta, we'll add some Spanish paella, some Norwegian creamed herring and a bottle of Portuguese Mateus. Although we still won't know the true nationality of old Chris, at least we'll have a fine meal.

In Casablanca, we took a taxi to visit Rick's Café Americain inside the Casablanca Hyatt Regency Hotel. Of course, none of the famous characters were there in person. But the walls were covered with posters that were used back in 1942 to advertise what is arguably one of Hollywood's finest films. They still have a piano player.

But he isn't named Sam. Sam's replacement is called: Big Joe.

While we were in and out of the Lisbon Airport twice, there was no trace of Ilsa and Victor there either.

On a serious note, our voyage had two real highlights. One was a day-long tour of the Rock of Gibraltar. Gibraltar is one of those fascinating places where it would be prudent to spend several weeks.

The other highlight was to witness a Christmas Day High Mass celebrated in the world's third largest cathedral. Even for two Protestants, the Mass as celebrated in the Cathedral of Seville on Christmas Day was a profoundly moving religious experience. The liturgy spoken and sung, partly in Latin and partly in Spanish, was not a barrier to our understanding because the celebration of the birth of the Christ Child transcends the limitations of human speech. What began as a light-hearted look at some parts of the world which we had not seen before came to an uplifting climax that Christmas Day in Seville.

But we couldn't resist one last bit of frivolity. All the barbershops were closed that day in Seville. Fortunately, Wonder Wife remembered to bring a comb and some scissors to trim my hair. An obliging fellow cruiser used our video camera to record Wonder Wife as the Barber of Seville.

©2000. 927

EMILY'S BIG JOURNEY

Once upon a time, there was a little Denver girl named Emily Hanrahan. She was very pretty, very nice and, if you couldn't tell by her red hair, fair skin and blue eyes, her name told you she was very Irish.

One day, when she was old enough to travel by herself, she flew, for the first time, in a Douglas DC-3 airliner out to western Colorado to visit a girlfriend. At some point in the flight (long before we worried about sky-jackers) the flight attendant asked Emily if she would like to see what the pilots were doing in the cockpit.

Emily took one look at the dazzling array of dials and switches and the aircraft controls and it was love at first sight. At that moment, she vowed she would become a pilot. Little did she and the world know that Emily Hanrahan would someday make American aviation history.

While in high school, she worked in a big Denver department store. She saved every penny so she could buy flying lessons. In those days, it was almost unheard for young girls to do such a daring thing.

Out at the flight school, the owner was so impressed with Emily's winning personality and her obvious gifts for flying that he offered her a job as the school's receptionist. Soon, Emily had her private flying license and, not long after that, she went from private pilot to flight instructor.

In fact, after 15 years of instructing, she became head of the flight school and its chief pilot. During that time, she amassed over 7,000 flying hours. One of her duties at the flight school was to provide instrument flight instruction to young airline pilots.

In those days, the airlines would only hire males to fly their aircraft. Emily was told women could never be airline pilots because passengers wouldn't get on an airliner flown by a woman.

Then, Emily noticed that many of her former students were being hired by Frontier Airlines. She knew she had taught those males everything they knew about flying. She decided to apply to Frontier Airlines for a job as a pilot.

She filled out an application form, attached her more than impressive flying resume, mailed it in and she waited. And waited and waited.

As she gained more and more flying credentials, she updated her resume. Then, she took to sitting quietly in the waiting room at the headquarters of Frontier Airlines in the hope of talking with one of their executives.

Late one day and out of the blue, she was summoned to Frontier for an interview. She hurried over expecting only to be asked some questions. Instead, she was greeted by their chief pilot who threw her into an instrument flight simulator she had never seen before and he asked her to perform dozens of instrument approaches. The "test" took hours and, when it was over, both she and the chief pilot were exhausted. But Frontier's chief pilot knew he had just "flown" with a great pilot.

In 1973, Emily Hanrahan Howell, became the first woman to be hired as a pilot by a scheduled U.S. airline. In 1976, she became the first female airline captain. Today, her Frontier Airlines uniform hangs in the Smithsonian Air and Space Museum. Her list of aviation "firsts" fills an entire page.

At 11:00 a.m., on Saturday, March 11th, 2000, a permanent display honoring Captain Emily Hanrahan Howell Warner will be unveiled inside the Wings over the Rockies Air and Space Museum at the former Lowry Air Force Base. Looking as pretty as ever, Emily will be there. The event and parking are free and everyone is invited.

And what does the Irish girl who was told that only males could fly airliners do today? She works for the Federal Aviation Administration as an airline pilot flight examiner. Today, Emily Warner decides who can fly and who cannot.

NB: The Emily Warner Field Aviation Museum is located at the Granby/Grand County Airport -- Emily Warner Field. See: www.grandcountyhistory.org
©2000. 936

GETTING TOUGH ON TOFU

Recently, three U.S. cabinet-level officials were seated on a stage in Washington as they prepared to speak at a worldwide conference on nutrition. As you probably know, your top elected and appointed officials are protected by well-armed security personnel. Millions of your tax dollars are spent each year to pay, arm and train these bodyguards so those under their protection can make speeches urging that the rest of us not be allowed "to keep and bear arms" for our own protection.

Despite the phalanx of armed guards surrounding U.S. Secretary of Agriculture, Dan Glickman, a woman armed with a Tofu Cream Pie was able to break through the concentric circles of armed protection, climb up on the stage and hurl her Tofu Cream Pie at Secretary Glickman. Fortunately, Secretary Glickman ducked and the Tofu Cream Pie only struck a glancing blow to his shoulder. An alert aide immediately took his Tofu-soiled suit coat away to be dry-cleaned with a solvent that was, no doubt, approved by the Environmental Protection Agency (EPA) and will be disposed of in accordance with EPA guidelines.

Just how many people, not to mention high government officials, are killed or maimed by Tofu Cream Pies is unknown at this time. But in its unending quest to achieve a risk-free society, you can bet the Clinton Administration will launch a crusade to keep these potentially dangerous weapons out of the hands of ordinary citizens.

While this observer was not privy to the interrogation of the Tofu-tossing attacker, one can imagine how the questioning went. But due to the respect the White House and the Department of Defense have shown for individual privacy rights, we can only bring you the questions and not the answers.

"All right, young lady. Where did you purchase the Tofu you tossed at Secretary Glickman?

"Was the Tofu merchant a licensed Tofu dealer or did you purchase the Tofu from some unregulated Tofu street vendor?

"What was your state-of-mind when you bought the Tofu?

"Did you buy the Tofu with the intent of inflicting harm upon an official of the U.S. Government?

"Young lady, we have your Tofu Cream Pie over at the FBI laboratory right now. If the FBI finds that you were using that Tofu to culture some kind of infectious bacteria, you are in big trouble.

"Do you know what the penalties are for failure to register bacteria-infected Tofu as a Weapon of Mass Destruction? Well, the penalties are even worse than the penalties the Clinton Administration imposes on criminals who use firearms in the commission of crimes such as murder, rape, kidnapping and robbery.

"Why, if convicted, I'll bet you'll be required to undergo two, maybe even three, slaps on the wrist and forced to say six, maybe even seven, 'I'm sorrys.' So, young lady, do you think this is funny? Wipe that smile off your face! We are not fooling around here nor have other governments gone easy on the likes of you in the past.

"In 1922, Turkey disarmed the Armenians and eliminated 1.5 million of them between 1915 and 1917.

"In 1929, Stalin imposed mandatory weapons control and between 1929 and 1953 was able to eliminate 20 million Ukrainians who were using up too much precious food.

"China disarmed private citizens in 1935. Between 1948 and 1952 over 20 million anti-Communists were eliminated.

"Hitler installed weapons control in 1938 and by 1945 eliminated 13 million unarmed people, to include six million Jews.

"In 1956 private gun ownership was banned in Cambodia and between 1975 and 1977 over one million Cambodians were taken to the 'killing fields.'

"Uganda established weapons control and between 1971 and 1979, over 300,000 unarmed Christians were slaughtered.

"So, if you think we'll stop at just confiscating your pitiful, little Tofu Cream Pie, you've got another think coming. No ma'am, no one is going to be able to accuse Bill Clinton, Al Gore and Janet Reno of being soft on Tofu."

©2000. 949

LOSS OF CIVILITY: OUR ACHILLES HEEL?

The great aviation writer and humorist, Rod Machado, opened a column this way: "Recently, I read Virgil's *The Aeneid* in its original Latin form. I enjoyed it. I would have enjoyed it more if I understood Latin." Recently, yours truly re-read a translation of Homer's *The Iliad*. But with even less enjoyment.

While some of us do not remember all that happened in Homer's epic re-telling of the wars between Athens and Troy, many do remember that, as a protective measure, Thetis held her son, Achilles, by one heel as she dripped him into the River Styx. Unfortunately for Achilles, the heel by which he was held did not receive the river's protective armor.

Achilles started out as a great warrior for the cause of Athens. But when his advice was not always taken as gospel by the Athenian powers-that-be, Achilles became angry, directed hate speech against his comrades, and dropped out.

In fact, Achilles even refused to fight for Athens against Troy. Even worse, Achilles prayed that his Athenian comrades would be slaughtered by the Trojan forces and that Athens would lose the Trojan War.

Does this start to sound familiar? Does this begin to sound like the position taken by the Bush-haters in Hollywood Left such as Michael Moore and the like?

Of course, not everyone on the far Left wants us to lose the War on Terror. But virtually everyone on the Left side of the debate has thrown civility out the window. If political hate speech were a crime, some rather famous names might be getting to bunk with Martha Stewart.

In his commencement address at Hillsdale College, Heritage Foundation president, Ed Feulner, recounted a psychology experiment that bears on our loss of civility in political discourse: A Stanford psychologist arranged for two cars to be abandoned – one on the streets of the Bronx, the other in a posh neighborhood in Palo Alto, California.

Within ten minutes the Bronx car was stripped by vandals. In three days, it was totally trashed and destroyed. The Palo Alto car sat for a week unmolested. Then, the psychologist took a hammer to the Palo Alto car and smashed a window. Soon, passersby were taking turns with the hammer until the car was demolished.

So, what's the point? The broken window, like graffiti, like the presence of panhandlers, like public drunkenness and littering, sends the signal that no one is in charge -- that community norms have broken down or been abandoned.

So, Dr. Feulner's point is this: Political civility is broken in this country. While the first windows, if you will, were broken by the far Left, the far Right is beginning to break a few windows of its own. Book stores are filled with books with titles such as the Leftist: *The Lies of George* W. *Bush* or, from the Right, Ann Coulter's *Treason: Liberal Treachery from the Cold War to the War on Terrorism.*

Founded in fact or not, this lack of civility has the pernicious effect of driving those in the middle away from the debate. In the last two presidential elections, over half of the eligible voters failed to vote. More votes were cast for the most recent "American Idol."

For example, this observer once subscribed to an Internet chat room devoted to a particular brand of sailboats. But one of the chatters dominated the exchanges with hate speech directed against the sailboat manufacturer to the point I asked to unsubscribe. I had joined to learn maintenance techniques, not read his baseless diatribes.

In the end, Achilles put aside his anger and rejoined the battle against Troy. But had Achilles not prayed for their defeat, Athens might have won sooner, with less bloodshed and without resorting to trickery. Today, our nation cannot afford for one side to substitute hate speech for reasoned debate and to wish for our defeat. This loss of civility may be our Achilles heel.

©2004. 1168

FRACTURED HISTORY: TEST YOUR KNOWLEDGE

What was the Boxer Rebellion? That was a revolt by reform-minded military officers who were jockeying for better support for their Privates.

What were the Articles of Confederation? Those were a series of articles written by Jefferson Davis.

What were The Federalist Papers? First, there were the federal papers, then came the more federal papers and, finally, the federalist papers.

What was the Missouri Compromise? That was a deal whereby Kansas City got the Chiefs, St. Louis got the Rams, and Los Angeles got nothing. *NB: Later, the Rams went back to L.A.*

What was the Kansas-Nebraska Act? That's when the Jayhawks and the Wildcats pretend to be able to play at the same level as the Nebraska Cornhuskers.

What was the Zimmerman Telegram? That was used by Pedro Zimmerman-Castillo to wire money from the U.S. back to Mexico.

What was the Treaty of Guadalupe-Hidalgo? An agreement whereby Hidalgo had to promise to stop his sexual harassment of Guadalupe.

What was the Dred Scott Decision? (1) The U.S. Supreme Court ruled Mr. Scott wasn't a person and (2) Mr. Scott had to return to the *dreaded* South.

What was decided in *Plessy vs. Ferguson*? That Mr. Scott was a person after all; however, Plessy and Ferguson had to have separate, but equal, water fountains.

What was the ruling in *Brown vs. Board of Education*? That Plessy and Ferguson could use the same water fountain. But they had to reach the fountain by bus.

What was the Miranda Decision? While making arrests, police officers may not disguise themselves with fruit-laden headgear.

What was decided in *Roe vs. Wade*? That a bridge would be better.

What is a Fabian Socialist? That is someone belonging to a cult centered on a popular singer of the 1950s and '60s.

What does Cher mean? That is the Armenian word for slut.

Who is Madonna? See Cher above.

Which Hollywood actor added a letter to his last name in order to appear more rational? George Clooney.

What was the Stamp Act? An Irish dance group led by Michael Flatley.

Who were the Big Four? Ringo, George, Paul and John.

Who was the King who served in the U.S. Army? Elvis.

Name the Strait involved in the Pig War between the U.S. and Canada? George.

With regard to immigration, what was the effect of the Simpson-Mazzoli Act? Simpson got to stay here, and Mazzoli was deported.

What was the French Resistance? An oxymoron.

On *Cinco de Mayo,* whom did the Mexicans defeat? See French above.

What did Montezuma tell the U.S. Marines? Knock off that singing in the halls!

Where is Hong Kong to be found? On top of the Empire State Building.

What was the Gettysburg Address? After he left the White House, that is where President Eisenhower lived.

What was the New Deal? An early version of Texas Hold 'em.

What is the name of the falls so revered by honeymoon couples: Viagra.

What was decided in *Lewinsky vs. Clinton*? That U.S. Presidents, when acting outside the realm of their official duties, are liable for dry-cleaning bills.

What was the meaning of "Remember the Alamo?" A reminder to turn in your rental car.

Essay question: What is the name for readers who do not recognize the above as satire? Note: Neatness counts. Take your time...

©2006. 1297

MEXICO, 2010: THE OBAMA TELEGRAM

The year was 1917. Germany, France and England were stalemated in the trenches of World War I. Casualties on both sides were horrific. But the carnage wasn't limited to Flanders Fields where the Germans summarily executed Nurse Edith Cavell and rounded up entire Belgian villages to feed their firing squads. German U-boats killed thousands of men, women and children by sinking, among others, the passenger ships: *Lusitania*, *Housatonic* and *California.* President Woodrow Wilson kept apologizing to Germany. No. Wait. Wrong President.

To break the stalemate, Germany decided to sink even more ships. But, if Wilson responded by getting the U.S. Congress to declare war, Germany needed to divert America's attention and war supplies to a second front in Mexico. If Mexico would invade the U.S., and help Germany defeat England and France, the victorious Germans would award Arizona, New Mexico and Texas to Mexico.

German foreign minister, Arthur Zimmermann, sent a coded telegram to the German ambassador in Mexico, instructing him to offer Arizona, New Mexico and Texas to Mexico in return for a Mexican invasion of the United States. But British intelligence intercepted the Zimmermann Telegram and showed it to Wilson. In 1917, an invasion of America's southern border was unthinkable. President Wilson got Congress to declare war on Germany.

Now, the year is 2010.The understaffed U.S. Border Patrol is in the trenches with the Mexican drug cartels, with the Coyotes smuggling in kids to work in U.S. brothels, and smuggling in poor, illegal aliens seeking U.S. jobs. It is a stalemate. State treasuries are being drained by the costs of law enforcement and welfare. Hospital emergency rooms are overwhelmed delivering Hispanic babies and treating gunshot wounds. Each day, some innocent person is kidnapped in Phoenix.

But wait. The Obamessiahs have Plan A and Plan B. Plan A is to drive down the U.S. economy to the point no one wants to come here. Plan A, however, takes time. Plan B, The Obama Telegram, is quicker:

The Obama Telegram, saying the U.S. plans to give Arizona, New Mexico and Texas to Mexico, is sent to the American ambassador in Mexico, using an easy-to-break code.

Mexican intelligence breaks the code and shows The Obama Telegram to the President of Mexico. He is outraged. Having just exported his most pressing social and economic problems into Arizona, New Mexico and Texas, there is no way Mexico is taking them back.

Mexico declares war on the United States. Mexico invades Arizona and New Mexico. (You don't mess with Texas.) Caught off-guard, the understaffed U.S. Border Patrol is overwhelmed. Joyous people waving sombreros cheer the Mexican Army all the way to Phoenix. Not clued in on Plan B, an illegal alien mistakenly kidnaps the Mexican commander.

Finally, U.S. troops arrive from Afghanistan and Iraq. The Mexican Army begins a well-planned retreat that leaves U.S. forces in occupation of the northern Mexican States of Sonora, Chihuahua and Coahuila.

Appalled by the Mexican government's neglect of its people, the Obama Administration recreates the Marshall Plan that rebuilt the defeated Germany of World War II. After a few years of massive, taxpayer-funded aid from the United States, northern Mexico becomes an economic miracle -- just like post-war Germany.

Mexico's economy becomes so strong not even the poorest peon wants to be an illegal alien in the USA. The U.N. orders Obama to return Sonora, Chihuahua and Coahuila to Mexico.

Thus, Plan A and Plan B worked together to solve everyone's problems. Well, except for the devastation to Arizona and New Mexico and to the families who lost loved ones due to Plan B.

The Mexican and American Presidents share the Nobel Peace Prize. ACORN figures out a way for the people of Sonora, Chihuahua and Coahuila to vote for Obama. Even Michelle is proud.

©2010. 1476

PRESIDENT OBAMA AND THE TALE OF THE TROJAN HORSE

During the presidential campaign of 2008, this writer never thought Barak Hussein Obama or John Sidney McCain were "Manchurian Candidates" in the sense of John Condon's 1959 novel. Recall, *The Manchurian Candidate* was about an American POW being brainwashed to be a sleeper agent for the purpose of clearing the way for a covert communist to become President of the United States.

Granted, McCain did spend over five years in a communist prison camp. Granted, Obama was mentored (according to his own words and associations) by the communists: Frank Davis and Saul Alinsky; by the Pentagon bomber, William Ayers; and by the race-baiting, America-hating, Rev. Jeremiah Wright.

While McCain's post Hanoi-Hilton behavior may seem goofy to some, he remains intensely patriotic. The better analogy for Mr. Obama comes from Pulitzer-Prize-winning historian Barbara W. Tuchman's non-fiction work: *The March of Folly: From Troy to Vietnam*. She ponders how supposedly rational men can make irrational decisions despite obvious evidence that they are about to do something really stupid.

Mrs. Tuchman wrote: "All human experience is in the tale of Troy, first put into epic form by Homer [No, not Simpson] who lived between 850 and 800 B.C." The Trojan Horse gained entrance to the Fortress of Troy because the opinion leaders of Troy (read today's mainstream media) decided, out of fear of offending the Gods of cultural correctness, to dismantle Troy's main gate and roll the Greek gift-horse inside.

During the night, the Trojans, thinking they had beaten the Greeks and were free to spend their Bill Clinton-like "peace dividend" on wine, women and song, were slaughtered by 30 Athenian Special Forces-types who were hidden inside the Trojan Horse. Also, there was the usual "mole," who signaled the Greek Army to come back to Troy and join in the slaughter.

By analogy, Obama plays the role of the Greek general who devised the Trojan Horse. His Special Forces are the 30 or so key appointees who are helping Obama spend the nation into unsustainable debt. Also, there were those who read Candidate Obama's two autobiographies and recognized the Marxist-Leninist belief system of Candidate Obama's mentors. They argued it would be folly to allow Candidate Obama (mostly, on the basis of political/racial correctness), to roll his entourage through the gates of the White House. Like Cassandra, they were not believed.

In his 1964 book, *From Colonialism to Communism*, former North Vietnamese communist official, Huong Van Chi, revealed how Ho Chi Minh (after exterminating the upper class that had "collaborated" with French colonialism), saddled the remaining common folk with crushing debt, making them beholden to and fearful of the central communist regime. Those who resisted the confiscation of their land, via Uncle Ho's heavy taxation, were made to confess theirs "crimes" and executed.

Today's massive federal debt and the redistribution of wealth via taxes that will hit after January 1, 2011, could be analogous to what happened to the people of North Vietnam. The good news is: much of the Obamessiahs' socialization of medicine and commerce can be reversed by legislation. The bad news is: the massive debt already incurred cannot be undone by congressional action.

Those who bought our trillions of dollars of debt (largely, the Red Chinese in the form of U.S. Bonds and U.S. Treasury Bills) can rightfully demand full payment. But the U.S does not have the money to cover its indebtedness to foreign powers and/or to private investors unless it confiscates the money from its citizens in the form of higher taxes. Unlike U.S. Bonds or U.S. Treasury Bills, taxes do not have to be paid back. The party in power simply takes them.

What happens if the U.S cannot honor its debt and declares bankruptcy? The entire international monetary system collapses. Maybe we would be happier just watching Homer Simpson.

©2010 1484

WHAT IF: THE WAY THINGS MIGHT HAVE BEEN

Ever wonder about the "first causes" of major world events? "What if" this had happened or "what if," that had not happened? Let's examine some "what ifs."

"What if" the French monarchs had not treated their people so shabbily? How could a maritime nation blessed with such abundant natural resources have a food shortage, leading to bread riots? The French Revolution led to Napoleon's conquest of Western Europe and, for a time, his occupation of Moscow to the North and of Cairo to the Southeast.

After defeating the Prussians in 1806, Napoleon imposed a 42,000-man limit on the Prussian Army. That created a dilemma for General Gerhard von Scharnhorst, the mentor of the great strategist Carl von Clausewitz. Prussia could train the same 42,000 men over and over into a model army of professional soldiers. Or, Scharnhorst decided, he would retain a small cadre of his most professional officers and NCOs and have them train and indoctrinate class-after-class of short-service military conscripts who, after leaving active service, would comprise a "secret" reserve.

Thus, by 1813, the Prussians "secretly" trained an additional 33,000 men and resumed the fight against Napoleon. By 1815, those "added" forces gave Prussian General Gebhard von Bluecher the military might he needed to help the British Duke of Wellington defeat Napoleon at the Battle of Waterloo. So, "what if" Scharnhorst had not used conscription to train an additional 33,000 troops? A lot more people would be speaking French.

"What if" Russian Czar Nickolas II had not waged war so ineptly against Japan in 1905, a naval and land warfare disaster that suggested the yellow races could whip the white races and, thereby, gave encouragement to the Japanese militarists eager to slake their thirst for empire? Would we have had World War II in the Pacific in 1941?

"What if" the Treaty of Versailles had actually been based on President Wilson's 14 Points for Peace? "What if" the sickly Wilson had not caved in to the demands of the French and, to a lesser degree, the British? "What if" Wilson had accepted the minor compromise offered by Senator Lodge that would have resulted in Senate ratification of the League of Nations? Would an American-backed League have stopped the aggressions of Mussolini, of Japan, of Hitler, and avoided World War II?

In 1918, in Paris, instead of being rebuffed, "what if" Ho Chi Minh had been allowed to ask the writers of The Treaty of Versailles for Vietnamese independence? In the 1960s and 70s would over 58,000 Americans have died in Southeast Asia?

Following the defeat of Germany in World War I, the Treaty of Versailles limited the German Army to 100,000 officers and men. So, the clever Germans cut a secret deal with Soviet Russia that allowed the German Army to train troops and test weapons, in secret, inside the USSR. Meanwhile, the German Army encouraged the formation of, and even helped equip, a la Scharnhorst, some off-the-books irregular "reserve" forces such as the *Freikorps*. A combination of regular and irregular forces, to include the thuggish Brown Shirts, gave Hitler the military power to hold the dithering Allies at bay as Hitler threw the Treaty of Versailles into the trash.

"What if" former Secretary of State, Dean Acheson, had not made a speech in early 1950 suggesting South Korea was outside the American sphere of defense? Would the North Koreans have invaded South Korea on 25 June, 1950?

In 1998, Osama bin Laden topped the FBI's Most Wanted List. "What if" the Clinton Administration had taken advantage of the well-documented, multiple opportunities it had to kill or capture Osama bin Laden? Would we have suffered the atrocities of 9/11?

Yes, what might have been? That's the problem with playing the "what if" game. They say "guilt" is the gift that keeps on giving. We can say the same about "regret."
©2011. 1528

USA: THE LAST SALUTE?

In the opening paragraph of Barbara W. Tuchman's *The First Salute*, the Pulitzer Prize-winning historian describes the very first time that the fledgling United States was recognized as a sovereign nation by another sovereign nation.

The year was 1776. One of the four warships belonging to the newly-created U.S. Navy approached the harbor of St. Eustatius, a seven-square-mile, Dutch-owned island in the West Indies. In accordance with naval custom, the American ship fired a salute to the Dutch flag flying atop Ft. Orange. Then came the magic moment: Johannes de Graaf, Governor-General of St. Eustatius, ordered the Dutch saluting cannon to fire an answering salute to the American ship.

As Barbara Tuchman wrote: "In its responding salute the small voice of St. Eustatius was the first officially to greet the largest event of the century -- the entry into the society of nations of a new Atlantic state destined to change the direction of history." It was the dawn of America as an emerging world power.

In 1776, no one could have known that, by 1945, the United States would possess the world's most powerful navy, would take on the role of guarantor of freedom-of-the-seas for all nations desiring to engage in peaceful trade with other nations, and would continue to carry out that historic role until the year....well, that remains to be seen.

President Reagan's almost 600-ship U.S. Navy is now only 284 ships. A reduction of over 50-percent. The Obama Administration plans to cut $400 billion from defense and shift that money to non-defense spending. At some point, the freedom-of-the-seas mission will become unsustainable.

Currently, four of the Navy's ten aircraft carriers are docked side-by-side in Norfolk harbor doing maintenance. T*he Eisenhower* and the *Stennis* are in the Mediterranean and Arabian Seas, respectively. Lack of funding delayed the scheduled deployment of the *Harry S. Truman* from Norfolk to join the *Stennis*. Three carriers are docked in other home ports performing maintenance.

The *Abraham Lincoln* is due to have its nuclear reactors refueled; however, there is no money. Failure to refuel the *Lincoln* on time throws the entire nuclear refueling schedule out of alignment and could result in having more aircraft carriers awaiting refueling than those capable of operating at sea.

Just how important are our aircraft carriers? In 1993, President Bill Clinton said: "When word of a crisis breaks out in Washington, it's no accident that the first question that comes to everyone's lips is: 'Where's the nearest carrier?'"

Unless the current downward trajectory in our naval strength is checked by the election of 2016, the day may well come when a ship of the United States Navy might fire a salute upon entering a foreign port and the salute will be met with...well, a revealing silence.

©2013. 1668

FOREIGN AFFAIRS: THROUGH A LOOKING GLASS

In his best-seller: *Things That Matter*, Dr. Charles Krauthammer includes an essay entitled: "The Mirror-Image Fallacy." The former psychiatrist explains how some people look in the mirror and then assume the rest of the world thinks and acts the same as they do.

Some successful salespersons use "mirroring" to advantage by a subtle mimicking of the facial expressions and body gestures of their potential customers. Done artfully, the potential customer starts to feel warm and fuzzy as if he or she is conversing with himself or herself.

Recent studies of both Twitter and Facebook patrons reveal when people write about themselves -- their favorite subject -- dopomine flows to the brain's pleasure center, giving the Tweeter or the Facebooker a pleasant feeling. Like a shot of booze. Some over-achievers release dopomine simply by the accomplishment of their goals.

They achieve the pleasurable "runner's high" without the harmful side effects of illegal drugs or alcohol.

Sometimes, the mirror-image fallacy has disastrous effects in world affairs. Prior to WWI, when French defense planners looked into their mirror, they assumed the Germans had the same lack of confidence in their Reserve troops as the French did in theirs.

Actually, in 1914, the French and German active-duty armies were roughly equivalent. But the French failed to factor in the German Reserves which were, in fact, very large and quite well trained.

The French, looking at their stolen copy of Germany's von Schlieffen Plan, decided the Plan's manpower requirements were too great for the Germans to succeed unless the Germans used their Reserves as front-line troops. Something the French would never do. Surprise! The Germans threw their Reserves into the Schlieffen effort, making the Plan eminently workable and -- except for their own mirror-image fallacy -- the Germans would have won WWI in less than 40 days.

Just before the Germans attacked through Belgium in August, 1914, the Germans -- looking in their own mirror -- decided, if they were the French, that they would mass the French Army on the border with Alsace-Lorraine and execute French Plan 17 (they had a stolen copy) and try to recapture Alsace-Lorraine. Then, when the French forces were deep enough into Lorraine, the "center" of the German line would fall on the French from behind. But to do that, the German "center" would need a lot more troops which the German planners took away from the Schlieffen Plan.

Result: Although successfully ravaging little Belgium, the reduced Schlieffen Plan forces were insufficient to overrun the newly-arrived British blocking force. The French, sensing the trap in Lorraine, turned toward the German "center" and survived. Both sides, having lost their chance for a speedy victory, dug down into trench warfare that lasted for four horrible years. American troops from the New World had to break the stalemate and rescue the Old World from mutual suicide.

Sometimes, American foreign policy falls into the mirror-image trap. As Dr. Krauthammer relates: President Carter thought the Iranian Ayatollahs would enter into rational negotiations when the Ayatollahs simply wanted the Shah of Iran's head mounted on a platter. That fallacy got our embassy staff imprisoned in Iran for 444 long days and shattered Carter's chance for reelection. And maybe his mirror, as well.

©2014. 1715

HISTORY 101: DON'T CRY FOR ME, CRIMEA

As every Russian schoolchild knows, Catherine the Great annexed the Crimean Peninsula to Mother Russia in 1783. Today, the population of the Crimea is 12.1-percent Tatar, 24.3-percent Ukrainian, and 58.5-percent Russian. Ninety-seven percent of the population speaks Russian.

While few westerners like to see Russia's Vladimir Putin throw his weight around, Putin has history, demographics, and geo-politics on his side. One does not need to be Admiral Alfred Thayer Mahan, to understand that it is a vital national interest for Russia to have a warm-water port on the Black Sea and, from there, to be able to access the rest of the world's seas and oceans.

For 171 years, the Crimean Peninsula was part of Mother Russia. In 1954, then Soviet Premier, Nikita Khrushchev, inexplicably gave the Crimea to the Soviet Republic of Ukraine; however, the USSR retained possession of its naval base at Sevastopol, Crimea.

Khrushchev's gift of the Crimea -- with Russia's only warm-port port -- was just one of Khrushchev's several dumb ideas that caused his Politburo comrades to force him to "retire" in 1964, to become a "non-person." In 1971, *"Pravda"* (the main Soviet newspaper) devoted just one sentence to the death of Nikita Khrushchev.

In Moscow, in July of 1989, Wonder Wife and I, and ten other American journalists, interviewed Sergei Khrushchev. Unfortunately, none of us thought to ask Sergei why his father had given the Crimea to Ukraine. Mainly, we asked: Why did your father risk putting those missiles in Cuba? He said President Kennedy did not impress his father when they met in Vienna and Kennedy's generally weak responses to Soviet initiatives, such as the Berlin Wall, led his father to think the U.S. would allow Soviet missiles to be stationed in Cuba. Wrong.

Recently, Sergei told reporters that the Crimea was given to Ukraine which, at the time, was part of the Soviet

Union; because another massive hydro-electric dam was being built in Ukraine and his father thought it would be more efficient for the entire area downstream from the dam, to include the Crimean Peninsula, to be under Ukrainian control.

Obviously, Nikita Khrushchev did not foresee the end of the USSR or he would not have given the Crimea to Ukraine, which officially broke away from the USSR in 1991. Nevertheless, Nikita Khrushchev continues to make trouble even from the grave. Had Khrushchev kept the Crimea inside the USSR, we would not be reading today about the fruitless diplomatic charge of Secretary John "Swift Boat" Kerry's Lightweight Brigade.

Even though the remote Crimea is virtually unreachable for U.S. ground and naval forces, the current dust-up over the rejoining of the Crimea to Russia can have an upside for the United States. It brings to the public mind that our armed forces are being cut in half just when Russia and Red China are more than doubling the size of their military forces.

Attempts to relate the Crimea to Hitler's 1938 annexation of Czechoslovakia's Sudetenland are misplaced analogies. There is no canine-American in this fight. While western Europeans may mutter in their Chablis or their Guinness about Vladimir Putin, the return of the Crimea to Mother Russia will soon be forgotten.

©2014. 1722

SUCKING SOUNDS: IRAQ & IMMIGRATION

Unlike religions, such as Islam and Global-Warming, which will eventually Peter-out, the Laws of Geo-Politics are immutable. They abhor power vacuums. Recall, during the period between World War I and World War II, Great Britain, France, and the United States allowed a geo-political power vacuum to form that was filled by three well-armed totalitarian powers: Nazi Germany, Soviet Russia, and Imperial Japan.

In fact, the United States, by itself, did not have enough military power to defeat Nazi Germany or Soviet Russia. Only because our ancient aircraft carriers were on maneuvers away from Pearl Harbor on December 7, 1941, was America able to defeat Imperial Japan. Even then, it took two atomic bombs to subdue the slaughter in the western Pacific.

During World War II, the only way for the western democracies to survive the onslaught by the totalitarian powers, was for one of the three totalitarian powers to join in on the side of the western democracies (the Allies). Fortunately, on June 1, 1941, Hitler made the mistake of attacking the Soviet Union.

At that point, even though millions more would die or be wounded, the Allies were virtually certain of victory. But, if Hitler had attained a nuclear-weapons capability prior to D-Day, the 6th of June, 1944, the Allies would have been forced to sue for peace, leaving Western Europe and the rest of Hitler's territorial conquests in Nazi hands.

Today, one of the totalitarian powers of World War II is on the geo-political rise again. Just how far west Vladimir Putin will roll a rampant Russia remains to be seen. The Islamists of an irrational Iran are on the verge of attaining the nuclear weapons Hitler sought and almost achieved.

Red China thinks it has a vital fossil-fuel interest in doing what FDR would not allow Japan to do: Secure the oil of Indonesia and control the flow of oil through the Strait of Malacca. Just when the United States military is undergoing its largest reduction in 40 years, Russia and Red China are creating aircraft carrier task forces and developing undetectable submarines and unstoppable anti-ship missiles. A madman rules a nuclear North Korea.

Ever since World War II, the indispensable role of the United States has been to provide the leadership and military power necessary to preserve the freedom of the western democracies and to offer hope to the millions still living under totalitarian regimes. Today, statesmen around the world hear the sound of Russia, Red China, India, North Korea, Iran, and even illegal immigrants, being sucked into the geo-political space being abandoned by the Obama Administration.

President Obama's political base of: minorities, undocumented Democrats, mixed genders, Wall Street high-rollers, academics, Hollywood liberals, dot.com millionaires, and utopian socialists seems unconcerned by this geo-political power vacuum. But, when the next conventional war comes -- as history teaches us that it sadly will -- our diminished volunteer military, with its politically purged leadership, will be too weak to avert defeat. A return to conscripted service (the Draft) will be necessary and the great irony is that much of the fighting and dying will be done by the least fortunate among Mr. Obama's political base.

©2014. 1734

TODAY'S AMERICA AND PLATO'S ALLEGORY OF THE CAVE

What we read in the major media and what we see on the broadcast TV networks these days raises the question: What is reality? For example: Why do the Obama White House and State Department insist we are defeating the terrorists when ISIS is taking control of more and more territory in Iraq, Syria, and Yemen? Can we keep our current health insurance or not? Can we keep the physician we like or not? Was "Hands up, don't shoot" real or something fabricated to undermine law enforcement? A lot of things do not add up.

Actually, the struggle to know reality has a long history. Around 380 B.C., Plato, in his main work, "The Republic," told of a cave in which children were chained to a wall in such a way that they could only stare at the cave wall in front of them. Moving right behind the children was a parade of humans holding a variety of everyday items. Sunlight spilling in from the entrance of the cave plus a large fire cast the shadows of the parading humans and the objects they carried onto the wall seen by the children.

Overtime, the children came to believe that the shadows represented reality. Then, one day, one of the children broke free and was able to turn around and see the parade of humans and the objects they carried. Conditioned to believe that the shadows were real, the child concluded that the actual humans and the objects they carried were not real. That was Plato's famous "Allegory of the Cave."

Okay. So how does this ancient allegory apply in today's world? Studies done with laboratory rats have found that experiments designed, like the "Allegory of the Cave," to confuse reality with illusion, produce a state of confusion. Rats, placed in an environment where rising waters would spell their doom wanted desperately to rise above the waters. The experimenters provided the rats with a series of sticks which "appeared" to offer a way of climbing out of the rising waters. But each stick either led the rats nowhere or collapsed under their weight.

Eventually, a sturdy stick the rats could have used to climb out of the rising waters was introduced to the rats. But, by then, the rats had been conditioned into a state of "learned helplessness." They ignored the stick that could have saved them and all of them drowned.

The political pollsters of today report that ignorance and apathy are found all-too-often among the people they attempt to poll. Could it be that the talking points of the current administration, as echoed by the main-stream media, have confused the voting public into a state of "learned helplessness?"

Instead of being engaged in the public affairs that determine the reality of how we actually live our lives, have we thrown up our hands and turned to watching video games, sports, and other entertainments as an escape from the main-stream media messages that do not square with what we perceive as reality?

What if one of the presidential contenders proposes a path that would lead America up out of today's troubled waters. Would the path to prosperity be recognized or ignored? We report. You decide.

©2015. 1783

PRESIDENT WILSON: THE PEACE TO END ALL PEACE

On December 4, 1918, President Woodrow Wilson, the first American president to depart the United States while still in office, sailed toward France on a captured German luxury liner converted to be the *USS George Washington*, From overseas, President Wilson was viewed as the American "savior" who was sailing from the New World to rescue the Old World from its follies and show the Europeans how to manage their affairs without killing each other. Accompanying President and the new Mrs. Wilson on the *USS George Washington* were dozens of academics whose expertise covered almost the entire spectrum of human endeavor. They were supposed to be the data bank for the negotiations to take place in Paris, to provide the fine print for the Treaty of Versailles.

A war-weary world was in love with Woodrow Wilson. The adoring cries of "Veelson! Veelson!" could almost be heard on shipboard as Wilson crossed the Atlantic, further fanning the already out-sized ego of the American president who saw no need to share credit with the Congress that gave him a Declaration of War against the Central Powers, that raised the funds to create sufficient armed forces to turn the tide against the Kaiser, that passed the unpopular Selective Service Act that provided the men needed to fight in the trenches. In fact, when Wilson spoke in England, he failed to mention the great suffering and sacrifices of the peoples of the British Empire.

When Wilson and his entourage arrived in France, British Prime Minister, David Lloyd George, and French Prime Minister, Georges Clémenceau, were still at home shoring up their domestic political bases and making sure they understood the peace-treaty demands of their electorate. But Wilson, like President Obama, had his "pen and his telephone." Wilson had his 14 Points for Peace and his vision of a collective-security agreement to be called: The League of Nations. For Wilson, that was more than enough.

In February, 1919, Wilson made a brief trip back home which should have alerted Wilson that the newly Republican-controlled U.S. Senate might not ratify a peace treaty about which it had not been consulted. But with the adulation of the European masses ringing in his ears,

Wilson felt the concerns of the American Congress could be safely ignored.

Wilson even ignored the vast array of academic minds assembled in Paris to provide the technical advice that would be needed to adjust geographical boundaries, to adjudicate and resolve ethnic and religious differences among the peoples who were going to have to live under the dictates of the Treaty of Versailles which, as history would eventually record, set the stage for World War II, Vietnam, Kosovo, and Iraq.

Ironically, and with tragic consequences for future American war dead, wounded, and their families, when Nguyen Tat Thanh (later, Ho Chi Minh) tried to plead the case for Vietnamese independence to Wilson, Lloyd George, and Clémenceau, he was ignored. Thus, the peace treaty that was to end all wars ended up as the peace treaty to end all peace. And yes, with just a "pen and a telephone," a president who ignores the elected representatives of the people can do a lot of harm.

©2016. 1817

WORDS MATTER

In this Atomic Age, which presidential candidate has temperament to be Commander-in-Chief? In a world of fingers hovering near nuclear triggers, rash words, taken seriously, could plunge the entire planet into nuclear winter.

In the world of domestic politics, there is no better exposition of this reality than Dr. Frank Luntz' *"Words That Work: It's Not What You Say, It's What People Hear"* (2008). In the world of foreign relations, there is no better example than the Ems Dispatch that led to the Franco-Prussian War of 1870-72. Another example is the diplomatic bumbling that led to World War I and is described so well in Barbara Tuchman's Pulitzer Prize winning, *"The Guns of August"* (1962).

In 1870, France and Germany got into a diplomatic tiff because a German Prince was offered the vacant Spanish throne, causing the French to fear a German-Spanish axis. At the spa town of Bad Ems, the French ambassador interrupted the morning walk of Kaiser Wilhelm I to voice the French complaint. The Kaiser's actual response was civil, yet non-committal.

But Chancellor Otto von Bismarck had his eye on the coal fields of Alsace and the Quiche fields of Lorraine. Bismarck re-worded the official German reply to the French complaint in a way that Bismarck knew would call in question the honor of France. Predictably, the French declared war on Germany and got their derrieres handed to them by the Germans at the Battle of Sedan. By 1872, the Germans occupied the coal mines of Alsace and were dining on quiche in Lorraine, setting the stage for World War I to follow.

Another example of words gone wrong followed the assassination of Arch Duke Ferdinand of Austria and his wife in Sarajevo on June 28, 1914. Sarajevo was an incident that should have been readily resolved with a few measured words between the Central Powers, Serbia, and even Russia. Although the Austrian government in Vienna wanted to punish little Serbia -- a client state of Russia -- well thought out diplomatic language coming from France, Great Britain and the other European states should have been able to cool any war fever in Vienna and Moscow.

Instead, confusion over the intentions of what the parties were going to do about Sarajevo set in motion the mobilization of the armed forces of Austria-Hungary, Russia, and Germany. Ever fearful of a mobilized Russia, Kaiser Wilhelm II and his Prussian generals decided to secure Germany's west flank by attacking France via Belgium. Paris in hand, the Germans planned to then secure Germany's eastern flank from possible Russian attack. Only it did not turn out that way. By 1918, 17 million people were dead and another 20 million had been wounded.

Bear in mind, the diplomatic missteps leading to the Franco-Prussian War and to World War I were taken at a relatively leisurely pace. In both cases, the parties had ample time -- weeks or even months -- to dial back any harsh words and avert war.

Today, a U.S. president has roughly 30 minutes to erect whatever we have in terms of an anti-missile defense and order our nuclear triad to launch a counter strike. In this election, words matter.

©2016. 1831

THE ONLY THING WE HAVE TO FEAR IS HOPLOPHOBIA ITSELF

In the wake of all the recent murders of innocent men, women, and children in gun-free zones, hope springs eternal that even the most mentally challenged in Hillary's village will come to understand that gun-free zones work to the advantage of the radical Islamist killers and to the disadvantage of innocent people trying to go about their individual pursuits.

But "understanding" depends on overcoming irrational fears. First, there is the fear by some of being called an Islamophobe. Secondly, there is an irrational fear of firearms which has been given the name: Hoplophobia which combines the Greek word "hoplon," meaning "arms" with the Greek word "phobos," meaning "fear," which is then anglicized as Hoplophobia. The confirmed Hoplophobic believes that firearms have a will of their own, that firearms can commit crimes absent human involvement. In Congress, many Democrats and even a few Republicans, think that guns, rather than violence-prone humans, should be controlled.

But is it really irrational to fear Islam? Some people, in the wake of, yet another, Islamic jihadist atrocity are careful to say the atrocity was committed by "radical" Islamists, not by run-of-the-mill Islamists. What those people do not understand is that "radical" Islam is not the problem. The problem, ever since the Islamists tried to overrun France in 732 A.D, Spain in 1571 A.D. and Vienna in 1529 and 1683 A.D is (drum roll) Islam -- a violent, totalitarian political movement that wraps itself in the trappings of a religion. See: *The Looming Tower: Al-Qaeda and the Road to 9/11* by Lawrence Wright (2006), and *Islam Unveiled* by Robert Spencer (2003).

Islam is what it is. Judeo-Christians wishing for Islam to turn against its violent members are not going to change Islam. The so-called peaceful Islamists are not going to interfere with Islam's violent members. As Mao Zedong famously said, "The guerrilla must move amongst the people as a fish swims in the sea." The violent jihadists swim in a sea of non-violent Islamists who believe as they do and will not lift a finger to stop their violence. Ergo: The Islamic war against Judeo-Christian Western Civilization that began in 732 A.D. and has continued in fits and starts ever since 732 A.D. is not going to abate. That is the reality. Thus, there is every reason to be unashamedly Islamophobic

While it may not be possible for Islam to be defeated, it can be contained. As the French proved in 732, the Spanish in 1571, and the Viennese in 1529 and 1683, the Islamists can be beaten back by the use of armed force. But not if we continue to allow Hoplophobia to prevent us from exercising our inherent right to self-defense and our Constitutional right to "keep and bear arms."

While many think the Islamist terrorists are crazy, they are not stupid. In the typical hostage situation, they pretend to negotiate so they can stay on world-wide television for as long as they can before they kill their hostages. They think that is the way to win recruits to ISIS or other Islamic terror groups. Apparently, it works.

While Islamophobia may hurt some feelings on the Left, Islamophobia will not kill us. But Hoplophobia, if allowed to persist, most certainly will.

©2016. 1843

PRECEDENT: WIRE TAPPING HIGH-PROFILE PEOPLE

Tipped off by GCHQ, the British mid-wife of our National Security Agency (NSA), the Obama Administration's Intelligence Community may have monitored the electronic communications of members of the Trump campaign staff and the communications of the Trump transition team. Now we learn there is a British precedent for government electronic surveillance -- even of Britain's Royal Family.

According to an article by Peter Stanford in the April 10, 2017, edition of "Financial Review," in early 1936, an ailing King George V learned that his son, Edward, Prince of Wales, was consorting with the pro-Nazi, Oswald Mosley, and the pro-Hitler U.S. Ambassador to the Court of St. James, Joseph P. Kennedy. Moreover, that the Prince of Wales spent $11.5 million dollars on jewels for the American divorcee, Wallis Simpson, who was also suspected of sleeping, not only with the Prince of Wales, but also with the German ambassador to Great Britain, Joachim von Ribbentrop.

An alarmed, King George V turned to Prime Minister Stanley Baldwin. Baldwin tasked MI-5 to monitor communications between the King's heir and Mrs. Simpson. Initially, MI-5 director, Sir Vernon Kell, refused, just as current NSA director, Admiral Michael S. Rogers, is presumed to have resisted orders to monitor Candidate Trump.

Apparently, Roger's resistance prompted then Secretary of Defense Carter and then CIA director Brennan to ask President Obama to fire Admiral Rogers. On November 17, 2016, (nine days after the election) Admiral Rogers had a private meeting with President-Elect Trump inside Trump Tower. Note: Admiral Rogers has been retained by President Trump as his NSA director. Carter and Brennan have been replaced. We report. You decide.

During the first weekend of December, 1936, MI-5 agent, Thomas Robertson, tapped the telephones inside Buckingham Palace and recorded the newly enthroned King Edward VIII telling "Bertie," his stuttering younger brother and future King George VI, that he, Edward, was going to abdicate and marry the twice-divorced Mrs. Simpson. Upon assuming the throne, "Bertie," King George VI, made his brother, Edward, and his bride, Wallis, the Duke and Duchess of Windsor.

In 1940, after Germany, France, Poland were at war with Germany, the Duke and Duchess of Windsor were given a tour of the Maginot Line by French General Maurice Gamelin (whose additional military blunders belong in the Guinness Book of Records). According to Charles Bedaux, later revealed as the Nazi's agent handler for the Duchess, she reported to Bedaux the major weak point of the French defense. On May 10-14, 1940, that was exactly where the Nazi forces poured through, defeating the French and British forces in just six weeks.

According to Rob Evans and David Hencke, writing in the "UK Guardian" of June 29, 2002, Prime Minister Winston Churchill was aware of the duplicitous Duchess. Churchill arranged for the Royal Couple to be posted to the British Bahamas where the Duchess complained the natives were "lazy N-words." When the Royal Couple visited Florida, President Franklin D. Roosevelt had them followed and their communications monitored.

If former President Obama needed a precedent for spying on high-profile Americans, he needed to look no further than the spying done by King George V, Prime Ministers Baldwin and Churchill, and by FDR.

©2017. 1885

TIME FOR A MODERN-DAY BONFIRE OF THE VANITIES?

Satire: An imaginary phone call: "Mr. President, honey, I tried to call y'all today; however, and I got yawl's voice-mail system. So, I'm leavin' y'all this message: I'm a 95-year-old white woman. A college-educated former history teacher livin' in West by God Virginia. Mr. President, bless your heart, y'all must learn to speak out more forcefully. Y'all were too even-handed during that riot in Charlottesville. While blamin' both sides for being hateful was fair, y'all missed a chance to nail -- pardon my French -- some real racist bastards.

"If the statue-smashers and name-changers want to take down buildings and monuments named after racists, they can start right here in West Virginia with former KKK Kleagle and Exalted Cyclops, Senator Robert C. Byrd. In 1941, Senator Byrd wrote his fellow segregationist Senator Theodore Bilbo this here letter and I quote from it: 'I shall never fight in the armed forces with a negro at my side...Rather I should die a thousand times and see Old Glory trampled in the never to rise again than to see this beloved land of our become degraded by race mongrels, a throwback to the blackest specimen in the wilds.'

"As the Democrat Majority Leader in the U.S. Senate, Byrd funneled millions of taxpayer dollars into 36 buildings, five highways, two bridges, one lock and dam, and one Interstate interchange. All named for himself. He got 9 centers and buildings named for his wife. So, right there's over 50 things needin' to be renamed.

"Mr. President, darlin', if y'all don't hold with this history erasin', renamin' when it is ignorant and unfair, like in the case of Robert E. Lee, y'all need to call out all those hypocritical, linguistic PC fascists. Make 'em put up or shut up. Get yourself a copy of Professor Steven Wilder's Ebony & Ivy: Race, Slavery, and the Troubled History of America's Universities. Y'all will read how the early Ivy League colleges thought slavery 'stood beside church and state as the third pillar of a civilization built on bondage.' Mr. President, graduates of Harvard, Princeton, Columbia,

Yale, Dartmouth, Pennsylvania, William and Mary and even Oxford are holdin' some slavery-tainted diplomas.

"Mr. President, y'all are probably surrounded with Fulbright Scholars. Senator J. William Fulbright signed The Southern Manifesto opposin' Brown vs. Board of Education. Fulbright voted against the Civil Rights Act of 1964 and against the Voting Rights Act in 1965. Princeton graduates should be ashamed of Woodrow Wilson who ordered the "colored" signs put back on the water fountains and restrooms in the White House. Cecil Rhodes, founder of Oxford's Rhodes Scholarships, worked blacks to death in the diamond mines of South Africa.

"Mr. President, y'all need to send out a Tweet callin' for folks with college degrees from universities founded or funded by slave owners and racists to burn their diplomas like the hippies burned their draft cards in the 1960s over Vietnam. Have 'em do it on your south lawn over Charlottesville. A modern-day bonfire of the vanities. But I'll bet those hypocrites won't do it. Oh, oh, I hope I'm not runnin' out of time 'cause I'm fixin' to tell you how to build that (click)..."

©2017. 1906

CHAPTER SEVEN

MILITARY AFFAIRS

These particular columns do not necessarily appear here in the order in which they were published in "Central View."

YOU WERE A GREAT DOG, SNOOPY BEAGLE

Some Americans do not readily confess to the reading of comic strips. One suspects they do not wish to appear shallow or superficial. But, in the case of "Peanuts," by the late Charles Schulz, few people seem to suffer from such inhibitions. The essential goodness of the man, Charles Schulz, came through to readers in the form of the adventures and misadventures of Charlie Brown, Linus, Lucy, Snoopy and all the rest.

Since the passage of Charles Schulz to that great Heaven where there is no shortage of ink, paper and ideas, our world has been a poorer place. Personally, this observer mourns the loss of Snoopy the Beagle most of all.

Charlie Brown never did much to hold my attention. I suppose he was such a klutz that he was a painful reminder of all the klutzy things we all do from time-to-time. I never read the strips featuring Lucy. She was such a difficult person and I took no joy in either her antics or even in her inevitable comeuppance. But Snoopy the Beagle was an entirely different matter. Maybe it is because I think many dogs I know are better than some people I know.

Snoopy played two roles near and dear to those who fly airplanes and to those who have served their country in peace and war. In fact, I would be hard pressed to choose between Snoopy, the intrepid World War I Aviator and Snoopy of the French Foreign Legion defending Fort Zinderneuf from being overrun by hordes of scimitar-swinging men on camels. Both of Snoopy's roles have something to teach us about the human condition.

Snoopy, the World War I flying ace, spoke to us about courage. Given the primitive state of aviation technology in World War I, just taking flight was a major risk. Those early aircraft engines were very unreliable, and frankly, even the flight instructors of that era were possessed of highly imperfect knowledge of just what made a fixed-wing aircraft fly and which flight attitudes were inherently dangerous. It was truly a time of trial and error and, all too often, error won.

Add to the twin risks of imperfect machines and imperfect knowledge the risks of air-to-air combat and ground fire and one must conclude that the World War I fighter pilots were extremely brave or foolish and, probably, a bit of both. Whenever I saw Snoopy flying his doghouse against the Red Baron and his cronies, I always felt Charles Schulz was reminding us about something important.

Yet Snoopy's defense of Fort Zinderneuf is, perhaps, even more inspiring. But to really understand what Charles Schulz was telling us one needs to read or reread *Beau Geste* by Percival Christopher Wren in which the author tells the story of three brothers with overactive chivalry genes.

Michael "Beau" Geste joins the French Foreign Legion to protect the name and reputation of a favorite aunt. In a classic failure of intra-family communications, his brothers: Digby and John follow "Beau" into the French Foreign Legion and all but John are killed either in the defense of Fort Zinderneuf or after its fall.

Every time I saw Snoopy manning the battlements of Fort Zinderneuf, I was reminded of a time when chivalry, gallantry and dogged (no pun intended) determination were more prized than today.

Actually, we have no way of knowing what Charles Schulz was thinking when he sent Snoopy out to do battle in the skies over Flanders Fields or set him in the grim defense of Fort Zinderneuf, but I like to think that Schulz was using pen and paper to give us a subtle reminder of the brave men who were willing to risk all for God and family and country and for their fellow aviators and soldiers.

It is too bad that we won't see Snoopy again. But we are grateful for the times we had.

©2000. 945

VIETNAM: WHY MEN FOUGHT SO WELL

If ever the history of a war was like nine blind men trying to describe an Elephant and each coming up with a different description, then the Vietnam War is it. For those who spent all their time out in the "boonies," the war was about as sweaty, grimy and dangerous as war can be. For those who lived and worked in the larger base camps or in Saigon, life was relatively comfortable and far less dangerous.

Those who served only with U.S. Forces, have one view of the war. Those who served as advisors to the South Vietnamese have another. But, in both cases, the quality of the experience depended on the leadership available to the soldiers.

This observer had occasion to spend two years in Southeast Asia and the honor to serve with the 1st Air Cavalry Division as an infantry company commander, and later, as a battalion and a division operations officer. Sometimes, I ask myself: How did we compare with those who fought in World War II and Korea?

Well, for one thing, there is not one recorded instance of an American unit surrendering to the enemy. This was not the case in World War II and Korea. In nine years of fighting not one American platoon ever surrendered. On those rare occasions when an American unit was overrun, the men chose to fight to the death rather than surrender.

Today, the North Vietnamese generals talk and write openly of what the war was like from their perspective. A theme that runs throughout their memories is the "fanaticism" with which the Americans fought. But communists are trained to see the world in political terms. Our troops fought and fought well, but it was not due to "fanaticism."

Thanks to the helicopter, we never had a sense of being "cut-off." While bad weather and bad visibility might delay the arrival of the "cavalry" to save us, we knew they would eventually come. It was just a matter of holding on. Moreover, we always had tons of indirect-fire support from tube artillery, aerial-rocket artillery, helicopter gunships, the U.S. Air Force and, depending on our location, even naval gunfire.

We never wanted for food or water or medical evacuation, weather and enemy fire permitting. During the dry season, my company ran out of potable water one day when we were in a position where helicopters couldn't land. But I was able, via radio, to "flag down" a passing cargo helicopter. It was carrying a pallet of beer originally destined for some rear-area Post Exchange. Obligingly, the pilot dropped the pallet. Many of the cans burst open; however, we were able to salvage enough liquid to keep from going mad with thirst. And, they say: War is hell.

Yet, despite these logistical and fire-power advantages, the main reason our troops fought so well had to do with good leadership, training and equipment and the miracle ingredient: unit cohesion. In the heat of combat, men do not fight for some political system, be it democracy or communism. They fight because of their buddies to the left and right of them. They fight because of a sense of duty and of obligation to those around them and to their unit.

They obtain this sense of duty and obligation from the way they were raised, from good leaders who set the proper example, from learning their unit's history and traditions, from drill and ceremonies, from martial music, and yes, from military chaplains. Pride may be one of the seven deadly sins, but unit and individual pride played an enormous role in the exemplary combat record of our troops in Vietnam.

This has to be the answer because we sure weren't fighting to thank President Johnson and Secretary McNamara for keeping us from winning a war that was eminently winnable.

©2000. 960

USA Today, November 11, 2004

MISTY EYES FOR ONE OLD SOLDIER

When this old soldier was growing up in small-town Oklahoma, Veterans Day was very special. Only we called it Armistice Day back then. It seemed like the entire town of 5,000 and all the farmers, ranchers and oil field hands came to the town square to share one special moment followed by a parade.

The special moment was when the courthouse clock struck 11:00 a.m. on the 11th day of the 11th month of the year. A hush fell over those assembled as the minute hand inched toward the top of the hour. We held our breaths as the clock chimed the magic moment.

Then, off in the distance, from a seemingly secret place, we heard a trumpet playing the first plaintive phrase of Taps, answered by another trumpet echoing the first phrase of Taps from some other secret place. I swelled with pride because I knew the first trumpet player was my own Navy veteran Father.

When the last notes died off in the distance, women were sobbing into their bandanas. Men found it necessary to polish their glasses or wipe some mysterious insects from their eyes.

Then, off we went to line both sides of Broadway in anticipation of what we thought of as The Big Parade. One of my uncles marched wearing his American Legion cap. He was in World War I. My father marched wearing his Veterans of Foreign Wars cap. He was in World War II. My mother, my younger brother and I swelled with pride. I thought: if I have to go to war and come home safely, maybe my dad will still be playing Taps on Veterans Day and, later, we'll march together down Broadway.

A different time for veterans

But that wasn't to be. During a 20-year career as an infantry officer, I came back from Vietnam twice. The first time, I detected coolness from some I thought would be more welcoming. A few years later, I came back from Vietnam again, and the reception was downright hostile. Hurrying to catch a plane to be rejoined with loved ones, a hippy-looking youth stepped in my path and spat right in my face and all over my uniform.

Needless to say, the images of those Veterans Days of long ago were not restored on my return from serving our nation in uniform. But then, came the Gulf War. I tried to return to active duty; however, I was over 60 and got a polite "thanks, but no thanks."

At the end of the Gulf War, my wife helped organize a huge welcome home parade in Lincoln, Nebraska. Veterans of all previous wars were invited to march. I found I could still wear an old set of jungle fatigues and boots and my paratrooper's red beret. I was proud to line up in the parade marshalling area with all kinds of veterans wearing bits and pieces of whatever military apparel they could find or still fit.

Of course, there were a handful of the seemingly obligatory bogus Vietnam veterans with their old fatigue jackets covered with patches from units with which they had never served and other indicia from countries they had never seen. It only takes a few pointed questions to know which ones are bogus. But, what the heck, maybe they had some nascent feelings of patriotism and just wanted to march in the company of men and women who had actually served their country in time of war.

Now, from Afghanistan to Iraq and wherever freedom is threatened or struggling to take root, young Americans face implacable forces determined to replace our way of life with theirs. If there is ever a time for all Americans to honor the sacrifices being made by our young soldiers, Marines, sailors, airmen and special operations forces, this Veterans Day should be it.

Something we can all agree on

Now, we live high in the mountains of what the coastal elites like to think of as fly-over country. It's a place where we all still assemble to be struck silent at the 11th hour of the 11th day of the 11th month. It's a place where they play Taps, where the veterans march in a parade, where Old Glory flies and total strangers get in your face. Not to spit, but to say some kind words of thanks and praise.

And, off in the distance, I can still hear my late father beginning the first plaintive notes of Taps. My wonderful wife suggests I must have gotten something in my eye and hands me her handkerchief. She has to drive us home.

NB: The above article won the Valley Forge Freedoms Foundation Medal.

COMMUNICATIONS: LESSONS LEARNED

Lessons can be learned from the sad end to the legendary football coaching career of Joe Paterno. Long ago, First Sergeant Lee F. Cobble -- one of those characters you never forget, -- taught a then brand-new infantry officer many valuable lessons.

Serving as our rifle company's executive officer, it was a joy to work closely with 1SGT Cobble who, like our other Korean War-veteran platoon sergeants, took the training of young officers as a serious responsibility.

1SGT Cobble was meticulous about adhering to the chain-of-command. He advised "his" lieutenants to do so as well; however, when sending any kind of written communications to higher headquarters, he always figured out a logical way for someone, in addition to the communication's main addressee, to be entitled to a copy. At the bottom of the page, he always listed any additional addressees. That way, he reasoned, the chance of your correspondence being lost or ignored by higher headquarters was greatly reduced.

Cobble had another rule that served us well. When he heard a young officer complain about higher headquarters, he would say: "Lieutenant, we have a rule around here that until everything at Charlie Company, 2d Battalion, 47 Infantry, is in perfect order, we do not complain about higher headquarters – no matter how stupid we know them to be."

He told us hiding bad news does not make it better. He said bad news only gets worse for those who knew about the bad news and did not report it. At Penn State, an assistant coach witnessed a retired assistant coach in the commission of a felony. He reported what he saw to Coach Paterno. Coach Paterno sent him to tell then athletic director, Tim Curley. Now, both Curley and former finance official, Gary Schultz, are charged with failure to report a felony to law enforcement.

No doubt, Nebraska football fans are as appalled by any kind of child abuse as anyone, but do not expect Nebraska fans to be too broken up over the demise of Coach Paterno. Many of them still remember a 1982 game in Penn State's Beaver Stadium. The game took place before it was possible for rulings on the field to be reversed by review officials armed with "instant replay."

In the closing seconds, Penn State quarterback, Todd Blackledge, threw a pass to tight-end, Mike McCloskey, who caught the ball so far outside the field of play that even the severely-visually-challenged could see McCloskey was clearly out-of-bounds. The blatant wrong call put Penn State on Nebraska's two-yard line. Penn State went on to hand Nebraska a 27-24 loss, costing the Cornhuskers a national championship.

Later, Mike McCloskey admitted to the media that he knew he was out-of-bounds when he caught the ball. In fact, the call was so outrageous that Nebraska tee-shirt shops immediately reproduced the Beaver Stadium gridiron on the front of tee-shirts depicting a nine-square-foot extension appended to the Beaver Stadium gridiron at the two-yard line. While one would not expect Coach Paterno to refuse the win (no matter how tainted), some kind of apology would have been nice.

Graham B. Spanier, the Penn State president who was fired along with Paterno, used to be the chancellor at Nebraska. Interestingly, Spanier was the chancellor who fired Bob Devaney, Nebraska's legendary former football coach and, at the time, was serving as Nebraska's athlete director. Is there a pattern here?

A military commander is responsible for all his or her unit does or fails to do. Apparently, the president "commander" at Penn State took no action against the felon. Coach Paterno directed his subordinate to report what he saw up the chain-of-command. Apparently, that was not enough.

©2011. 1556

THE DAY I LEARNED THE MEANING OF FREEDOM

To truly understand what freedom means, one must be deprived of it. This is how I lost my freedom on a day in late 1961:

I was ordered to fly from New York to Frankfurt Rhein/Main Airport, change into civilian clothes, purchase a train ticket to Bremerhaven (but get off the train early in the town of Iserlohn) and await pick-up by a fellow intelligence agent for a ride to my new duty station in Luedenscheid. Fluent in German and with some ability in French and Spanish, I thought: Europe, here I come. Ian Fleming, you ain't seen nothin' yet.

As I waited outside the Iserlohn Bahnhof, a VW beetle skidded to a halt in front of me. A biggie-size American said only: "Throw your bag into the trunk and get in!" Forty kilometers later, he skidded to a halt at a former German Army barracks (Kaserne), guarded by Belgians.

Suddenly, two burly Belgian policemen carried me down a set of stone steps into a dungeon and threw me into a cell where I was searched and stripped of my wallet, cover ID, cover civilian passport and money.

By then, I had been traveling for over 24-hours with almost no sleep. I had an eight-hour case of jet lag, was in a foreign country, unaccustomed to civilian clothes, speaking a foreign language, had ridden two hours on a German train, had survived a terrifying ride down mountainous German roads to be thrown into a dank dungeon, searched, stripped of my ID and money and left there alone to ponder my fate. Things were not going well. While in "solitary," I thought a lot about home and family and America and the meaning of our Bill of Rights.

Finally, a Belgian, who looked like the actor David Niven, took me to an interrogation room. He said he was M. Van den Plaas, of the Belgian Counterintelligence Corps. He said I was a KGB agent. If I did not confess, I would be tortured. And, if that did not produce the truth, I would be taken out into the courtyard and shot. M. Van den Plaas was amused when I protested that my 1st, 4th, 5th, and possibly, my 8th Amendment rights were being violated.

Fortunately, I had had Military Code of Conduct training and been subjected to mock POW torture at Ft. Benning, Georgia. So, all M. Van den Plaas got from me was my name and my cover story. Period.

Finally, in desperation, M. Van den Plaas called the guards and they threw me back into my cell. In French, I heard him order a firing squad to be ready at dawn. I was left alone and, I might add, scared.

Then, from the top of the stairs leading down into the dungeon, a procession of six Americans came down the stone steps singing: "For He's A Jolly Good Fellow." Only the lead American was in uniform. He introduced himself as Major Reed, my new boss, and then introduced me to the other members of the hush-hush team with whom I would serve for the next two years.

I had just been the victim of an elaborate practical joke and security test conceived by Major Reed and his

Belgian counterpart, M. Van den Plaas. I would like to tell you what we Americans, Belgians and Germans were working on in that remote area of northern Germany. But then, I would have to .... You know the rest.

That day, back in 1961, was when I came to know what American Freedom means and how wonderful it is. I wouldn't wish that dismal day on anyone. But I do wish more Americans would take about five minutes, read our Bill of Rights and then, on September 11th, thank God for them and offer a prayer of grateful thanks for all those who have been killed or wounded in the defense of American Freedom.

© 2002. 1067

COLD WAR: MR. HAMILTON GOES TO DENMARK

Early in the Cold War, the United States negotiated top-secret agreements with some of the NATO nations to allow the U.S. military to store nuclear weapons on their soil.

After spending time in a plain-clothes counterintelligence assignment in the four northern German States and in the Netherlands, yours truly was promoted to captain and transferred to an intelligence outfit near Frankfurt. One day, the boss told me to go back into civilian clothes, fly to Copenhagen, meet with the Danish Minister of Defense, and work out the final security arrangements for the storage of U.S. nuclear warheads on Danish soil.

Yeah, right. A junior officer from a small town in Oklahoma is going to sit down elbow-to-elbow with the Danish Minister of Defense? No way.

The boss instructed me to cover my civilian suit and tie with a military flight suit and report to a nearby airstrip where a single-engine aircraft would be waiting to fly me though the night to Copenhagen. To my surprise, one of the pilots was my next-door neighbor – a naval officer who, unknown to me at the time, was working for the CIA. He and his buddy were Navy commanders.

In Copenhagen, I told the pilots to have a good time and meet me back at the aircraft the next morning at 0800 hours. I shed the flight suit, used my official U.S. Government passport to clear Danish customs, took a taxi to the Ministry of Defense (MOD), and presented my credentials as: Mr. Hamilton.

Holy protocol, Batman! The Minister of Defense himself (the same rank as U.S. Secretary of Defense Robert S. McNamara) ushered me into a conference room. Talk about shock and awe!

If the minister knew my true rank, he gave no sign. Apparently, I was just a young official representing the government of the United States of America. Naturally, I was in awe of someone who spoke all the Scandinavian languages plus French, German and English. Recalling the brutal Nazi occupation of Denmark, I did not make the mistake of suggesting that we use German.

Working without any of his staff, he and I went page-by-page through the top-secret engineer drawings detailing the construction and physical security arrangements for the nuclear storage sites. When it came time for lunch, the minister sent out for Smørrebrød – those delicious Danish open-face sandwiches.

We labored right on to suppertime. We worked out the arrangement for the Danish Army to provide the external forces to protect the sites. We even discussed some of living arrangements for the families of U.S. forces which, at all times, would be in actual physical possession of the nuclear weapons.

The minister sent out for more Smørrebrød. Long after dark, we finished and we each applied our signatures to the solemn security agreement between Denmark and the United States. I checked into a nearby hotel.

The next morning, at 0800 hours, I detected the two commanders had taken my "good time" instructions too literally. I sent them back to their hotel with instructions to return the next morning fit to fly. Meanwhile, I looked at Edvard Eriksen's statue of the Little Mermaid. Noon found me at the Amalienborg Palace watching the changing of the guard. Then, I went to Tivoli Gardens to people-watch the afternoon away. Finally, I checked into the five-star Hotel D'Angleterre for the night. The next morning, we flew back to West Germany.

In 1971, after picking up a new VW in Norway, I was driving to another duty assigment in Germany, But I could not pass through Denmark without driving by the Danish MOD and recalling the heavy and, sometimes, even fun, responsibilites that make military service so appealing.

©2010. 1509

COLONEL BILL LACEY: OUR LOSS, HEAVEN'S GAIN

Last week, one of America's most gallant and inventive soldiers went to join his band of brothers who have already earned their place in Heaven. Colonel William J."Bill" Lacey, Jr., U.S. Army (Ret.), who never shied away from any fight, lost his battle with a blood disorder caused by Agent Orange.

Bill began his illustrious military career as an enlisted soldier in Berlin, the place where Bill became absolutely fluent in German.

"Soldier Bill," as he was known, never really retired. Appalled by the carnage inflicted by the Islamic terrorists' improvised explosive devices (IEDs), Bill spent virtually every waking moment inventing devices to defeat the IED menace.

We first met in 1969 in Phuoc Vinh, South Vietnam, where Bill was one of several highly decorated captains working in the G-3 (Operations) section of the 1st Air Calvary Division. Operations are the around-the-clock heartbeat of any division. Bill liked the shift that started at midnight and ended at 0700 hours when Bill gave the division's three general officers the G-3 portion of the morning briefing.

The briefing order began with the G-2 (Intelligence) briefer, followed by Bill briefing for Operations, followed by G-4 (Logistics), then G-1 (Personnel), and G-5 (Civil Affairs). One morning, we noticed the G-2 briefer was telling the generals about operations that should have only been known to the G-3 Section, namely, to Bill and to me.

Ah ha! The G-2 had a spy in the back of the tent where Bill and I rehearsed his portion of the briefing and the spy was stealing Bill's stuff, leaving Bill with virtually nothing to report.

Bill's solution was simple. Since both of us were fluent in German, we did our morning rehearsals in German. The G-2's efforts to steal our stuff were from that moment, *Kaput.*

Bill, a practical joker in the tradition of M*A*S*H, invented the mythical Phuoc Vinh University. He had a Vietnamese shop make up T-shirts that read: "Phuoc U!" Bill helped invent the mythical Phuoc Vinh Flying Club. A M*A*S*H-type story for another time.

Months later, as a fledgling member of Toastmasters International in Newport, RI, I had to produce and introduce a guest speaker. Soldier Bill (by then, in the Pentagon) had an amazing ability to speak a mix of German and English that was comically understandable to both German and English listeners.

Bill agreed to be my guest speaker, appearing as a retired German U-boot captain. So, Bill flies up to Newport in a double-breasted blue blazer over a white turtle-neck sweater, looking and speaking exactly like the German film actor, Curd Jűrgens. *NB: Curd, not Curt, was how Jűrgens spelled his name.*

Following my fulsome introduction, Bill had his audience of senior naval officers convinced that he was, indeed, a retired German U-boot captain. Then, on purpose, Bill started making mistakes of knowledge about submarine operations. As the audience of naval officers caught on to the hoax, the room started to ring with gales of laughter. Bill earned me an "A" from Toastmasters.

For decades now, we have e-mailed each other almost daily. Lord, I can't tell you how much I'm going to miss him. But, to borrow from Bill's favorite, Rudyard Kipling: *I'll meet him later on at the place where he has gone, where it's always double shots of Guinness ale. He'll be on a cloudy hill, doing his act as Soldier Bill, and telling tales as only Bill can tell.*
©2013. 1697

TWO DIFFERENT CULTURES: SOLDIERS AND DIPLOMATS

Recently, while reading *The Kennan Diaries* (2014), the almost-daily diaries of George F. Kennan (the father of the Containment Doctrine with regard to the Soviet Union), another book was brought to mind.

When this soldier entered the Army in 1958, *The Soldier and the State* by Harvard's Samuel P. Huntington was hot off the press. While the fine ROTC instructors at the University of Oklahoma gave us a good start with regard to Army life, the relationship of the military to civil society begged for Professor Huntington's explanation. For the next 20 years, a dog-eared copy of *The Soldier and the State* was either in my backpack or my briefcase.

Taken together, these two books remind me why some soldiers don't care much for diplomats and why some diplomats dislike soldiers. You see, both soldiers and diplomats are, at heart, Pacifists. When the soldier has to go to war, he blames the diplomats for failing to preserve the peace. The carnage of war constantly reminds the diplomat of his or her failure to avoid war.

The diplomat reflects on his or her failures in opulent surroundings over a glass of fine wine. The soldier reflects on the failure of the diplomats while, say, humping an 80-pound backpack, under enemy fire, up a monsoon-rain-soaked, slippery-clay-soil Hill 534 in Vietnam in 95-degree heat and 100-percent humidity while hoping his canteen has enough iodine-treated water left to assuage his adrenaline-caused thirst.

Cultural differences abound, as well. George F. Kennan was your quintessential, Ivy-League educated Eastern Establishment snob who looked down on his fellow humans from the lofty perch of his own towering self-esteem. That said, Kennan was also a gifted linguist, writer, and geo-political thinker.

As a general rule, Kennan and his follow Foreign Service Officers constitute a unique class which is very different from the work-a-day Americans they are supposed to represent. But then, the foreign diplomats with whom our diplomats must interact are not representative of the work-a-day people of their nations, either. So, in effect, you have highly educated elites lavishly entertaining each other at government expense in the hope that alcohol will cause someone to let slip some state secret that can be reported back home in the next day's cables.

While a surprisingly high percentage of our military personnel have earned advanced degrees, they rarely -- and especially, after the advent of the Vietnam War -- have come from the elite Eastern Establishment. As a general rule, the racial/ethnic make-up of our military is reflective of our population while, historically, our Foreign Service Officers (and even career CIA officers), have been Lily-white and pro-Arab. See: *America's Great Game* by Hugh Wilford (2013).

That said, our military has a certain regional bias. The American South produces the majority of those who risk their lives in uniform. So, it is not surprising that some diplomats look down on the military as a bunch of southern red-necks and some military look at the diplomats as a bunch of wimps. The current "Swift Boat" Secretary of State is a case in point.

But as the Obama Administration gelds, gentrifies, trans-genders, and makes our military more "politically-correct," these two groups will have much more in common. Just how that will serve our national interest remains to be seen.

©2014. 1723

VETERAN'S DAY: SALUTE *THE CENTURIONS*, PAST AND PRESENT

During the week surrounding Veteran's Day, we give thanks for those who lost their lives or have been grievously wounded in defense of the freedoms we enjoy here at home. But this Vietnam veteran's thoughts go back to 1961 and the publication of Jean Lartéguy's classic war novel, *The Centurions*.

In the mid-1960s, a generation of Vietnam-bound Army and Marine lieutenants and captains were eager to learn something about the people, the land, and the culture of Vietnam and why the French colonials had failed so miserably in Vietnam -- even if such understanding could only be found in the pages of fiction written by a former French paratrooper who served in French Indo-China, fought in Korea, and later became a journalist making his home in Saigon.

By 1966, this soldier had owned and given away to fellow officers at least a dozen paperback copies of *The Centurions*, to include, unfortunately, my very last copy. Recently, as she often does, Wonder Wife came to the rescue and found, on-line, an original, collector's copy of this classic. She intended the novel as a secret Christmas present; however, once it came, she could not resist giving it to me. It now resides next to my copy of Professor Samuel P. Huntington's *The Soldier and the State*.

Back in the mid-1960s, *The Centurions* became a cult-like classic at Ft. Benning's Infantry School. In 1965, as LBJ started landing regular Army and Marine divisions in Vietnam, many *"Centurions"* were riding along inside footlockers and rucksacks. In our air-mobile infantry battalion, Lartéguy's characters were so vividly reborn in our minds that we started calling each other by the names of Lartéguy's characters.

Until the division's signal officer put a stop to it, we often substituted our *"Centurion"* names for our official radio call signs. Years later, when Wonder Wife and I got around to writing *The Grand Conspiracy* by William Penn, we devoted an entire chapter to a fictional annual reunion of Lartéguy's mythical 10th Colonial Parachute Regiment.

Just for fun, one year after the publication of *The Grand Conspiracy*, we put an advertisement in the local papers that the 10th Colonial Parachute Regiment would be holding its annual reunion at a certain time and date at a certain local watering hole. The advertisement invited the public to attend.

On the advertised date and time, we walked into the local watering hole, not expecting to see anyone; however, we were astonished to be greeted by a saloon full of local readers who had gotten caught up in the spirit of the 10th Colonial Parachute Regiment. And, one might add, some other "spirits" as well.

In 1966, Hollywood made "Lost Command," which was intended to be based on *The Centurions*. While Anthony Quinn was good as Colonel Raspéguy, the film was not nearly as good as the novel.

So, how is a 1961 novel relevant in 2015? The French paratroopers, who had to do the actual fighting in Indo-China and in Algeria, understood what was necessary to win; however, their political masters in Paris were just as clueless about how to win wars back then as are the civilians in charge of the White House and the Pentagon today.

©2015. 1808

SNIPERS: HISTORY'S OFTEN UNSUNG HEROES

When diplomacy fails and it seems necessary to engage in violent, armed combat, this former infantry officer has often thought it wasteful to send masses of young men to kill and maim each other. If two or more nations cannot resolve their differences by diplomacy, why not have each side select their best warrior and let the two warriors decide the outcome? Or, maybe let their top leaders duke it out?

Imagine Abraham Lincoln and Jefferson Davis with dueling pistols. Between the former frontiersman, Abraham Lincoln and West Point-graduate, Jefferson Davis, that would have been an interesting contest. Or, how about General William C. Westmoreland (who always stayed in top physical shape) versus North Vietnamese General Vo Nguyen Giap? I'd bet on "Westy." Or, how about former KGB agent, Vladimir Vladimirovich Putin, versus former community organizer, Barack Hussein Obama. Stop. Let's not even go there.

There is, however, a middle way: the sniper. People who know their Holy Bible might recognize David as history's most-storied sniper. When the Philistines (later known as the Palestinians) were led by the giant Goliath, the young boy, David, volunteered to go up against Goliath. Armed with the single-shot sniper weapon of the day -- the slingshot -- David picked up a stone (today, known as ammunition), put the stone inside the "pocket" (today, we would call it the rifle chamber), and let fly with the sling shot. With one smooth stone, David slew Goliath and saved the Israelites from defeat at the hands of the Philistines.

During the American Revolution, General George Washington defeated the British Red Coats -- the world's most powerful and battle-experienced army. Rag-tag American frontiersmen used their long, squirrel rifles to pick British officers off their horses, leaving the British foot soldiers leaderless, terrified, and in disarray.

In 1815, General Andrew Jackson, with only 4,732 troops, used his snipers to defeat 11,000 British troops and win the Battle of New Orleans. This author's sainted Mother was a Rennie. So, this passage from *"Shock Factor"* by Gunnery Sergeant Jack Coughlin, USMC (Ret.) is of special interest: "...a British colonel named Rennie led an assault on an isolated American redoubt... He struck an impressive figure at the head of his men, coaxing them forward... Rennie pressed forward...with two of his officers by his side...several shooters from the New Orleans Rifles...opened fire. All three officers went down. The leaderless British soldiers froze, then fell back, pell-mell, their ranks savaged by the American fire..."

Over 150 years later, we used snipers to good effect in Vietnam. Not only did our snipers pick off Viet Cong and North Vietnamese Army leaders, they sometimes had a terror effect, as well. As a security precaution to keep us from creeping up on them from behind, enemy patrols routinely had one member trail the rest of their column by many yards -- often out of ear shot. If we were fortunate enough to have sniper team with us, they would pick off the trail-behind member. Later, when the remainder of the enemy patrol discovered one of their own was inexplicably missing, their panic turned to terror. Just like at the Battle of New Orleans.

©2014. 1758

VETERANS DAY MEMORIES

"Captain Hamilton!" barked Major General 'Jumpin' Jack' Norton. "You still wannabe a rifle company commander?" "Yes sir!" "Grab your weapon. By sundown, you'll likely be a company commander in the Second Battle of the Ia Drang."

Newly arrived in Vietnam, I had yet to be issued jungle boots. Fortunately, II Corps Headquarters (forward) was nearby. The late Bobby G. Porter, a friend from Ft. Benning, was in charge over there. Bobby took off his jungle boots and gave them to me, leaving Bobby in his stocking feet. I never saw him again. Bobby retired as a lieutenant general.

After flying us through torrential rain, General Norton dropped me off near the base of Hill 534 of the Chu Pong Massif where I met Captain Richard N. McInerney, headquarters company commander for the 2d Battalion, 5th Cavalry. We huddled under a make-shift shelter. Dick was eating a C-ration with a white plastic spoon. "Hungry?" asked Dick, as he handed me the spoon we shared back-and-forth until the can was empty. Friends, forever. Later, another Huey dropped me off up on the side of Hill 534 to take over from a fallen rifle company commander and to rescue a platoon surrounded by the North Vietnamese.

Then, it was six months of doing combat air assaults and patrolling along the Cambodian border. We never suffered a KIA out in the jungle, a few wounded. But, back at base camp, the 2d Brigade operations officer, a major who thought he knew more than our troops, selected my 1/4-ton Jeep to lead a supply convoy. Proven practice was to lead convoys with a sand-bagged five-ton truck. The major would not listen to my enlisted men who pleaded for the proven procedures to be followed. PFC Johnny M. Hairston, our supply clerk, was killed when my jeep, leading the convoy, ran over an improvised explosive device (IED).

Six months later, I turned over command to Dick McInerney who, a few months later, was killed in a fire fight. Dick earned the Silver Star. 1SGT Mel Rand was seriously wounded. At the Vietnam Wall, I always do pencil rubbings of the names of Dick and Johnny, plus one more:

Four years earlier, in West Germany, my neighbor was then Lt. Commander George K. Farris, a naval aviator on shore duty in Frankfurt. Sometimes, as a member of the 513th Intelligence Corps Group, I needed "covert" transportation at night to European parts best left unknown. George would fly me in a U.S. Army DeHavilland "Beaver" (U-6A). We became close friends. In 1966, when George was flying missions off of the *USS Oriskany*, a fire killed George and 43 others. Along with Dick's and Johnny's, I do pencil rubbings of George's name and think of his widow and their two children.

So, when millionaire NFL players, who never served in uniform, disrespect our National Anthem and our Flag, I think about Dick, Johnny, and George. The sight of a white plastic spoon, just seeing a Jeep, or watching a back-country "Beaver" in flight -- all of those things -- bring back a flood of memories of some really fine men who deserve our respect, forever and ever. Even at NFL football games.

©2016. 1862

COMBAT AIR ASSAULTS: A VIETNAM MEMOIR

Imagine the year is 1966. You are commanding an airmobile infantry company in South Vietnam. The dawn is coming up like thunder; however, the thunder is from Air Force fighter-bombers and Army artillery prepping the landing zone (LZ) your company is about to assault. Soon,

21 helicopters will arrive in a long, single-file formation to pick up your company and fly you into the cauldron of fire known as: the Combat Air Assault.

In the gathering light, you and your First Sergeant visit quietly with each man in each squad. Although we have done dozens of these combat air assaults, everyone is scared, but tries not to show it. You check to see that each man has his "buddy." The "buddy system" makes foxhole-buddies by combining a soldier with more time in-country with a "newbie." The "buddy system" helps "newbies" become "oldies."

Demographically, your skytroopers match the national norm: About 13-percent Black, about 12-percent Hispanic; the vast majority White, although a high percentage of the NCOs are Black or Hispanic. Of your four platoon leaders, one is Black.

You look each trooper in the eye and wonder why some of these fine young men may be dead or wounded within the hour? (You may be, too; however, you can't think about that and do your job.) Why can't a sniper or a bomb take out the malefactors who set up this conflict? Why is political assassination taboo? Yet, it is open season on young conscripts trying to stay alive amidst poisonous snakes, malaria-bearing mosquitoes and the jungle rot that comes with horrific heat and humidity.

Preceded by their gunship escorts, the lift birds hover in to pick up your company. Within moments, seasoned sergeants have their squads on board and we all lift off, flying toward the LZ. From your place in the lead chopper, you see the black smoke from the artillery barrage prepping the LZ. You pray the barrage continues until the very last moment and is then lifted in time so you don't take any "friendly-fire" casualties.

Alongside your chopper, the aerial-rocket artillery (ARA) helicopters are launching rocket-after-rocket into the edges of the LZ. Then, the ARA birds, their rockets expended, break away to be replaced by the gunships that fine tune the edges of the LZ with machine-gun fire.

The cauldron of flame and smoke that envelopes the LZ makes you feel like you are descending into Dante's Inferno. The noise is deafening. At one minute out, to minimize the time the lift birds will be sitting ducks on the LZ, everyone wiggles down off the cargo deck and holds onto the landing skids, ready to jump. The slipstream dries your sweat. You are as cool as you are going to be until the chill of night when, hopefully, all will have survived to form a defensive perimeter of two-man foxholes.

When the choppers are about five feet above the ground, everyone jumps off the skids. The sudden weight reduction causes the choppers to pop almost straight up as they flee the LZ.

You hear the clacking sound made by a few AK-47s. Green tracers fly overhead. A handful of the enemy survived the LZ prep. Most did not. Your men pick off a couple of the retreating enemy. They've taken a POW. He is questioned for immediate tactical intelligence. The LZ now secure, you get a chopper to fly the POW to higher headquarters.

While you've taken no casualties so far, you still face another grueling day of cutting through the dense jungle in pursuit of an elusive enemy. That was daily life and death in the 1st Air Cavalry Division.

©2010. 1465

THE PIG FAT DETERRENT: WHOSE IDEA WAS THAT?

A primary motivation of the Islamic suicide bombers is to achieve instant entry into Islamic Paradise where they believe they will be embraced by Allah and the Prophet Muhammad and then rewarded by the gift of seven-two virgins. But what would be the point of being blown to bits if, in the end, one is ineligible to enter Islamic Paradise?

Muslims believe the ingestion or infusion of any part of a pig's body or blood into their bodies will deny them entry into Muslim Paradise. For that reason, Israeli officials have a plan to hang bags of pig lard on buses, in train stations and other public places which might be the target of suicide bombers. Along with that will be a public relations campaign telling prospective suicide bombers how their exploded blood and body parts will be mixed with exploded pig lard. With their bodies defiled by pig particles, they will be ineligible for entry into the Muslim Paradise.

Although Jews have somewhat similar views about swine being unclean, Rabbi Eliezer Moshe Fisher, of the Jerusalem Rabbinical Court, stated there is no Jewish law that would forbid placing bags of pig lard in buses and other places where so doing might save Jewish lives.

Apparently, Jews can be atomized along with the pig lard and still, after meeting certain other conditions outlined in the Old Testament, attain Heaven.

This real-life pig lard situation in Israel is of more than passing interest to this observer and his co-author of *The Panama Conspiracy* by William Penn. In that work of fiction, which first appeared in April 2003, we created a way for the CIA to cause the death of Osama bin Laden so that bin Laden's death could not be directly attributed to the U.S. Government. Why the deception? So as not to further inflame the Islamic radicals.

Like all good fiction, we worked from a basis of actual facts: It was widely believed that bin Laden suffers from both diabetes and renal disease. Therefore, for many years, bin Laden has received injections of Insulin. Until just a few years ago, Insulin was manufactured from the pancreas of both cattle and swine, in combination. Today, Insulin is made from recombinant DNA. But because the bin Laden family has a history of both heart disease and diabetes, the odds are that bin Laden developed diabetes long enough ago that he received injections of Insulin made, in part, from the pancreas of pigs. Bingo! Osama bin Laden, the leader of al Qaeda and Muslim fanatic, doesn't have a Muslim prayer of entering the Muslim Paradise.

But it was bin Laden's need for periodic dialysis treatments to rid his blood of the impurities his failing kidneys cannot eliminate naturally that provided the opportunity for him to be killed without leaving the fingerprints of the United States.

Back to scientific fact: Without a municipal power supply, dialysis machines must rely on gasoline-or diesel-powered generators for electricity. Diesel fuel is notoriously susceptible to contamination by microbes called: *Cladosporium Resinae*, which are commonly found in bread mould. Unless diesel fuel is treated with a microbe killer, such as Biodor JF, the presence of microbes will quickly turn diesel fuel into an unusable jelly-like substance.

No diesel fuel, no electric generator. No electricity, no dialysis. No dialysis, no bin Laden. Thus, part of the plot is devoted to getting into bin Laden's Tora Bora headquarters to infect the diesel fuel supply. But the finishing touch is to let bin Laden know his earlier Insulin supply was made from pig pancreas. If you read the novel, you learn how all this works out in the end.

Meanwhile, it is the authors' Walter Mitty dream that the scheme we cooked up back in April 2003 may have inspired the Israelis to festoon their buses, trains and public places with bags of pig fat. *NB: Osama bin Laden was killed by Navy SEALS on May 2, 2011.*
©2004. 1147

MALAYSIAN MEMORIES

Seminal events like the Indian Ocean Tsunami of 2004 or the 1963 assassination of President John. F. Kennedy record themselves in our mental calendars. We may recall, not only what we were doing at the time, but other memories as well.

Word of the horrific Tsunami caused this observer to say a prayer for the people living on the island of Penang, Malaysia where, in 1967, this soldier spent an idyllic week on R&R. A computer search revealed Penang lost 52 souls, with five still missing. In comparison to the devastation of other nations bordering the underwater earthquake, the loss of life, while still tragic, was relatively light.

That is because the island is mostly mountainous with a relatively narrow fringe of beaches around its circumference. Georgetown, the main city, is located on the eastern side of the island, facing the mainland. The Tsunami hit the west side and the northern tip of the island.

After commanding an infantry company in Vietnam, I was due for R&R. I really didn't care where. At the R&R processing center north of Saigon, I ran into an Army Chaplain who told me he was being reassigned from Vietnam to be the resident Chaplain at Penang's R&R center. Figuring an Army Chaplain could keep me out of trouble, I signed up to go along with him to Penang. Talk about serendipity.

We flew from Vietnam to the U.K's Royal Air Force Base at Butterworth, Malaysia. Back then, the only way to Penang was by ferry. Now, Penang is also connected to the mainland by a 13.5 kilometer suspension bridge. The longest in Asia, and the world's third longest.

Our ferry load of GIs was greeted by the officer-in-charge (OIC) of the Penang R&R Center. Because the

Chaplain and I were now buddies, I was serendipitously included in all the orientation activities the OIC had planned for his new Chaplain.

The Chaplain and I literally got the royal tour of the entire island. One of the many highlights was a bus ride around the narrow mountain road that circumscribes Penang. Our driver's other job was as a member of Penang's parliamentary delegation.

His English was excellent, so I got into the jump seat beside him and proceeded to learn all I could about the island's history and how parliamentary democracy was practiced in Malaysia. Several times, we dismounted to visit some temples and shrines.

One temple was devoted to pit vipers. The vipers were festooned all over the temple in a writhing array of venomous critters. I kept looking down at my feet trying to make sure a stray viper wasn't intent on wrapping itself around my leg.

But what that Penang R&R gave me, besides a chance to heal some wounds and rashes in the salty waters off Penang's sandy beaches, was hope. Atop one of the most modern high-rise hotels I had ever seen was a pleasant watering hole. At sundown, the bar filled with Malaysian businessmen dressed in three-piece suits that looked like the best of London's Savile Row.

Their talk was of stocks and bonds and of a bright economic future for the region bordering the Straits of Malacca. I thought: *Wow, this kind of nascent capitalism should not fall prey to the Red Chinese or North*

Vietnamese communists. It did not and Penang retains its reputation as the "Pearl of the Orient."

We also saw a bitter-sweet moment. We watched as the British Royal Howard Regiment, the Green Jackets, marched from their barracks down Penang's main street and into the ramped maw of a waiting Royal Navy troop transport. In 1967, they were the last British troops to be stationed east of Suez. We saw history made that day.

If you want to help the Penang islanders recover, vacation there, someday. A Tsunami cannot hit Georgetown on the island's east side. Stay on that side. Meanwhile, I pray for my parliamentarian friend and his family.

©2004. 1192

CHRISTMAS: A TIME FOR REMEMBERING

Like Charles Dickens' "the Ghost of Christmas Past," the memory of a particular Christmas in Vietnam haunts me to the degree I'm compelled to write about it once again. The place was Fire Support Base "IKE," about ten miles south of a downward dip in the Cambodian border called: "the fishhook." The time was Christmas Eve, 1969. Earlier that day, my request to rejoin the 2d Battalion, 5th Cavalry Regiment had been approved.

While lugging my rucksack from the shell-pocked helipad toward the battalion headquarters bunker, a line from the King James Version of the 23d Psalm came to mind, *"Yea, though I walk through the valley of the shadow of death, I will fear no evil..."*

Actually, there was no shortage of bravery. The North Vietnamese Army (NVA) had attacked IKE so many times that seeing a sign that read: "FSB IKE, The Fire Base Too Tough to Die," came as no surprise.

Shortly, one of the finest men I have ever known met me: Lt. Colonel John R. Witherell. In the failing light, the battalion commander and I walked the inner perimeter together, pausing at each firing position to exchange Christmas greetings with each trooper. IKE's location was no secret to the North Vietnamese, so small warming/cooking fires were permitted. Some of the troops were reading the Bible. As we moved along, a refrain sounded in my head, *"I have seen Him in the watch-fires of a hundred circling camps. I can read His righteous sentence by the dim and flaring lamps."*

Some of the sand-filled ammo boxes surrounding the firing positions were decorated with the Cross and with the symbols of Christ's birth. *"They have builded Him an altar in the evening dews and damps."*

Our tour finished, Colonel Witherell introduced me to "Red," our intelligence officer and to Doug, our artillery liaison officer. We descended into the sand-bagged and timbered bunker where I would lodge with Colonel Witherell, Red, and Doug until February, 1970, when we closed IKE in preparation for the battalion's eventual move into Cambodia. As we huddled together around a candle, the battalion commander led us in prayer. *A cappella*, we sang some Christmas hymns. Our four radio operators, with whom we shared the command bunker, joined in.

Colonel Witherell, Red, Doug and I spent an hour or so getting acquainted. We recited where we were from, previous places of service. We spoke of those back home. I thought especially of my son, John, and others whom I might not see again. I recalled singing: "Oh, Danny Boy," to John, only I had changed the lyrics to "Oh, Johnny Boy." One of the verses came to me: *"And if you come, when all the flowers are dying and I am dead, as dead I well may be, you'll come and find the place where I am lying, and kneel and pray and say an 'Ave' there for me. And I shall hear, tho' soft you tread above me, and all my dreams will warm and sweeter be..."*

Sometimes, if an Army Chaplain choppered in with a field organ, we would request Kipling's "Recessional." *"God of our fathers, known of old – Lord of our far-flung battle line beneath whose awful hand we hold dominion over palm and pine. Lord God of Hosts, be with us yet, lest we forget – lest we forget."* We were long on palms, but short on pines.

This Christmas, as the winter sun dies in Iraq or Afghanistan or South Korea or whatever our far-flung troops happen to be, imagine, if you will, the sound of a lonely and far-off bugler playing the haunting notes for: *"Day is done, gone the sun, from the hills, from the lake, from the sky. All is well, safely rest; God is nigh."* During this Christmas season, let *us* not forget them.

©2010. 1507

GRAND OPERA: A FAREWELL TO PORDENONE

Recently, in a store that sells pots and pans, my eye was drawn to a product with "Panini" printed across the box in bold letters. As someone who attended (albeit only once and poorly) a live performance of Grand Opera in Italy, I made amends by buying a Panini.

When it comes to Grand Opera, Italians are a tough crowd. So, it came as no surprise that the work of Panini has been panned. Were it not for his Uncle Giacomo, the publisher of the Panini Press, it is doubtful that we, here in America, would have ever heard of Panini. Seriously, your faithful observer actually attended a performance of Giacoma Puccini's "Tosca" in Pordenone, Italy.

Although our airborne battalion was based in Germany, we were scheduled to parachute onto a drop zone north of Pordenone, about half way between the famous ski resort at Cortina d'Ampezzo and Venice. Once we hit the ground, we were to maneuver under live machine-gun fire toward our mountain-top objectives.

Safety requirements mandated some detailed advance planning and coordination. Our battalion operations officer, Joe Spencer, and his assistant, Roberto Miller, and I flew down to Italy to hold meetings with the Italian Alpine Brigade and the Bersaglieri, the elite Italian troops who wear a veritable volcano of black, capon feathers erupting from their hats.

Roberto, born in post-war Italy of a U.S. Counterintelligence Corps agent and an Italian beauty spoke, well… native Italian. The three of us got along famously with the Italians. In fact, our Italian counterparts liked us so much that they took us to downtown Pordenone where they hosted us to the best lunch I have ever had, anywhere, ever. I think the place was called: *Al fresco,* or something like that. But, in any event, we can't go back.

After a week of negotiations, we found ourselves alone in Pordenone on a Friday evening with nothing to do until Monday. Unfortunately, the resourceful Roberto produced three, front-row tickets to "Tosca."

Even Italians of meager means dress up for the Opera. So, we decided to wear our best American uniforms. Also, prior to "Tosca," we decided to enjoy a large Italian dinner.

The opera was moving along just fine until we got to the part where Mario caresses the hands of Tosca, who had just committed murder for Mario. Then, as the firing squad, that was "supposed" to conduct a "fake" execution of Mario, marches on stage, yours truly fell into a wine- and pasta-induced sleep.

Moreover, just when Tosca learns: that she has been tricked, that the firing squad switched from the promised blanks to real bullets, that Mario is actually dead; and just as Tosca (singing, of course) is leaping to her death -- I began to snore. We were lucky the firing squad did not reload and turn its guns on the three Americans in the front row.

While Italians can interrupt an Italian opera company to applaud a well-sung aria or even boo and hiss at the singers for missing notes, it is not acceptable to snore. At the desk of the Pordenone Arms the next morning, I fully expected the hotel clerk to hand me a telegram from the American Embassy in Rome telling us that we had all been declared *persona non grata*. Fortunately, that did not happen.

The following month, we dropped over 700 paratroopers without a hitch. With machine-gun bullets zipping overhead, our troops scaled their objectives in record time. The Bersaglieri, seeing the up-mountain charge of our superbly-conditioned airborne troops, started jumping up and down and cheering so hard that black capon feathers were flying everywhere.

Despite the all-around acclaim, we decided the better part of valor was to bid a farewell to Pordenone. For the return flight to Germany, we had Italian Army trucks convoy us directly to the U.S. Air Force Base at nearby Aviano.

©2009. 1432

ADVENTURE TRAINING: WINNING FRIENDS AND SAVING TAX DOLLARS

In 1956, my second cousin, Admiral Tommy Hamilton, stopped by the Volvo plant in Goteborg, Sweden, to pick up a new car. By chance, he bumped into Countess Madeline Hamilton – a former *Life Magazine* writer and photographer -- who, at the time, was director of public relations for Volvo. That is what began a shirttail relative connection.

It seems that during the 30 Years War, the Swedish King hired two regiments of Scots to come fight on the side of the Protestants. Hamiltons commanded both regiments. But, by war's end, the King was dead, the treasury was flat broke and the Hamiltons had to be paid in farmland and noble titles. Today, about 400 Hamiltons still live in Sweden.

In 1972, when he learned I would be returning to Europe, Cousin Tommy urged us to go see "Cousin" Madeline and her brother, Lieutenant Colonel Count John Hamilton, who was commanding a Swedish armored cavalry regiment. Between writing, photography and troop command, Cousin Tommy felt we would all have a lot in common. He was correct.

The Vietnam War was on going at the time and a number of our draft-dodgers had taken refuge in Sweden. "Cousin" John said he didn't think much of American youth because they took drugs and were thieves. I said Sweden was seeing the dregs of American youth and that the draft-dodgers were not typical Americans. I also countered by saying that many Americans thought that Swedish women were promiscuous.

This brought on a wager. So, I said I would send a squad of my men to Sweden on an Adventure Training exercise and Cousin John could judge the behavior of my young Americans for himself. John agreed on the spot to greet my troops and transport them in Swedish Army Lorries up to middle Sweden so they could canoe down river to John's country estate outside Kristianstad. There,

John would host them for a weekend and send them back to Germany.

Meanwhile, I was transferred to Fulda, West Germany, to command an armored cavalry squadron. Once settled in Fulda, John and I resumed our wager.

The most critical military occupational specialty in my squadron was avionics technician. Private firms offered big salaries for these highly trained specialists to leave the Army and work for them. This was costing the Army mega-bucks.

So I called in our avionics specialists and asked them if they would like to participate in an Adventure Training exercise in Sweden. Twelve bachelors volunteered immediately. Somehow, I forgot to tell Cousin John that my troops were handpicked from the smartest enlisted men in my squadron.

They flew by helicopter to Kiel and boarded the overnight ferry to Malmo. Cousin John's trucks met them as promised. The entire exercise went off like clockwork. But instead of having to camp out, my troops were taken into private homes almost every night. When they reached Kristianstad, John took them to his country estate where they had a royal time.

The helicopters returned some smiling troops to Fulda. After I debriefed them, I called Cousin John. "What do you think of American youth now?" I asked. "They are all splendid chaps," said Cousin John. "I apologize for what I said about American youth."

"That's good to hear," I replied. "But, I'm afraid I have some bad news for you about Swedish women." He was not amused.

All 12 of those avionics specialists reenlisted for their own positions, saving the Army hundreds of thousands of dollars in training costs. But I knew the Heroes (?) of Heidelberg would never have permitted such an exercise, so higher headquarters was never told. In fact, I had to get the troops to agree to use some of their annual leave to cover their absence. But, we showed them on the Morning Report as being on Adventure Training, which they were. On their safe return, I burned their leave papers.

©2001. 1015

THE HEROES (?) OF HEIDELBERG

Never doubt the physical courage of the American military in combat. But, in peacetime, senior officials are sometimes lacking in what I'll call: administrative courage. This true story illustrates my point.

On a moonlit winter night in 1943, nine Norwegian commandos parachuted into the snow not far from the town of Telemark and Norsk Hydro – the hydro-electric plant the occupying NAZI forces were using to prepare the heavy water essential to development of an atomic bomb. An American-born Norwegian named Knut Haukelid led the commandos.

After skiing to a point just below the heavy water plant, the commandos scaled an unscaleable cliff to reach

Norsk Hydro, blew up the plant and escaped into the night. Later, after the NAZIs rebuilt the plant and produced a railroad carload of heavy water. Knut Haukelid and other commandos infiltrated the ferryboat carrying the heavy water. They blew it up and sent it to the bottom of a fjord. Justifiably, Haukelid became a national hero. He served in the Norwegian Army reserve after the war, retiring as a three-star general.

In 1969, this observer had the honor of meeting and skiing with Knut Haukelid on winter maneuvers with the Norwegian Ski Brigade. We became friends and stayed in contact.

In 1972, when I was commanding an airborne battalion in West Germany, I decided a reenactment of the Telemark Raid would be wonderful training for some of my troops. Fortunately, the father of one of my platoon leaders was the U.S. Naval Attaché in Oslo. Both he and his Army lieutenant son were eager for the reenactment to happen. I contacted General Haukelid who agreed to have a Norwegian Army squad on the drop zone to greet my paratroopers, issue them cross-country skis and get them headed toward Telemark where they were to scale the cliff, plant dummy charges, and try to escape undetected. General Haukelid would be at Telemark to insure that nothing went wrong.

The entire plan was sent to U.S. Army Europe Headquarters in Heidelberg for review and final approval. Meanwhile, we arranged for the needed parachutes and a C-130 Hercules to fly the mission. Our troops practiced the scaling of steep cliffs and cross-country skiing.

If ever a peacetime training exercise was prepared in exquisite detail, this was it. We had Knut Haukelid, Norway's greatest hero of World War II, in charge of the arrangements for the drop zone and at Telemark. General Haukelid would be assisted by the U.S. Naval Attaché at the U.S. Embassy in Oslo whose son would lead his platoon out of the C-130 into the wintry night. Our troops were trained, fit and ready. Their morale was sky high and they had the physical courage to follow in the ski tracks of The Heroes of Telemark.

But their courage was not matched by the staff wimps behind their desks in Heidelberg. At the very last moment, our plans – which hitherto had been approved at each stage of development – were disapproved. The only reason given was some mumbo-jumbo about fears of causing an international incident in a foreign country. Hello. Norway was and is a member of NATO and U.S. airborne forces parachuted into other NATO countries such as West Germany, Italy, Greece and Turkey on joint NATO maneuvers.

But the real reason was probably concern that our West German allies would be offended by our reenactment of a daring raid against the German Army in occupied Norway. Moreover, the fact that Knut Haukelid's commandos got in, destroyed the heavy water plant and got out without a shot being fired would be a painful memory to our West German friends. It cost them the war. [Later, we learned it was our brigade commander who torpedoed the jump.]

Bottom line: the Heroes of Heidelberg [and Mainz] didn't have the administrative courage to allow us to train as hard as we wanted. They didn't even have the courage to contact General Haukelid themselves. I was ordered to give him their cockamamie excuse for the cancellation. Of course, he didn't buy it.

©2001. 1013

NATO: STILL ALIVE AND WELL

The United States just scored a diplomatic/military coup by getting the ministers of the North Atlantic Treaty Organization (NATO) to vote unanimously to station tracking-radar sites in the Czech Republic and interceptors in Poland. Although the missile defense system is designed to protect Europe and Israel from Iranian missile attacks, Russia's Vladimir Putin was put out by the NATO decision.

Another burr under Putin's saddle was the recent U.S.-backed independence of Kosovo. Indeed, post-Cold War, the U.S.-led NATO has steadily expanded its membership eastward into the heartland of the Eurasian landmass. Even so, following the NATO meeting, Putin was a gracious host to the U.S. President and First Lady at Sochi on the Black Sea --Russia's opulent version of Camp David.

Following World War II, the efforts by Hitler and Mussolini to turn Europe to a fascist form of national-socialism had literally gone up in smoke. From Norway to

Greece, Europe was a shambles. Only the victorious Allied military possessed any vigor. But the Red Army, which was not demobilizing, was poised to invade westward to fill the political vacuum created by the war weariness of the western democracies.

In 1950, to counter the Soviet threat, the Americans and the British conceived of NATO. General Dwight D. Eisenhower was placed in command of the first five nations to join. By the end of the decade, NATO had 14 member nations. Now, there are 26. *NB: the number is now: 29.*

NATO commands were interesting places to work. The top NATO commander is an American, his deputy is most often British, although some German generals have served as second banana. This layering of nationalities is a feature of all the various NATO headquarters. The official NATO languages are English and French. Later, when French President de Gaulle decided to withdraw France from the *military* portion of NATO, French faded.

At the British Army of the Rhine (BAOR) headquarters in Moenchengladback/Rheindahlen, the staff was jokingly instructed as to which languages to speak on which days: "Monday: English; Tuesday, Dutch, Wednesday, German; Thursday, French; Friday, Danish; Saturday, Norwegian; Sunday, AMERICAN (we are closed Sunday)." The sign was posted where visiting American intelligence agents could not miss it. We found it only mildly amusing.

But once all the "spooks" got to recognize each other as members of "the club," our joint efforts were, sometimes, hilarious. During the Christmas season, it was the custom for each nation's spooks to make a formal "call" on the others. The visiting group would come with gift-wrapped whisky or cognac bottles in hand. The bottles were presented with great ceremony. The host group would then lavish the visitors with fine drinks and food. This routine would be repeated until all the groups had called on each other. This took weeks.

But giving away tax-payer purchased booze presented an accounting nightmare. So, our office would place the bottles presented to it --unopened -- in a secure cabinet, to await the time when they would be "re-gifted" to some other intelligence agency. A covert mark was placed on each bottle to make sure it would not be given back to the original giver.

Eventually, it became apparent that all the intelligence agencies were playing the same booze-recycling game. Our marked bottles were being recycled to us. To avoid filling out the detailed forms demanded by the bean-counters at higher quarters, none of the NATO intelligence agencies were opening and drinking their tax-payer provided schmooze booze.

What was being consumed during those convivial holiday visits was being paid for out of the pockets of the host agents. Finally, the charade became so obvious that all the agencies confessed to each other. But the camaraderie was too enjoyable to stop.

We thought the accounting problem was solved. Then, higher headquarters sent a blistering cable: "Because you are not expending the gifts we have provided, you must not be conducting necessary liaison with your NATO counterparts!" Go figure.

©2008. 1365

ACTIVE MEASURES, LEAKS, AND TREASON

The cover of the Summer, 2017, issue of *The Intelligencer: Journal of U.S. Intelligence Studies,* the quarterly publication of the Association of Former Intelligence Officers (AFIO), proclaims in large, bold, yellow letters: "Leaks = Treason." Oh my! That means *The Intelligencer,* which serves as both the tribune and the conscience of the U.S. Intelligence Community (IC), is calling some of its anti-Trump members to task for leaking classified information to the main-stream media (MSM).

In her article "Keeping Secrets," AFIO Director Emeritus, Elizabeth Bancroft, urges her IC colleagues to *"...Be the mature adult who honors agreements and promises. If you deeply disagree with policies and find no institutional way to resolve the matter **internally,** quietly depart for other employment. Anything else is immoral and a betrayal of your agency, colleagues, and the country. Disregard all the self-serving, faux moral handwringing by prize-seeking journalists, and fellow conspirators, urging you to spill classified secrets, while dismissing your appropriate concerns over your about-to-be destroyed career and reputation. Like all traitors, you will have* *crossed over to the other side, with no passport for return."*

The pleas by Bancroft and other leaders of the IC to get their own house in order are not taking place in a vacuum. The broader problem faced by the IC and, for that matter, faced by all non-Russian nations since the time of the communist takeover of Russia, comes under the heading of "Active Measures."

Today's history challenged MSM would have us believe that Russian interference in the election of 2016 was unique. The history of Soviet, now Russian, Active Measures tells a far different story. Wikipedia tells us: "Active Measures is a Soviet term for the actions of political warfare conducted by the Soviet and Russian security services (Cheka, OGPU, NKVD, KGB, FSB) to influence the course of world events." Active Measures include, but are not limited to: political campaign disinformation, propaganda, assassinations, counterfeiting official documents, and the penetration of domestic political party organizations and campaigns.

According to retired KGB General Oleg Kalugin, Active Measures are "the heart and soul" of Soviet intelligence. The objectives are to create fissures among the Western allies, disrupt NATO, to sow discord within the United States, and to prepare the psychological battle ground in advance of actual war.

In addition to throwing the cat among the pigeons in U.S. elections, Russian Active Measures have been used, just to mention a few examples, to: discredit the CIA, discredit Martin Luther King, Jr., to stir up racial tensions by mailing bogus letters from the KKK, by saying fluoridated drinking water is a U.S. government attempt at population control, by claiming the moon landings were hoaxes, by asserting that the strategic defense initiative "Star Wars" would not work, and that AIDS virus was created by the U.S. Army at Ft. Detrick, MD.

The Senate Intelligence Committee, The House Intelligence Committee, and a Special Counsel are spending time and taxpayer money to investigate an alleged, yet unproven connection between Russia and Trump campaign operatives. The IC "leakers" who have "crossed over the line," are adding to the already overly partisan discord. So, how effective are Vladimir Putin's Active Measures? We report. You decide.

©2017. 1905

THE MISADVENTURES OF USARELMNAVWARCOL

Violent protests at America's universities are in the news these days. Whether or not to support free speech is the issue. Used to be that the common definition of a university was a bunch of faculty, staff, and students assembled around a common parking grievance. No doubt the burning issue of the day will change as it always does; however, the lack of parking spaces is likely to persist.

Which brings to mind the extreme lack of parking spaces when this writer was an Army officer student living in Bachelor Officers Quarters (BOQ) on Coasters Harbor

Island, the 92-acre home of the U.S. Naval War College (NWC). The island is in Narragansett Bay, attached to the mainland City of Newport, RI, by a narrow, U.S. Marine-guarded causeway.

As the cold winds of the coming winter started blowing off the Atlantic Ocean, the need to park close to the BOQ became apparent to someone who had just come off a second year in the steaming jungles of Vietnam. Noticing that the admirals had reserved parking places marked by signs bearing those long acronyms so beloved by the Navy -- with a gift-boxed bottle of rum in hand -- I drove over to the sign shop at the nearby naval base and got a thirsty sailor to make a very, very official looking sign in Navy blue and gold that read: USARELMNAVWARCOL. In Navy speak, that meant: U.S. Army Element, Naval War College.

In the dark of one late September night, the reserved parking sign for USARELMNAVWARCOL appeared right next to the entrance to the BOQ. For eight months of the nine-month-course, the USARELMNAVWARCOL enjoyed his prime parking spot. But one late spring day a visiting Naval Reserve Captain (in Army rank, a full colonel) yelled, "Major, do you realize you just parked in the place reserved for USARELMNAVWARCOL? You Army types cannot just ignore naval protocol. So, you take that car of yours and find somewhere else to park on this island!"

I responded, "Aye, aye, Sir. So sorry. The car will be moved immediately!" The visiting reservist was so intrigued by the identity of USARELMNAVWARCOL that he made some inquiries at NWC headquarters.

The next day, USARELMNAVWARCOL found himself standing at attention in front of the full Colonel Army senior advisor to the NWC who said, "Major, there is a rumor that someone made a fictitious parking sign and placed it next to the entrance to the BOQ. If true, that sign needs to disappear. Dismissed!" It was like a scene from "Casablanca." "There's gambling going on here?"

That night, the sign for USARELMNAVWARCOL found its way to the bottom of Narragansett Bay. But that was not the end of the story. On the day for leaving the NWC en route to assignment in Europe, a letter written on the made-up letterhead of USARELMNAVWARCOL was posted to the vice admiral president of the NWC.

The letter read, in part, *"Dear Admiral Colbert: This is to thank you for the courtesy of a reserved parking place next to the BOQ and to inform you that the parking spot reserved for USARELMNAVWARCOL will no longer be needed."*

Signed, *USARELMNAVWARCOL*

©2017. 1901

CHAPTER EIGHT

POLITICAL AFFAIRS

POLITICS: A TRUE "THIRD" PARTY?

The East Indians may be on to something that could clean up American politics. At least it might get rid of the sexual sleaze affecting the Oval Office. It seems there are over one million eunuchs living in India. Why so many? I don't know. But many of them are unhappy with the political corruption exhibited by India's non-eunuch, mainstream politicians. (I am not making this up.)

Recently, in Delhi, hundreds of East Indian eunuchs held a party congress which they hailed as an "All-India Eunuch Meeting." This meeting formalized a growing political movement in India that might, pardon the expression, become a "potent" political force.

Eunuch candidates have already stood for election in Madhya Pradesh and, Mr. Kamla Jaan, was elected the mayor of the town of Katni. Next Tuesday, Mr. Dhanno Bai, another eunuch, in the northern state of Haryana, is running for the state assembly.

In the Urdu language, eunuchs are called hijras or the "impotent ones." (It is amazing what you can learn reading this column.) Eunuchs, however, may not be so impotent when it comes to political and civil-service reform.

Historically, eunuchs have a long history of public service. In many Arab cultures, they were used as harem guards. But some of them got bored standing around all day looking at scantily-clad harem girls so, just to have more to do, they took on additional administrative duties around the palaces. Overtime, eunuchs were highly sought after as civil servants in Arab and Oriental cultures. Evidently, they had nothing else on their minds but work. Unfortunately, this cannot be said for a number of U.S. government officials. One **very** high official comes to mind.

Indeed, it would be safe to say that untold numbers of private citizens have difficulties with government bureaucrats. And, truth be known, only the fear of the F.B.I. keeps some irate taxpayers from introducing any number of government bureaucrats into eunuch-hood. That urge is usually strongest around April 15th.

But how does one form a viable political party where being a eunuch is a requirement for party membership? It would seem to this observer that recruitment of new members would be a real challenge. Can you imagine one of those political party phone-bank callers interrupting your dinner hour with this?

"Hello, I'm a volunteer with the National Eunuchs United To Elect Reformers. You may have heard of us referred to by the acronym N.E.U.T.E.R. We are conducting a drive for new members. We want to clean up government corruption. You know, stop those messy and expensive sex scandals. We are hoping you would like to join our party."

"Do you have any admission requirements?"

"Well, yes. You must be, shall we say, one of us; however, we can arrange that at no cost to you."

"Right." (click)

In a way it is too bad that N.E.U.T.E.R will probably never be able to attract enough members to elect reformers to occupy the highest office in our land. Just think of all the terrible problems that might have been avoided if N.E.U.T.E.R. could have elected some of our recent Presidents.

For example, if JFK had not been romancing the girlfriend of a Mafia boss who had connections to Castro, he might be alive today. If Bill Clinton had been a member of N.E.U.T.E.R., that might explain why he wouldn't go to Vietnam.

Even better, we would never have heard of Gennifer Flowers, Paula Jones, Kathleen Willey, Dolly Kyle Browning, Juanita Broddrick, Elizabeth Ward Gracen and, of course, Monica Lewinsky. Ken Starr would be a California law professor with a shot at sitting on the U.S. Supreme Court someday. Clinton wouldn't have bombed thousands of innocent people in the Balkans. And, Arkansas State Troopers would be writing traffic tickets instead of writing "tell-all" books.

Yes, there is something to be said for N.E.U.T.E.R. But one suspects their national party convention would be pretty dull.

©2000. 934

THE PARABLE OF THE GRACIOUS HOMEOWNER

With the advent of "no-call" legislation designed to prevent those annoying telephone solicitations from interrupting the dinner hour or your enjoyment of Monday Night Football, those who design and conduct political campaigns are relying less and less on political phone banks to get-out-the-vote. Instead, they are opting for greater use of direct mail appeals and for more door-to-door calling or "precinct walking" by party workers.

This gives rise to the age-old question: How should one respond when a party worker comes knocking on your door? Should you be gracious? Should you be rude? Should you not even answer the door? Perhaps, the best way to explain this is through The Parable of the Gracious Homeowner.

"Hello," begins the precinct worker. "I'm walking this precinct this evening urging concerned citizens to vote for my candidate, Mr. Karl Marx Lenin of the People's Progressive Party. Our motto is: Soak the rich, and down with the vast, right-wing conspiracy!"

As it happens, you are a member of the vast, right-wing conspiracy and your candidate is Adam Smith von Mises. So, your first reaction is to tell your caller to take a long walk on a short pier. Wrong. Be courteous. Be gracious. Be smart. The Judeo-Christian thing to do is to invite him or her into your home.

"Please come in. Tell me about your party and your candidate," you begin.

"Thank you, but I can't stay long. I'm supposed to call on 39 more homes before 9:00 p.m."

"Of course. But let me make some fresh coffee, so I'll be more alert. It won't take but a minute. And, while I'm at it, I think I'll whip up a coffeecake and slip it in the oven."

"That's very kind of you."

While the coffee and the coffeecake are making and baking, ask to see the campaign literature your caller is supposed to distribute. Insist on going over each piece of it in detail. Ask lots of questions that will allow your caller to demonstrate his vast (probably, half-vast) knowledge of economics and the great issues facing the nation, your state, your county, your town and your precinct. This will take some time.

"This coffeecake and your coffee are very good," says your caller. "But I really do have to get on my way."

"Yes, you do; however, I didn't quite understand your point about taking tax dollars from the filthy rich and giving the money to the poor. And, since the vast majority of the taxes are already being paid by a small minority of the population, I am wondering if it is fair to make them pay more?

"By the way, if you don't mind, I just happen to have some single-malt Scotch whiskey and no one to drink it with. While you are explaining the economics of socialism, I thought maybe we could share a taste. I would consider it a personal favor. Okay?"

"Well, okay. And, maybe, I could just leave some of our campaign literature so I can get on my way. It is getting very late."

"Quite right," you say, as you pour a couple of fingers of single-malt into his glass. "Actually, I was going to ask you to leave all of your expensive-looking campaign literature with me. I know I can find places to put it."

"I suppose I could do that. Anyway, there really isn't time for me to take it around the neighborhood this evening. If you would distribute it for me, it would save a lot of time. By the way, thissss whissskey is really good. May I have another taste?"

Eventually, it is 9:00 p.m. And, as your caller weaves his way to the door, he says: "Thank you; I really appreciate your hosssspitality. And ssshanks for taking all my campaign literature, Mr. Machiavelli."

©2002. 1070

OSTRACISM: SHOULD WE CAST OUR OSTRAKA?

When the political waters got too rough in ancient Athens, the people (the demos) had a way of pouring oil on troubled political waters by voting to "ostracize" one or more of their political figures – especially those suspected of tyrannical ambitions or, maybe, just for being contentious.

Paper (papyrus) being too expensive to use for ballots, the Athenians of the 5th Century B.C. used shards (ostraka in Greek) of broken jars and dishes onto which they scratched the name of the public figure they wished to be ostracized – exiled for ten years. If over 6,000 ostraka were "cast," then the way was cleared to ostracize the political figure or figures receiving the most ostraka. Failure of the ostracized to depart Athens was punishable by death. During the approximately 70 years it was practiced, ostracism served, in general, to reduce political tensions.

What if 21st Century Americans adapted ostracism to our system of political caucuses and primary elections? Even though the polling data collected at: **www.realclearpolitics.com** are too early to be meaningful, let's use those polls to examine the presidential contenders of today's two major political parties in terms of what their ostracism might do to calm our political waters:

If Hillary Rodman Clinton (36.3%) were elected President, that might be a way for taxpayers to get back some of the furnishings she carted off from the White House to her New York mansion. Since then, Hillary has probably thrown enough of our dishes at Bill to provide enough ostraka to hold a Greek-style election for the entire State of New York. If Hillary's attempt at a Restoration fail, she and Bill might be interned (bad word choice) on St. Helena.

For obvious reasons, Barack Hussein Obama (25.7%) cannot be ostracized. But when Hillary turns her attack-canine, James Carville, loose on Barack Hussein Obama, something Muslim is sure to surface. (Ironically, when John F. Kennedy (JFK) was running for President, we were told religion shouldn't be an issue.)

Mr. (anti-law-suit-abuse-reform) John Edwards (11.7%) could be ostracized for claiming there are two Americas: One for the poor and one for folks like lawyer Edwards and his wife who live in a brand-new, 28,000 square-foot mansion. That's larger than many office buildings!

Al Gore (no poll numbers yet) could be ostracized because his Nashville mansion consumes more energy every month than the average American home does in an entire year. But, like the pre-Reformation sinners, Gore has purchased global warming indulgences from the Our Lady of Kyoto Cathedral for High Carbon Dioxide Producers.

Rudi Giuliani (36.9%) may be ostracized by the evangelicals because he and his current wife have each been married three times. For that, the evangelicals could send them into a ten-year exile to some foreign place like, well, Staten Island. John McCain (21.3%) could be ostracized for wanting to grant amnesty to illegal aliens and for his denigration of evangelicals. McCain could be sent to manage a Big Macquiladora factory in Mexico. Newt Gingrich (10.6%) with his three marriages could be exiled to update his Contract With America. Unlike JFK, Mitt Romney (8.1%) might be ostracized to conduct a ten-year Mormon mission

Brought back to life in the 21st Century, the ancient Greeks might ostracize all of today's candidates. Unfortunately, others will come forward as in: "We child-proofed our house, but they keep getting back in."

Republicans should fear U.S. Senator Evan Bayh of Indiana who says he isn't running but has not done a

General Sherman: "If nominated, I will not run. If elected, I will not serve." But, should the Democrats deadlock in Denver, there may be no sitting Bayh.

Democrats should fear former U.S. Senator Fred Thompson. With only one divorce (amicable), strong on fighting the war on terror and a conservative voting record, Fred Thompson might be the one to bring "law and order" not just to our land, but to wherever our troops are fighting the Islamic fascists.

So, let he who is without sin, cast the first ostrakon (singular).

©2007. 1309

SHOPPING DECISIONS: LEFT VERSUS RIGHT

Many Americans dutifully make financial contributions to the political party they favor and/or to the political candidates whom they want to see elected and/or to charitable organization whose goals they favor. In the case of political candidates, campaigns and political parties at the national level, those financial contributions are reported to the Federal Election Commission (FEC) which, eventually, makes public who gave what and to whom. In a free and open society, that is as it should be.

Yet, when asked if they make financial donations to political parties, causes or candidates, there are other Americans who will flatly state that giving money to political parties, candidates or causes is something they do not do. And yet, they do. They just do not know it.

Here is how it works: Virtually, every organization in America, be it a labor union, or a business corporation or company, or any group seeking special-interest legislation or some kind of favored treatment by elected officials contributes dollars to certain political parties and/or candidates. As we will see in the upcoming presidential election cycle for 2012, billions of dollars will be amassed from union dues, from corporate profits, and from special-interest group fundraising

Back in 2001, after careful research of FEC records, a group of liberals published an online consumers' guide listing, by corporation, the percentage of corporate political donations that went to conservative candidates and causes and also the percentage of corporate political donations going to liberal candidates and causes. The idea, of course, was to get liberals to boycott the conservative-leaning businesses and to spend their money, instead, with liberal-leaning businesses.

But, by failing to recognize the Law of Unintended Consequences, the BuyBlue.org liberals were also pointing conservatives toward those businesses that contribute to the Republican National Committee and to conservative political candidates and causes. Eventually, BuyBlue.org failed.

But the data are still available. In, 2006, the liberal-leaning PoliPoint Press published *The Blue Pages: A Directory of Companies Rated by Their Politics and Practices*. According to *The Blue Pages*, if you are a dyedin-the-wool liberal who does not mind shopping at big-box stores, you should head for COSTCO which gives 99-percent of its political donations to Democrats and ranks nationally as one of the top-ten Democrat contributors.

If you are a true conservative, not a Republican-in-name-only (RINO), then head for Sam's Club which gives 100-percent to Republicans. Moreover, the parent corporation of Sam's Club is Wal-Mart which gives 78% to the GOP and 22% to Democrats.

Most of us do not have big bucks to give to our favorite political parties, candidates, or causes. Ergo: what few dollars we have need to count for our side. So, in a larger sense, the BuyBlue.org idea was sound. Why would any one of sound mind, armed with the data from *The Blue Pages*, knowingly hand their hard-earned dollars over to their political enemies?

Granted, some corporations use their donations to walk both sides of the political street. In The Blue Pages, you can find lots of corporations who give half to Democrats and half to Republicans. Interestingly, the big Wall Street brokerages and investment banking houses give most of their money to Democrats. Wonder if that is why the O'Bamessiahs bailed them out first?

The editorial content of The Blue Pages, suggests that the corporations that give most of their money to Democrats are on the side of sweetness and light while the corporations that give most of their money to Republicans are on the side of darkness and evil. That kind of editorial bias did not, however, prevent this researcher from buying a copy via Amazon.com (61% to the GOP and 39% to the

Dems). For people who care where their money ends up politically, *The Blue Pages* provide a handy shopping guide.

©2011. 1531

THE CASE OF THE BANISHED BUST

Making a steeple out of his fingers as Sherlock Holmes did so often when listening to the recital of a case, the famous sleuth said, "Tell me, my dear Dr. Watson, what are the available facts?"

"Up until the time that Mr. Obama began work in the Oval Office in January, 2009, the famous bust of former British Prime Minister Winston Churchill was a prominent artifact in the Oval Office."

"Dr. Watson, you are using the past tense with regard to this famous bust of someone who is regarded by many as Great Britain's greatest statesman. Surely, the bust is not lost, strayed, or stolen."

"I am happy to tell you the famous bust currently resides in the residence of the British Ambassador to the United States."

"Then how, pray tell, did this famous bust move from the Oval Office to the residence of the British Ambassador?"

"On the orders of Mr. Obama. One of his aides must have packed up the bust and taken it over or had it taken over to the British Embassy at 3100 Massachusetts Avenue, Northwest where, by the way, is a large statute of

Sir Winston Churchill. One of the statue's feet is inside the embassy grounds, the other rests within the District of Columbia. This was not the error of some surveyor. The statue was placed that way to symbolize that Churchill's mother was American, that his father was British, and that Sir Winston Churchill was made an honorary citizen of the United States."

"Well, Watson, if the bust of Sir Winston is not lost, strayed, or stolen, what's all this fuss about?"

"Inexplicably, Mr. Obama's communication director, a Mr. Dan Pfeiffer, took issue with a columnist for *The Washington Post* who reminded his readers that Mr. Obama banished the bust of Sir Winston from the Oval Office. In effect, Mr. Pfeiffer called the columnist a liar."

"With the facts so well-known, why would Mr. Pfeiffer do that? This seems like pulling a scab off an old wound right when Great Britain is in the limelight of the London Olympics."

"It turns out that former President Lyndon Johnson was a great admirer of Sir Winston Churchill. So, the British government gave President Johnson a copy of the famous bust and it was put in an upstairs room of the White House. Apparently, Mr. Pfeiffer found the copy of the bust and decided to make the claim that Mr. Obama never banished the bust of Sir Winston from the Oval Office. Almost immediately, the British Ambassador issued a statement that the original bust that had once graced the Oval Office is firmly ensconced inside his residence."

"Did Mr. Pfeiffer apologize to the columnist for disputing his veracity?"

"Yes, but only after being pilloried in the American press and, as you know, our Fleet Street press picked up the story of the banished bust, thus renewing the unpleasantness of January, 2009. The columnist graciously accepted Mr. Pfeiffer's apology."

"Well then, my dear Watson, it seems that all's well that ends well."

"By Jove, Holmes, that has a certain ring to it. Maybe you should also be a playwright," concluded Watson.

©2012. 1635

ARE ALL Y'ALL READY FOR SOME FANTASY POLITICS?

Lots of folks play Fantasy Football these days. How about some Fantasy Politics? A future White House press briefing might go like this:

"Ladies and gentlemen: I am the new president's press officer. If y'all think I'm some redneck you see on reality TV, then that's y'all's problem. The president directed me to tell y'all to expect some major changes. For notepaper, y'all can use the back of them Democrat National Committee Talking Points y'all rely on. They ain't nothing but male bovine excreta (MBE), anyway.

"First of all, the president ain't gonna be issuing a bunch of executive orders that's contrary to the U.S. Constitution. So, all them previous 900 or so executive orders are hereby null and void. As for all them 49 or so unconstitutional political czars, they is all lookin' for jobs.

"If the people want a particular action taken, they need to contact their members of Congress and maybe we'll git-er-done. In fact, the president has sworn to faithfully execute all the laws. No more pickin' and choosin'. Speaking of Congress, the president won't sign any legislation that does not apply to everyone in the United States, to include members of Congress.

"As for the Supreme Court, the president suggests they go back applyin' the Constitution to their decisions. Of course, being a separate branch of government, that's up to them. But the Supremes would be well-advised to stop inventin' stuff that ain't in the U.S. Constitution. You J-school grads, listen up. The Supremes ain't some Mo-town singin' group.

"Regardin' the Joint Chiefs of Staff and all them generals and admirals, the president is going to make some really stupid proposals that have nothin' to do with combat readiness but have to do with social and political correctness. The generals and admirals who tell him he is full of MBE will stay on. The wimps who tell the president his ideas are the greatest thing since von Clausewitz will join the previous president on the golf course. As for foreign and military policy: If it ain't a vital national interest -- such as freedom-of-the-seas -- it's just more MBE.

"Also, those Republicans-In-Name-Only (RINOs) might as well join the other party. No more White House dinners for them. The president needs men and women of principle. And no more usin' Air Force One as a political payoff machine.

"As for health care, the system installed by the previous president stuck all the taxpayers with the health insurance tab for all the non-taxpayers. But the new system doesn't provide affordable, quality health care. Meanwhile, until the president gets that sucker repealed, the poor folk are stuck with it.

"Notice the British Royals used a private clinic to birth their new prince, not their crappy National Health Service. As for our rich folk, they can fly off to Thailand or the Cayman Islands and get all the health care they need. Stand by for a plan that uses the forces inherent in the free-market to produce an affordable health-care system. Won't be no more death panels.

"On immigration, them who have been standin' in line the longest will get the consideration they deserve. If illegal immigrants want to stay here and they get caught, they go to the very back of the line.

"Okay. That's it. I know all y'all have deadlines. Please, no more MBE."

©2013. 1693

VALERIE JARRETT: THE WOMAN WHO STAYS FOR DINNER

Washington insiders are well aware that the key decision maker in the Obama White House is Valerie Bowman Jarrett. Washington lobbyists know that if they have an idea or project to push, unless it has the blessing of Valerie Jarrett, it is probably dead in the water.

Valerie Jarrett may have even more power than Mrs. Woodrow Wilson. Recall, in 1919, President Wilson suffered a debilitating stroke and, for the next 18 months, Mrs. Edith Wilson decided which papers President Wilson saw and which ones he signed. But, despite her influence on President Obama, Valerie Jarrett is not well-known outside of Washington circles.

As most everyone knows, the First Family lives upstairs in the White House in what is known as the presidential residence. What most people do not know is that Valerie Jarrett has her very own bedroom inside the presidential residence and she most often eats her meals with the First Family. Every matter of importance is discussed between the President, the First Lady, and Valerie Jarrett.

Some say that Valerie Jarrett is the *de facto* President of the United States, that the First Lady is actually the de facto Vice President of the United States and that Barack H. Obama is their skilled official spokesman. The three work together. They travel together. They even vacation together, albeit Barack and Michelle often take separate vacations. When that happens, Valerie usually goes on vacation with Michelle and the children.

So, who is this mysterious *l'éminence grise* of the Obama White House? She is the daughter of James E. Bowman, M.D. and Barbara T. Bowman. Valerie was born on November 14, 1956, in Shiraz, Iran. Yes, in Shia-dominated Iran, which is now the major self-proclaimed enemy of the United States and of non-Shia Muslims everywhere.

Valerie's first five years were lived in Iran where her cradle language was Persian and her second language was French. At age six, she lived in London for a year where her English was perfected. After that, her family settled in a wealthy African-American section of Chicago. She holds a B.A. from Stanford University and a law degree from the University of Michigan. She is a divorced single mother with a grown daughter.

Working quickly up the ranks of Chicago's Democratic Party politics, Valerie was the person who got Michelle a job in Mayor Richard J. Daley's office and who served as the Yenta or match-maker (Valerie has a Jewish great-grandfather) who brought Michelle Robinson and Barack Obama together in marriage.

Sometimes, Wonder Wife and I put together imaginary lists of famous dead people we would like to bring back to life and have over for dinner. Usually, Thomas Jefferson, James Madison, Benjamin Franklin, Alexander Hamilton, and the historians Barbara W. Tuchman, Daniel J. Boorstin, and Stephen E. Ambrose top the list. But we also make up lists of today's interesting people. Someone with the smarts and influence of Valerie Jarrett, despite our political differences, would be more than welcome. To find out why President Obama has been so painfully slow to provide arms and aid to our Kurdish allies (mostly, Sunni) would be worth serving filet mignon and some decent wine. Wonder if Valerie's background in Iran (mostly, Shia) plays a role?

NB: In 2017, Ms. Jarrett took up residence with former President Obama's family in Georgetown, D.C. ©2014. 1743

THE 2014 PHEME (FAY-MAY) AWARDS

Satire: These days, it seems like there is a TV show that presents awards for almost anything you can imagine, even advertising. According to Wikipedia, "...the Clio Awards are the world's most recognizable international advertising awards, presented annually to reward innovation and creative excellence in advertising, design and communication." (Clio was the Greek goddess/muse of History.)

Thus far, an Internet search does not reveal a TV award show recognizing the best and the worst 2014 TV political advertisements. Apparently, that's a niche that needs to be filled. We will start by giving it a name: In Greek mythology, the Goddess of Gossip was called: Pheme, which is pronounced: fay-may. If there were any, ah...dirt to be dug up concerning the Greek gods or even some of the mortals, you could count on Pheme to spread it around.

To hear gossip better, Pheme kept her hair short so it did not cover her ears. In order to keep an eye on everyone, she lived in a house with 1,000 windows. No, not Windows 1.0; however, Pheme was the NSA of her day.

Once Pheme dug up a piece of, well... you know, she would begin by whispering the gossip over and over and louder and louder. Apparently, Adolf Hitler was a follower of Pheme. In Mein Kampf Hitler proclaimed: "The greater the lie, the greater the chance it will be believed." In ancient Art, Pheme is usually depicted as having wings and a trumpet, giving rise to the practical advice: Toot your own horn before someone else uses it for a relief tube.

If this writer decided the winner of this year's Pheme Award for the best political campaign advertisement, it would go to Congressman Roger Williams who won reelection to the Texas' 25th Congressional District with "The Donkey Whisperer." The scene opens with Williams beside his pick-up truck, surrounded by about 40 donkeys, all wanting to be fed.

Congressman Williams talks to the donkeys as if they were human; castigating them for being welfare donkeys whose only labor is to show up when they want to eat. Williams tries to explain to the donkeys that he would like to take better care of them; however, he is so burdened with regulations coming down from Washington, D.C. that he doesn't have the money for better feed or even to fix their teeth.

Williams concludes by threatening to trade them all in for elephants, which, in a way, foretells the 2014 GOP election landside. Congressman Williams, an Anglo, won reelection in a heavily Hispanic congressional district versus a challenger named Montoya. Readers who go to: www.youtube.com and search for The Donkey Whisperer can enjoy this year's winner of the Pheme Awards Golden Trumpet.

One of the worst political advertisements occurred in Colorado's gubernatorial race. The GOP challenger was accused of being a corrupt banker. The incumbent's advertisement was so blatantly false that even the left-leaning *The Denver Post* editorialized against the advertisement's outrageous falsehoods. Undeterred, the Democrat incumbent's supporters continued to run the bogus advertisement over and over again. The incumbent governor narrowly won reelection and, of course, the 2014 Pheme Shield of Shame.

©2014. 1759

METRICS AND AMERICA

W. Edwards Deming (1900-1960), the dean of American management consultants, used to teach, "You can't manage what you can't measure." Professor Deming's lectures to Japanese industrialists set off the Japanese economic miracle of 1950-1960, causing Japan to produce high-quality cars that almost sank Detroit's automobile industry.

For measurement, it is necessary to have goals. Some readers may have seen the "nine rules for radicals" floating around the Internet which are attributed, inaccurately, to Saul Alinsky (1909-1972). But, over the years, Alinsky's thoughts have been transmogrified (to change or alter greatly often with grotesque effect) by radicals such as Bill

Ayers and others into rules or goals which someone wanting to fundamentally transform America into a Marxist-socialist society might find useful. We report. You measure and decide if any of these goals apply to today's America.

1. Control healthcare. That gives you control over the people. From "A" through "F," which letter grade would you assign ObamaCare? Please do the same for the remaining eight "goals."

2. Increase the poverty level as much as possible. Poor people are easier to control and will not fight back if you distract them, as did the Romans, with bread and circuses.

3. Increase government debt to an unsustainable level. That way you are able to increase taxes just to pay the Interest, and this will produce more poverty and more dependence on big government.

4. Impose gun control. Remove the ability of people to defend themselves from big government. That way you are able to create a police state and maybe even declare Martial Law.

5. By executive action, take control of every aspect of food, housing, income, and the environment. Self-explanatory.

6. Use some kind of one-size-fits-all common-core curriculum to take nation-wide control of what children learn in school. In the process, make sure to denigrate American achievements and emphasize American failures.

7. Remove religion from the public square. And, if possible, from private homes as well. Karl Marx said, "Religion is the opium of the people." By the way, if Marx is correct, should we be legalizing any green leafy products that act like opiates?

8. Promote class warfare. Divide the people into the wealthy and the poor. This will cause more discontent and make it easier to tax the "haves" and give what they have earned to the "have-nots."

9. Seize control over the Internet. Self-explanatory.

Please check your scores. Are we advancing toward the goal of a Marxist /socialist state? Or, as radicals might say: Are we still stuck in the free-market capitalism of those dead, white guys of 1776?

Finally, there is an added 10th Rule which those who oppose ObamaCare need to heed: *"The price of a successful attack is a constructive alternative. You cannot risk being trapped by the enemy in his sudden agreement with your demand and saying 'You're right — we don't know what to do about this issue. Now you tell us.'"*

Recent polls suggest the need for a bi-partisan effort to fix the "glitches" in the Democrat-only-passed ObamaCare legislation which few, if any, bothered to read before enactment. The legislation's co-creator, Professor Jonathan Gruber, says ObamaCare was designed to fool the stupid American voters. As Alinsky advised: Someone needs to propose a constructive alternative.

©2015. 1774

URBAN VIOLENCE: POVERTY AND POLITICS

In the early 60s, when yours truly was a student at the U.S. Army Intelligence School in Baltimore, the city was in the hands of corrupt white leaders. We used to run "covert" surveillance and counter-surveillance exercises along East Baltimore Street which was chock-a-block with strip clubs, sex shops, and drug dealers. It still is. In case we were apprehended by the Baltimore police, we had a special phone number to call off the cops. The police were allied with a gang of car thieves which would turn stolen cars over to the police who would demand a big tip for "rescuing" the car from the thieves.

Apparently, Baltimore has changed. The city is now in the hands of corrupt black leaders. They say the definition of insanity is doing the same thing over and over again while expecting a different result. African-Americans in America's major urban centers keep voting the same party into office and they keep getting the same result. If you know which party that is, go to the head of the class.

In the late 60s, yours truly was attached to the U.S. Air Force in North Carolina. In civilian clothes, I took part in some civil-rights marches sponsored by Dr. Martin Luther King, Jr. After Dr. King was assassinated, those marches proved to be a life-saver for me. Wearing a civilian suit and tie, I was headed for the memorial service for Dr. King when I got a cable from 3d U.S. Army Headquarters in Atlanta directing me to attend the memorial service in the Army Blue Uniform and to drive to the service in a clearly-marked military sedan.

Inside the church, I was greeted by the elders with great courtesy and seated in the front row with the mayor and a handful of other Caucasians. After the very moving service, I got back in the military sedan to drive away. Suddenly, the sedan was surrounded by a gang of young blacks who started rocking the car from side-to-side and were getting close to tipping the sedan on its side with me inside it when a large black woman came barreling down off her front porch. Whatever she yelled put the fear of God in the young men and they ran off. She said she remembered seeing me before, marching for Dr. King. Whew!

In 2008 and 2012, some people voted for Barack H. Obama based on his skin color. Apparently, they thought that would end racial strife in America. Readers can decide how that has been working out. But maybe the violence we see in urban streets today is not rooted so much in skin color but in big-city machine politics which have not focused on arresting the decay of the inner cities, but rather, perpetuating the decay as a means of staying in political power.

The list of American cities with the highest inner-city poverty rates includes: St. Louis (Ferguson), Newark, Cincinnati, Philadelphia, Milwaukee, Buffalo, El Paso, Cleveland, New York, and Detroit. Big cities facing possible bankruptcy are Detroit, Cincinnati, Camden, Baltimore, San Diego, San Jose, San Francisco, and Los

Angeles. One particular political party has controlled those cities for decades. If you know which one, raise your hand. ©2015. 1780

HACKER'S DELIGHT: UNPROTECTED "PRIVATE" SERVERS

For those not familiar with the handling of highly classified national security information, the investigations into Mrs. Bill Clinton's "private" e-mail server and whether or not she caused "exceptionally grave damage" to our intelligence and military services might seem like much ado about nothing.

So, let's take a fictional journey into the world of the fictional mortal enemies, Berzerkistan and Creta. We begin inside the Cyber Warfare Center of Berzerkistan where skilled hackers are reading the flow of e-mails between the Secretary of State for Creta and Sid, one of her outside advisors:

"Sid, I took your advice and invited the Berzerkistan Ambassador to our cocktail party. But I knew in advance that he would not accept because the big Nebbish had already accepted an invitation to dine with the King and Queen of Vulgaria. But his cow of a wife stayed out in the sun too long, sunburned her fat butt, and can't put on a dress. So, he's going alone to the Palace. Really, Sid, she is way too old to have a butterfly on her derriere."

"Well, Madame Secretary, you at least got credit for inviting the Putz. How did you know he was in no position to accept?"

"Sid. Let's just say a little birdie told me. Look, I have to go now. That special mission over in. Ah, you-know-where, is hounding me for extra security. I realize they are in a dangerous situation, but if we beef up their security too much, that would attract attention to what we are doing and we don't want that. If you know what I mean."

"Yes, Madame Secretary, I do. Meanwhile, I'm wondering why the Vulgarian Royals want the Berzerkistani ambassador to dine with them. Maybe you could get our asset working on that. An alliance between Berzerkistan and Vulgaria would be counter to our national interest."

"Sid, thanks for your advice. It is comforting to have a friend from outside this snake pit of a department. Signing off. XOXOXO."

Now, let's see what the Berzerkistanis have learned from their hacking of the Cretan Secretary of State's "private" e-mails: 1. Madame Secretary thinks the Berzerkistani ambassador is an inept, stupid person, a Nebbish. 2. Her friend, Sid, thinks the ambassador is, well... a jerk. 3. The ambassador's wife is unattractive. 4. Berzerkistan telephone communications are being tapped by the Cretans. 5. The "little birdie" probably refers to a Cretan NSA satellite. 6. To know about the butterfly tattoo, the Cretans must be flying a UAV over the area where the ambassador's wife does her sunbathing. 7.

Somewhere, there is a diplomatic mission that has inadequate security and would make an easy target for terrorist attack. 8. Something super-secret is going on at that location. 9. It appears the Cretans may have an "asset" inside the Vulgarian Palace who could monitor the conversation between the ambassador and the Vulgarian Royals.

In sum, this seemingly innocuous e-mail exchange compromised the "sources and methods" being used by Creta's own intelligence agencies. Berzerkistan counterintelligence will now take steps to nullify the covert actions of the Cretans. They will identify the diplomatic mission that has weak security and have surrogates attack it. Big deal or not? You decide.

©2015. 1796

NATIONAL POLITICAL CONVENTIONS: WHO ATTENDS?

Amidst all this talk about a contested Republican National Convention in Cleveland and the Democrats not even sure if their anointed one will be "free" to attend their convention in Philadelphia, the question arises: What kind of folks attend these quadrennial political gatherings?

Basically, they are mostly folks who have chosen politics as their avocation. An expensive hobby. Except for the very highest state and national party officials, they pay their own transportation, hotel, meals and other expenses.

Nor is it a spur-of-the-moment avocation. Like becoming good at golf, or bridge or fishing or hunting, or sailing, a lot of time and commitment is required. They are faithful attendees at their local precinct meetings. They attend meetings of their county central committee. They strive to be elected to their party's state convention where they lobby fellow delegates to elect them to be delegates to their national convention.

Some, but not all, are volunteer campaign workers for their favorite presidential candidate. As a condition for election, they are even willing to be "bound" to vote for the favorite of their state convention. Well, at least on the first ballot. So, in sum, these are by and large people who have paid their political dues down in the trenches and their coveted reward this year is to pay their own expenses to Cleveland or Philadelphia and back.

But, unlike the solitary golfer or fisher or hunter whose hobby is essentially a private quest, the delegates to national party conventions will leave for Cleveland or Philadelphia feeling like they are going to play a personal role in their nation's future.

On arrival, they will be bombarded by campaign staffers and candidates all vying for their votes. Suddenly amidst the red, white and blue glitter, someone, who may have a rather ho-hum job back home, has an important role to play in a grand political spectacle that is the envy of the world. Well, not in Cuba, North Korea, Red China, Iran or Russia.

But it is not all political maneuvering. Some of the political hobbyists from one state are long-time friends with political hobbyists from other states. Their families count on seeing each other every four years. For some, it is like one grand family reunion.

While naysayers may denigrate them as members of the "political class," even the naysayers should have the good grace to admit that these folks have done the heavy lifting at their precinct, county, and state levels and have earned the right to play their role in Philadelphia or Cleveland this summer.

But will the fateful votes they cast in Cleveland or Philadelphia be universally applauded back home? No way. Far too many interests converge at these conventions for the delegates to be able to please everyone. The mission of the delegates is to nominate the candidate who, in their collective judgment, has the best chance of defeating the candidate of the other party in November's general election.

Some will leave Cleveland and Philadelphia elated by their party's decision and eager to support their party's nominee. Those who end up disappointed in Philly or Cleveland, will find their commitment to party principles tested. Some avocations are more fun than others.

©2016. 1830

HILLARY'S "HOME-BREW" SERVER: WHY ALL THE FUSS?

Folks who have never had occasion to deal with sensitive national security information as found in classified documents, may wonder why all the fuss about former Secretary of State Hillary Clinton's unprotected, "home brew" e-mail server? Last week, on Hugh Hewitt's nationally syndicated radio show, former Secretary of Defense, Robert Gates, said "odds are pretty high" that Secretary Clinton's server was hacked by the Russians, Chinese, and Iranians.

Satire may be the best way to explain the uproar: "The Independent Counsel engaged by the U.S. Department of Justice (DOJ) to investigate Madame Secretary has hired the law firm of Dewey, Cheatham, and Howe (DCH) for advice on what information should be classified and at which level. DCH begins its report to the Independent Counsel with some properly marked, fictional e-mail examples, in ascending order of sensitivity:

Unclassified For Official Use Only:
Madame Secretary:
(UFOUO) Attached is a list of RSVP attendees for tonight's reception for the Ambassador of Lower Slobbovia. The dress for the evening is black tie for men and short formals or pant suits for women. See you there.-- Huma

Confidential:
Madame Secretary:
(C) Tonight, you will notice the Ambassador of Lower Slobbovia has a tick in his left eye, indicating he is under considerable stress, the cause of which we are trying

to determine. Suggest you try to ignore the tick. Please recall they always vote against us in the U.N. --Huma

Secret:
Madame Secretary:

(S) We must postpone your scheduled flight to Upper Slobbovia set for next week. The Pentagon says the anti-missile chaff dispenser in your aircraft is inoperative, making it unsafe for you to overfly Lower Slobbovia. --Huma

Top Secret:
Madame Secretary:

(TS) We have now learned that the anti-missile chaff dispensers for the entire fleet of Air Force Special Mission aircraft are inoperative. Even Air Force One is grounded for now. --Huma

Top Secret/Special Access Program
Madame Secretary:

(TS/SAP) When you greet the Ambassador of Lower Slobbovia tonight, please do not ask him how he enjoyed his trip to Monaco. The CIA bugged his office. The janitor works for CIA. So, we know he got a girl in Monaco pregnant and she is blackmailing him for millions which he is going to pay with counterfeit casino chips. --Huma

Finally, Dewey, Cheatham, and Howe forward these fictional examples of classified e-mails and, in return, collect a big fat fee for services rendered. Your tax dollars at work."

Back to reality: It should be noted that the Special Access Program (SAP) designation can be applied to any level of classification because SAP has to do with the sources and methods by which the sensitive information is obtained from electronic listening devices, human intelligence (our spies) and/or by NSA satellite communications interceptions.

It is an awesome responsibility to handle sensitive information which, if compromised, could expose the planting of a bug, could cause spies to be caught, tortured, and executed, and could cause our enemies to take extra measures to foil our communications intercept capabilities, leaving the United States blind to enemy intentions and capabilities. How big a deal is exposing sensitive national security information to potential hackers? We report. You decide.

©2016. 1820

THE CANDIDATES: CAN THEY "GENTLE THEIR CONDITION?"

Once upon a time (you can tell this column will be an allegory), just before the Battle of Agincourt (1415 A.D.), the English King Henry V decided to look in on the 2016 battle for the American presidency. Accompanied by Generals Gloucester, Bedford, Exeter, Westmoreland (no, not that Westmoreland), and Salisbury, King Henry was told tales of Queen Hillary, the heir presumptive, who was jousting with Sir Bernie, whose creed of taking from the rich and giving "free everything" to the poor, gave Sir Bernie the mantle of a modern-day Robin Hood.

The Queen, however, was beset by "a sea of troubles," not the least of which involved selling her office when she served as her Kingdom's Chief Envoy and charges that she let slip the Kingdom's most secret correspondence. Sir Bernie, who had never had a job save in government, was stuck in a time warp, reliving his honeymoon in the people's paradise of the Soviet Union from which his mind never returned. But, despite her troubles, the Queen was prepared to slay Sir Bernie with hundreds of the Super-Knights her political party held in reserve. That's assuming the Queen does not end up in the Tower of Club Fed.

After looking at the American Electoral College forecasts, General Westmoreland suggested the Republican candidates needed a lot more troops. Apparently, wanting more troops is a trait handed down in the Westmoreland DNA. But King Henry opined that a short-handed Republican victory would be all the more sweet. In fact, he said: "The fewer men, the greater share of honour."

Besides, said the King, noting that the Queen's lecherous Consort was a Vietnam-era draft-dodger, "That he which hath no stomach to this fight, let him depart; his passport be made, and crowns for convoy put into his purse; we would not die in that man's company..."

The idea of deporting the Queen's Consort brought to mind the candidacy of the wealthy peasant, Donald of Trump, whose battle cry is: "Deport them all, and let Allah sort them out!" Lord Salisbury drew the King's attention to Squire Kasich who seems to be riding off in all directions, left-and-right, trying to find a King under whom he could serve.

Opposing Donald of Trump was Sir Cruzader Cruz, who claimed the bumptious Donald of Trump's promise to build a modern-day Hadrian's Wall would trample all ore the Magna Carta. Besides, claimed Sir Cruz, the wealthy peasant Donald of Trump, who was having his garments made in foreign lands, was giving the nouveau riche a bad name. Hearing that, King Henry decided, no matter how much of his fortune that Donald of Trump poured into his campaign, it would not be possible to "gentle his condition."

Having heard enough American campaign rhetoric, King Henry V decided to return to northern France where the Battle of Agincourt awaited him. On the way, he worked on a speech to fire up his troops. He underlined this passage: "From this day to the ending of the world, but we in it shall be remembered. We few, we happy few, we band of brothers; for he today who sheds his blood with me shall be my brother..." (Although outnumbered five-to-one, the Brits won.)

©2016. 1833

NATIONAL ARCHIVES: THE DISAPPEARING DOCUMENTS

Even the most non-partisan observer would conclude that Bill and Hillary Clinton and their close associates have a problem with classified documents. For example: After 19 Islamic terrorists killed 2,996 Americans and injured over 6,000 others on September 11, 2001, the 9/11 Commission investigated the Islamic terrorist attack, hoping to discover how the attacks could have been prevented. Sandy Berger, President Clinton's former National Security Adviser, was slated to be a key witness. Beginning in October, 2003, while claiming a need to refresh his memory, Berger visited the classified documents section of the National Archives on four occasions.

During each visit, Berger stole classified documents relating to President Clinton's missed opportunities to eliminate Osama bin Laden in advance of 9/11. (See: Sean Naylor's Relentless Strike: *The Secret History of Joint Special Operations Command* (2015) reveals President Bill Clinton called off two Delta Force operations that could have nailed Osama bin Laden long before September 11, 2001.)

On his fourth visit to the National Archives, Berger was caught in the act. In April 2005, Berger pleaded guilty to a charge of unauthorized removal and retention of classified material from the National Archives. Berger was fined $50,000, sentenced to serve two years of **probation** and 100 hours of community service, and stripped of his security clearance. Facing disbarment, Berger surrendered his law license. After the Sandy Berger scandal, you would think the National Archives would keep a closer eye on documents related to the Clintons.

When investigators visited the National Archives in 1994 to review documents related to the July 20, 1993, suicide of Hillary Clinton's great good friend and aide, Vince Foster, they took note of two FBI agent reports (FB-302) that included information about a White House staff meeting during which Hillary Clinton ridiculed Vince Foster mercilessly in front of his peers for raising a legal objection to Hillary Clinton's proposed socialized-medicine legislation. A week later, Vince Foster committed suicide.

Fast forward to 2016: With Mrs. Bill Clinton running again for President, journalists delved into the National Archives to review, among other Clinton papers, the Vince Foster file. According to two FBI agents who filed the reports linking Mrs. Clinton's tirade to Foster's suicide, the FB-302s about the White House staff meeting during which Hillary Clinton ridiculed Vince Foster, are now (drum roll) missing! As of August 23, 2016, despite a Freedom of Information Request by former *Washington Post* and *Wall Street Journal* investigative reporter, Ronald Kessler, the National Archives cannot find the missing FBI agent reports.

Wait. There's more! Back in March 2009, the National Archives discovered an external hard drive containing classified information from the Bill Clinton White House had disappeared. Criminal investigators offered a reward of $50,000 for information leading to the recovery of the hard drive. But, unlike the Sandy Berger thefts, the Clinton-related crime was never solved.

Mrs. Bill Clinton's use of a private, non-secure e-mail server to conduct Department of State and Clinton Foundation business while she was Secretary of State offers more evidence that the Clintons and classified documents don't play well together. If Mrs. Bill Clinton is elected President, one wonders if either of the Clintons could obtain a security clearance?

©2016. 1851

♫ SOUTH OF THE FILTERS, DOWN MEXICO WAY ♫

The U.S. economy benefits from the flow of legal commerce and from legal immigration between the USA and our neighbors to the south and to the north. Therefore, we don't need a Wall that acts like a prophylactic barrier. A condom, if you will. What we need are "filters" that keep the criminals and narcotics out, and allow industrious people and useful commercial products in.

Besides, there are places along our border with Mexico where rugged terrain and winding rivers make it impossible to construct a truly-effective Berlin-like Wall. But that's where Mr. Trump's "the-art-of-the-deal" could work. If the Congress and White House would work cooperatively with the International Boundary and Water Commission that was established back in 1889, we could trade stretches of rugged, hard-to-fence terrain lying inside the United States for stretches of more easily fenced terrain lying currently inside Mexico, ending up with a re-aligned border that looks more like back-and-forth saw tooth than a 1,989-mile straight line. Again, we would need someone who understands the "art-of-the-deal," and how to create win-win situations to the benefit of both sovereign states.

Where it is physically possible to build a "Wall," by employing military experts who understand the "static defense," the U.S. has the skills and know-how to do so; however, a "static defense" should be backed up by a "defense-in-depth," using an array of aviation and electronic assets to direct the actions of mobile vehicular and even foot patrols.

But this need not be a grim business. For example, on the Mexican side, we could provide free marijuana where the kind of lazy, indolent people we do not need in this country could lie about "wasting away in Marijuanaville." And, at those "filters" where we want to slow the processing of people and goods, we could put the TSA in charge. The wait times would be so long that only the most industrious would eventually make it through. An indirect form of quality-control.

But, seriously, how do we pay for effective border control? That is where Title IX of the Racketeer Influenced and Corrupt Organizations Statute (18 U.S.C. §§ 1961-1968), commonly referred to as the "**RICO**" statute, comes into play. As Donald Trump suggests, we take the drug cartel assets seized under the RICO statutes and use them to pay for the "Filter" stations. And, if the drug cartel seizures are not enough, we can look for other criminal enterprises where civil forfeiture penalties can be applied.

For example: What if the Clinton Foundation is found to be a giant money-laundering scheme for the Clinton family? In other words, a criminal enterprise. Under the RICO statutes, the U.S. could seize over $2 billion dollars from the Clinton Foundation that could be used toward securing our borders with Mexico and Canada.

Moreover, according to *The Washington Post* of April 5, 2016, illegal immigrants transfer about $2 billion dollars each month back to Mexico, 98-percent electronically. A modest tax on those electronic transfers could go into a fund to secure our borders. Thus, as Mr. Trump suggests, Mexico, in essence, gets to pay for his "Wall." We report. On Tuesday, November 8, 2016, you decide.
©2016. 1852

NOVEMBER 8TH: REVOLT OR MORE OF THE SAME?

Technically, a "revolution" replaces one political system with another. The Russian Revolution was a true "revolution." The Czarist Monarchy was replaced by Communism -- a totally different political and economic system. But most other "revolutions" are not so "true." South Americans often have "revolutions" where one group of corrupt generals replaces another group of corrupt generals. Brutal African dictators rise, experiment with socialist economics only to fail and be replaced by another brutal dictator. Somehow, none of these "revolutions" improve the plight of those the "revolutions" were supposed to liberate from oppression.

The French Revolution was simply a bloody Revolt. In 1789, the impoverished 3d Estate (starving peasants, called: the sans-culottes) revolted against the corrupt 1st Estate (the Clergy,) and against the high-living 2d Estate (the elite Nobles). Pure hatred for the Ancien Régime -- not high-minded political theory -- impelled the starving sans-culottes to murder the priests, rape the nuns, loot the churches, and behead the King, the Queen, and as many Nobles as they could imprison in the Bastille. The 4th Estate (the American mainstream media) was yet to be invented.

Nor was the American Revolution, a true "revolution." Our Founders adored the rights, privileges, and freedoms of their English forefathers and mothers. Our Founders took up arms to secure those same rights, privileges, and freedoms for Colonial America.

On Election Day -- and setting their regrettable personalities aside -- voters have the choice between a woman who has lived her public life as an Alinsky/Fabian Socialist or a man who has lived his life as an Adam Smith/Milton Friedman Capitalist. But, as the late Will Rogers famously said, "There is only one redeeming thing about this whole election. It will be over at sundown, and let everybody pray that it's not a tie, for we couldn't go through with this thing again." (This grim election may be God's way of making Old Age more palatable, and Youth less attractive.)

But, if the losers can show that this particular election was "rigged," this election might not be over at sundown. According to the Columbia Journalism Review, American journalists (our 4th Estate) have given $382,000 to one candidate and only $14,000 to the other candidate. Could media bias "rig" an election?

To quote from the Declaration of Independence, what if the government elected on November 8th is NOT "...deriving it's just powers from the consent of the governed?" The Declaration says: "That whenever any Form of Government becomes destructive of these ends [life, liberty, and the pursuit of happiness], it is the Right of the People to alter or abolish it, and to institute a new Government, laying its foundation on such principles and organizing power in such form, as to them shall seem most likely to affect their Safety and Happiness...But when a long train of abuses and usurpations ... evinces a design to reduce them under absolute Despotism, it is their right, it is their duty, to throw off such Government, and to provide new Guards for their future security..."

Wow! Our Founders refused to accept King George III's "long train of abuses and usurpations..." Pray this election will be "fair and square" and, as Will Rogers hoped, "...over at sundown..."

©2016. 1861

AN OPEN LETTER TO THE 45TH PRESIDENT

Dear Mr. President:

Observing your first few months in office from out here in fly-over land, it seems like there ought to be a course called: Presidency 101. But first, I apologize for not seeing any episodes of "The Apprentice." Except for sports, plus we used to watch our Grand Lake neighbor's "Last Man Standing" on ABC-TV before the PC crowd cancelled it, we don't watch the big broadcast networks.

Anyway, you now have what is, arguably, the world's toughest job. But, even though you were a big TV star, it appears there are some things you need to know about dealing with the so-called mainstream media (MSM) and about dealing in-person with people in the world of domestic and international politics.

While it is swell that you can use social media to go around the MSM and communicate directly with folks in fly-over land, you would be well-advised to let someone on your side look over your Tweets in draft before hitting "send." Also, using a spell-checker is a good idea.

Like all US Presidents, you want to set the record straight. But, before you fire off a Tweet, please understand the MSM often get their initial reporting wrong. Apparently, the MSM would rather be first with a story than have the facts. So, do not respond to something that is going to turn out to be untrue. Also, do not trust stories that come from anonymous sources. Watch out for news organizations that, instead of doing their own on-scene reporting, quote other news organizations. That shoddy practice can give a story that has no basis in fact a life of its own.

Beware that *The Washington Post* is now owned by an American billionaire who does not like you. *The New York Times* is controlled by a Mexican billionaire who does not like you. Both papers have abandoned any vestige of Joe Friday's "just-the-facts-ma'am" reporting. So, at the start of each day, give your staff the "message-of-the-day," get everyone singing off the same sheet of music, and hope for the best.

US Presidents, except for with their spouses, should never meet alone with anyone. Have your own note-taker present. If you want candid advice, do not record Oval Office conversations unless recording is agreed to in advance by those present. Although JFK and LBJ did some recording as well, President Nixon was foolish to try to record eight years of Oval Office chit-chat. As Dr. Kissinger asked "Who has eight years to listen?" Besides, human nature tells us that anyone who visits with you is going to head for their word-processor and write a Memorandum for Record (MFR). Have a trusted aide do that for you and stick it in a file of your presidential papers. We historians will thank you for that.

Finally, the folks who voted for you expect you to field a team devoted to "Making America Great Again." Apparently, there are some folks left over from the previous regime, both Democrat and Republican, who do not share your vision for America. Won't hurt to add a "thank you" to their pink slips.

Good luck, Mr. President. If you need more advice, the NSA knows where to find me.

Sincerely,

Bill

©2017. 1890

ACKNOWLEDGEMENTS

Without the encouragement of Penny (AKA Wonder Wife) and that of Patricia Shapiro Book Publishing, Dale Talkington, and Jenette Leblang, this project would not have gone forward. Penny and Trish took it upon themselves to rough out a concept and presented it to me as a *fait accompli*, along with an ultimatum: Either get this project done yourself or they would select about 200 columns from the universe of almost 2,000 "Central View" newspaper columns published over the past 35 years and go to press.

The appellation "Sage," in the title of this book, was inspired by our late, dear friend, Judith Wright Dawkins, who, during our 52 years of confiding in each other over a host of matters, conferred upon me the nickname: "Sage."

For the newspaper columns and articles selected, I am solely responsible. Just as I am for any errors of fact, spelling, syntax, and grammar.

William Hamilton

ABOUT THE AUTHOR

Nationally syndicated columnist, William Hamilton, is a laureate of the Oklahoma Journalism Hall of Fame, the Nebraska Aviation Hall of Fame, the Colorado Aviation Hall of Fame, the Oklahoma University Army ROTC Wall of Fame, and is a recipient of the University of Nebraska 2015 Alumni Achievement Award.

While on active duty with the U.S. Army, he was awarded the Silver Star, Legion of Merit, Distinguished Flying Cross, Purple Heart, Bronze Stars (4), Air Medals (20), the Army Commendation Medal with Combat "V," the Air Force Commendation Medal, the Expert Infantry Badge, Combat Infantry Badge, and the Master Parachutist Badge.

Dr. Hamilton was educated at the University of Oklahoma, the George Washington University, the U.S Naval War College (distinguished graduate), the University of Nebraska, and Harvard University. He and his wife, Penny R. Hamilton, Ph.D., are co-authors of four espionage novels. They write under the name: William Penn. The Hamiltons live in Colorado on the side of Sheepdog Hill, overlooking Lake Granby.

www.ingramcontent.com/pod-product-compliance
Lightning Source LLC
Chambersburg PA
CBHW052119270326
41930CB00012B/2684